£1.49

KU-545-624

Baedeker's
Tuscany

Baedeker's
TUSCANY

Imprint

100 colour photographs
26 maps, plans and sketches
1 large regional map

Conception and editorial work:
Baedeker Stuttgart
English Language edition: Alec Court

Text:
(part) Dr Hans-Joachim Fischer, Rome
Arrangement and completion: Peter M. Nahm (Baedeker)

General Direction:
Dr Peter Baumgarten, Baedeker Stuttgart

English translation: James Hogarth, Wendy Bell

Cartography:
Gert Oberländer, Munich
Franz Kaiser, Sindelfingen
Mairs Geographischer Verlag, Ostfildern-Kemnat (regional map)

Source of illustrations:
Baedeker (2), Campeggi (1), dpa (1), ENIT Rome/Frankfurt am Main (19), EPT Arezzo (5),
EPT Florence (4), EPT Pisa (4), EPT Pistoia (5), Fischer (26), Giovannini (1), Historia-Photo
(6), Kolb (1), Kranawetter (4), Merisio (2), Nahm (10), Nova Lux (1), Pfander (4), Prenzel
(1), Rogge (2), Romboni (1)

Following the tradition established by Karl Baedeker in 1844, sights of particular interest and
hotels of outstanding quality are distinguished by either one or two asterisks.

To make it easier to locate the various sights listed in the "A to Z" section of the Guide, their
co-ordinates on the large map of Tuscany are shown in red at the head of each section.

Only a selection of hotels can be given: no reflection is implied, therefore, on establishments
not included.

In a time of rapid change it is difficult to ensure that all the information given is entirely
accurate and up to date, and the possibility of error can never be entirely eliminated. Although
the publishers can accept no responsibility for inaccuracies and omissions they are always
grateful for corrections and suggestions for improvement.

3rd Edition (1992)

© Baedeker Stuttgart
Original German edition

© Jarrold and Sons Ltd
English language edition world-wide

© The Automobile Association,
United Kingdom and Ireland

Licensed user:
Mairs Geographischer Verlag GmbH & Co., Ostfildern-Kemnat bei Stuttgart

Reproductions:
Gölz Repro-Service GmbH, Ludwigsburg

The name Baedeker is a registered trademark

Printed in Italy by G. Canale & C. S.p.A. - Borgaro (TO)

ISBN 0 7495 0415 3

Contents

Abbadia San Salvatore · Abbazia di Monte Oliveto Maggiore · Abbazía di San Galgano · Abbazía di Sant'Ántimo · Ansedonia · Arcipélago Toscano · Arezzo · Asciano · Bagni di Luca · Barberino Val d'Elsa · Barga · Bibbiena · Borgo a Mazzano · Borgo San Lorenzo · Camáldoli · Capraia · Caprese Michelángelo · Carrara · Castelfiorentino · Castelnuovo di Garfagnana · Castiglione della Pescaia · Castiglion Fiorentino · Certaldo · Chianciano Terme · Chianti · Chiusi · Colle di Val d'Elsa · Cortona · Crete · Elba · Émpoli · Fiésole · Florence · Forte dei Marmi · Giannutri · Giglio · Gorgona · Grópina · Grosseto · La Verna · Livorno · Lucca · Maremma · Massa · Massa Maríttima · Montalcino · Monte Amiata · Monte Argentario · Montecatini Terme · Montecristo · Montepulciano · Orbetello · Pescia · Pianosa · Pienza · Pietrasanta · Piombino · Pisa · Pistoia · Pitigliano · Poppi · Populonia · Prato · San Gimignano · San Giovanni Valdarno · San Miniato · San Quírico d'Orcia · Sansepolcro · Siena · Valdichiana · Vetulonia · Viareggio · Volterra

Air services · Bathing beaches · Camping · Car ferries · Car hire · Coach tours · Conducted tours · Currency · Customs regulations · Diplomatic and consular offices · Emergency calls · Events · Food and drink · Getting to Tuscany · Hotels · Information · Insurance · Maps and plans · Motoring · Motoring organisations · Opening times · Postal, telegraph and telephone services · Public holidays · Rail travel · Restaurants · Roads · Souvenirs · Spas · Time · Tipping · Travel documents · Walks · Water sports · When to go · Wine · Youth hostels

The Principal Sights[1] at a Glance

[1] Not included in the above are the many sights in the regional capital of Florence (Firenze); these are summarised in this guide on pages 85–102 and are also comprehensively dealt with in the *Baedeker's Florence*. If all these sights were included in the list above it would unnecessarily distort the general survey of the highlights of Tuscany.

Preface

This pocket guide to Tuscany is one of the new generation of Baedeker regional guides.

Baedeker pocket guides, illustrated throughout in colour, are designed to meet the needs of the modern traveller. They are quick and easy to consult with the principal sights being described in alphabetical order with marginal headings.

The guide is divided into three parts. The first part gives a general account of Tuscany, its climate, economy, history, history of art, etc. Suggested itineraries introduce the second part in which the towns, villages, monasteries, etc. of tourist interest are described. The final part contains practical information arranged in alphabetical order.

The new guides are abundantly illustrated and contain many newly drawn plans and numerous colour photographs. In a pocket at the back of the book is a large regional map. Each entry in the main part of the guide gives the co-ordinates of the square on the map in which the particular feature can be located. Users of this guide, therefore, will have no difficulty in finding what they want to see.

Note on pronunciation. – In Italian the stress is usually on the last syllable but one of a word. Where it falls on the last syllable this is always indicated by a grave accent (as in Trinità). Where it falls on the third-last syllable an accent is not officially required except in certain doubtful cases; in this Guide, however, an acute accent is used as an aid to pronunciation (as in Camáldoli).

Facts and Figures

General

Tuscany belongs geographically and politically to central Italy, of which it forms the north-western part. It is bounded on the west by the Tyrrhenian Sea and on the north and east by the Arno and Tiber basins, beyond which rises the chain of the Apennines. To the south, beyond Monte Amiata (1738 m – 5702 ft), Tuscany merges into the hills of Umbria and Latium.

Situation

Tuscany (Toscana) is one of the 20 regions into which Italy is divided. The regional capital is Florence. The region of Tuscany is divided into nine provinces: Arezzo, Firenze (Florence), Grosseto, Livorno, Lucca, Massa-Carrara, Pisa, Pistoia and Siena.
The region has an area of 22,992 sq. km (8877 sq. miles) and a population of some 3·6 million.
The adjoining regions are (clockwise from the north-west) Liguria, Emilia-Romagna, Marche (the Marches), Umbria and Lazio (Latium).

Political structure

The great arc of the Apennines, with its open side to the west, encloses the old heartlands of Italy – Tuscany, Latium and Umbria. The Apuan Alps, rugged hills which form a kind of Anti-Apennine, represent in their dazzlingly white marble (a Triassic limestone recrystallised under the pressure of folding movements) a "geological window" near the area of origin of the overlying Tertiary rocks of Tuscany.
The products of the faulting which accompanied the first upthrusts of the Apennines were the basins, reaching deep into the upland regions, which are so characteristic of central Italy. During the Pliocene and Early Quarternary they were filled by lakes, the deposits from which can still occasionally be identified, as in the tabular Cerbaie hills in the Lucca Basin or the bizarrely hewn spurs of rock on a terrace in the Valdarno Basin. The Arno and the Tiber captured these basins, one after the other, by retrograding erosion; but the Arno, with a shorter course and a steeper gradient, encroached on the territory of its rival, tapping a river flowing through the Casentino and the Chiana Depression into the Tiber and converting it into its own upper course.
The fertile basins of Tuscany, dotted with villages and isolated farms, are excellently situated from the point of view of communications, lying as they do immediately below the Apennine passes. With their luxuriant *cultura mista* (vines, corn, fruit, sunflowers and tobacco) and their silver-grey fringes of olive trees they are in striking contrast to the hills of the Apennines, which are mostly bare of vegetation. The old-established towns such as Arezzo, Chiusi and Fiésole (Florence's predecessor), which are mainly of Etruscan origin, are built on the high ground above the valley floors, a situation

Topography

◄   *In the hills near Volterra*

Italy

- - - Regional boundaries

which offered security and freedom from malaria and was advantageous from the defensive standpoint.

The landscape to the south of the Lower Arno is very different. In the Tuscan Uplands, which rise in the Colline Metallífere ("ore-bearing hills") to a height of 1059 m (3475 ft), the eye ranges over an apparently formless pattern of rolling hills, steeply scarped in places but never of genuinely mountainous aspect. They do not form connected chains but are broken up into isolated massifs. The frequent variations in rock type and in altitude produce a very attractive diversity of landscape pattern and scenery. Here, too, the fertile soil is predominantly devoted to a *cultura mista* (olives, vines and corn). This was the

The region of
Tuscany is
divided into nine
provinces

MASSA-
CAR-
RARA

Carrara

Massa

LUCCA

PISTOIA

Pistoia

FIRENZE

Lucca

Firenze

Pisa

AREZZO

Livorno

PISA

Arezzo

Gorgona

Siena

A r c i p e l a g o

LIVORNO

SIENA

Capraia

GROSSETO

Elba

Grosseto

T o s c a n o

Pianosa

Montecristo

Giglio

Giannutri

Provincial boundaries ———

land of *mezzadria*, a share-cropping system with a tradition
going back many centuries, in which the landlord supplied
smallholders with farm buildings, equipment and stock as well
as land. This system proved increasingly less profitable,
however, and died out in the 1960s. All over the region, but
particularly around the hill towns, conspicuous on their
commanding heights, ancient farmsteads, handsome country
houses and churches, often with sturdy campaniles, are
scattered about the green countryside, variegated by the silver
foliage of the olive trees and the darker colouring of tall
cypresses. Tuscany is a land marked everywhere by the labour
of men's hands.

Climate

Cypress trees

The stony soil of the higher ridges supports meagre stands of oaks and pines and expanses of aromatic Mediterranean heathland (tree heaths, arbutus, cistus, etc.). In the Colline Metallífere and the Chianti hills this vegetation becomes denser, forming the evergreen Mediterranean *macchia* (scrub). Around Volterra and south of Siena the landscape becomes different again; here there are few trees, and the land is given up to fields of corn slashed by bizarre grey rifts caused by the continuing erosion of the soil. Even towns and farmsteads built on hills are threatened by deeply eroded gullies (*balze*).

The strip of land along the coast of Tuscany known as the Maremma (=*maríttima*), between the mouth of the Cécina (with the town of that name) and the town of Civitavecchia in Latium, has a character of its own. For centuries this area was shunned as the haunt of malaria, transmitted by the mosquitoes which infested the marshy coastal regions. In Etruscan times, however, the southern Maremma was densely populated, the heartland of an empire which extended over half of Italy; and the remains of Rusellae (now Roselle) and Populonia and the rich Etruscan material recovered at Orbetello. Massa Maríttima and other places bear witness to the prosperity of the area between the 8th and the 4th c. B.C. Thereafter the Roman system of latifundia, the abandonment of the drainage installations and the consequent spread of malaria condemned it to depopulation for more than 2000 years. It was not until the 18th c. that a beginning was made with the process of draining the land and reclaiming it for agriculture which was completed under Mussolini.

Valley basins

The principal concentrations of population are in the basins which thrust into the hills. The main valleys, from north-west to south-east, are the Lunigiana, Garfagnana, Mugello, Casentino, Valdarno, Valdelsa and Valdichiana. Between the Chiana Valley and the Maremma are the Colline Metallífere, with rich deposits of ore which have been worked since ancient times.

Rivers

All the rivers of Tuscany flow west into the Tyrrhenian Sea. In addition to the Arno, the largest river in Tuscany, the main rivers, from north to south, are the Magra, the Serchio, the Cécina, the Ombrone and the Albegna.

Climate

Mediterranean climatic region

Tuscany lies on the northern fringe of the Mediterranean climatic region. It shows a characteristic feature of the Mediterranean area in the presence of olives, which farther north grow only in particularly favoured areas.

Although there are certain differences between the coastal and the inland regions of Tuscany, the pattern of the seasons is broadly similar.

Seasons

The winter is generally mild. Snow falls regularly but rarely lies long except in the hills.

In spring the weather is changeable, with moderate rainfall, decreasing markedly in June.

The summer is warm and generally dry, with occasional showers.

A farm in Tuscany

In autumn the rainfall increases, but the weather is predominantly fine.

Average annual temperatures increase from south-west to   Temperatures
north-east from about 16 °C (61 °F) on the south coast to about
12 °C (54 °F) in the valleys in the hills. The lowest temperatures
are in January (Livorno 7 °C (45 °F), Pisa 6 °C (43 °F), Florence
4·7 °C (40·5 °F), Arezzo 4·4 °C (39·9 °F); the temperature falls
below zero only at altitudes of over 1000 m (3300 ft). The
winter is particularly mild on the islands of the Tuscan
Archipelago (Portoferraio 9 °C (48 °F) in January).
The warmest month in Tuscany is July (Livorno 24·4 °C
(75·9 °F), Pisa 23·5 °C (74·3 °F), Florence 24·6 °C (76·3 °F),
Arezzo 24·2 °C (75·6 °F), Camáldoli, alt. 816 m (2677 ft),
17·9 °C (64·2 °F).

There are considerable differences in rainfall within the region: Rainfall
while in the middle section of the Tuscan coast the annual
average is barely 500 mm (20 in), in the Apennines and Apuan
Alps it rises to 2000–3000 m (80–120 in). Examples: Viareggio
965 mm (38 in), Florence 840 mm (33 in), Siena 860 mm (34
in), Monte Amiata 1170 m (46 in). Most of the rain falls in
April–May and October–November. The driest month is July,
and rainfall is also low in January–February. The summer is for
all practical purposes totally dry only on the islands of the
Tuscan Archipelago and at certain points on the coast.
Snow is rare in low-lying areas. In Florence, for example, there
is usually a little snow every winter, but it does not lie. The
Apennines and Apuan Alps, on the other hand, have a
permanent covering of snow from December to April.

Economy

The prevailing winds in Tuscany are mainly from the west and south. Prominent among them are the moisture-bringing *scirocco* and the violent *libeccio*.

In winter and early spring the *tramontana*, blowing from the north or north-east, brings in a flow of surprisingly cold air.

Economy

Agriculture plays a major part in the economy of Tuscany, the principal products being olives, wine (Chianti), vegetables, corn, sunflowers and tobacco. Stock-farming is of lesser importance. In the coastal regions there is fishing, but the catches are barely sufficient to meet local consumption; the main fishing port is Livorno.

The marble-working industry of the Apuan Alps, and particularly of Carrara, is of international importance. Other old-established industries are the smelting of iron ore from Elba and the ores of the Colline Metallifere (copper, lead, mercury, etc.). At Larderello geothermal energy is harnessed to produce power.

Florence and Prato are important centres of the textile industry; the *alta moda* (haute couture) of Florence once world-renowned has been superseded by that of Milan.

The tourist trade is a major source of income. Apart from Florence, with its abundance of art treasures, the principal magnets for visitors are other historic old towns including Pisa, Siena, Arezzo and Lucca, together with Italy's two leading spas, Montecatini Terme and Chianciano Terme, and the numerous popular seaside resorts on the Tuscan coast.

Some Notable Tuscans

Born in Arezzo, from which he took his name, the young Pietro Aretino went to Rome, where he found favour at the Court of Pope Leo X. His satirical writings, however, made him enemies, and he was compelled to leave Rome in the reign of Adrian VI. Later he attached himself to the *condottiere* Giovanni de' Médici (of a junior branch of the Médici), known as Giovanni delle Bande Nere, and after Giovanni's death made his way to Venice. The best known of his many works is the "Ragiona-menti", a bawdy account of the life of the courtesan.

Pietro Aretino
(1492–1556)

The birthplace of the great humanist and writer Giovanni Boccaccio has not been established with certainty; the honour is claimed both by Florence and by Certaldo, where he died. Originally destined for a commercial career, he soon turned to literature and scholarship. His interest in classical antiquity foreshadowed the basic idea of the Renaissance. He instigated the first translation of Homer into Latin, and together with Petrarch he did much to promote interest in Greece and Rome. A great admirer of Dante, he was appointed in 1373 to a teaching post in Florence concerned with the reading and interpretation of the "Divine Comedy". His best-known work, however, is the "Decamerone", a series of 100 stories set in a country house outside Florence where the narrators have sought refuge from the 1348 plague. The individual stories cover a wide range, from pious legends to popular tales and current anecdotes. Boccaccio's language had a great influence on Italian writing.

Giovanni Boccaccio
(1313–75)

The composer and cello virtuoso Luigi Boccherini, born in Lucca, was appointed to a post at the Spanish Court in 1769. His music, most of it written for small ensembles (trios, quartets, quintets), was in the spirit of the Viennese pre-classical school. Perhaps his best-known piece is the "Menuet célèbre" from his string quintet Opus 13 No. 5.

Luigi Boccherini
(1743–1805)

Carlo Lorenzini, a native of Florence, is better known under his pseudonym of Carlo Collodi, a name he took from his mother's birthplace, the village of Collodi near Pescia. A theatrical critic and founder of the "Lampione", a satirical journal, he published in 1878 "Pinocchio", the children's book which made him famous. The book describes the adventures of the wooden figure, Pinocchio, who wants to become a real boy. Its novelty lies in the realism with which the characters and their qualities, good or bad, are delineated.

Carlo Collodi
(real name Carlo Lorenzini,
1826–90)

The son of a family of the lesser nobility, Dante (shortened form of Durante) Alighieri received a good education and devoted himself to the study of philosophy, the classical languages and poetry. A key event in his life, at the age of nine, was his meeting with Beatrice, probably daughter of the patrician Folco dei Portinari, whom, after her early death, he celebrated in his poems.
In the conflict between the Guelfs who supported the Pope and the Ghibellines who were for the Emperor, Dante at first took

Dante Alighieri
(1265–1321)

the Guelf side, and indeed went to Rome as the Envoy of the White Guelfs. In 1302 he was accused of maladministration as a member of the Florentine Council of One Hundred and as Prior of the city government and condemned to death for his failure to appear before the tribunal. This marked the beginning of a life of wandering, and after the death of the Emperor Henry VII he could no longer hope to return to Florence. He died in Ravenna.

Dante is Italy's greatest poet, his work of encyclopaedic range. He laid the foundations of literary Italian, which was rooted in his native Tuscan. His principal work, the "Divine Comedy" ("Divina Commedia"), symbolically presents in its 100 cantos man's path through Hell and through Purgatory to Paradise. His guides are Virgil, representing reason and knowledge, and Beatrice, the personification of love and divine grace.

St Francis of Assisi
(Giovanni Bernardone,
1181/82–1226)

The son of a wealthy merchant, Francis spent his youth in thoughtless pleasure, but at the age of 24 he had a profound experience of conversion, and thereafter lived a life of extreme humility and renunciation.

The principles of his conduct were those given by Christ to the Apostles (Matthew 10, 6–14). These led him in 1210 to found the Order of Minorites, and soon communities of Franciscans were established in Italy and other countries. With St Clare of Assisi he established the Order of Poor Clares in 1212, and this was followed in 1221 by the foundation of the lay Order of Tertiaries.

After giving up the leadership of his Order Francis withdrew to La Verna, where on 17 September 1224 he received the stigmata (the marks of Christ's wounds). In the same year he wrote his "Cántico di Frate Sole" ("Hymn of Brother Son") glorifying all created things – the first great work in the Italian language.

Galileo Galilei
(1564–1642)

Galileo Galilei was born in Pisa, the son of an architect, and at the age of only 25 became Professor of Mathematics in the University of Pisa. Here he is said to have made the observations and carried out the experiments which led to his epoch-making discoveries: the candelabrum in the cathedral gave him the idea of the movement of the pendulum, and the Leaning Tower served for his study of falling bodies. In 1609 he constructed a telescope and used it in his astronomical investigations. He refined Copernicus's view of the Universe as centred on the sun and in consequence came into conflict with the Church. He was brought to trial and condemned in 1633 to indefinite imprisonment (later commuted to exile). After his sentence he is said to have muttered, sotto voce, "Eppur si muove" ("It [i.e. the earth] *does* move"). Galileo is held to be one of the greatest masters of Tuscan prose.

Leo I
(St Leo the Great,
Pope 440–461)

Leo I, who may have been of Etruscan descent, was the greatest Pope of the Early Christian period. He established the primacy of the Pope as the supreme authority in the Church and secured its recognition from the Emperor Valentinian. A man of great resolution and courage, he saved Rome on two occasions when it was in great peril: in 452 he faced up to Attila, leader of the Huns, and compelled him to withdraw from Rome, and three years later put a stop to the plundering of the city by Genseric's Vandals.

Leo was canonised, and is commemorated on 11 April. In

Giovanni Boccaccio

Dante Alighieri

Galileo Galilei

paintings he is often depicted with Peter and Paul, who are said to have supported him against Attila.

The Renaissance produced numerous many-sided personalities, but none but Leonardo showed such superlative and varied talent as painter, sculptor, architect, engineer and scientist. Leonardo was a pupil of Verrocchio's, and at the early age of 20, in 1472, was admitted to the Florentine Guild of Painters. From 1482 to 1498 he worked at the Court of Duke Lodovico Sforza in Milan, then came back to Florence and later went to Rome. In 1517 he was invited to France by King Francis I, and died there two years later.

Leonardo da Vinci
(1452–1519)

The works created by Leonardo in the last 20 years of his life have almost all been completely lost or are preserved only in copies by his pupils. A few fragments survive in the Uffizi in Florence. He designed a wall-painting of the Battle of Anghiari for the Palazzo Vecchio in Florence, but the painting was never executed and even his cartoon is lost.

Leonardo was active as a military engineer, investigated human anatomy, carried out experiments in flying and studied botany and geology. His numerous drawings and notes (mostly in mirror writing) demonstrate the universality of his genius.

Machiavelli, the son of a Florentine lawyer, devoted himself to humanist studies and then became Secretary of the Council of Ten which ruled Florence. In this capacity he travelled widely – to France, to the Court of the Emperor Maximilian and to Rome as Envoy to the Pope. When the Médici returned to Florence in 1512 Machiavelli was dismissed from his post and spent some time in prison, accused of involvement in a conspiracy. Thereafter he retired to his country estate and gave himself up to literary work (among his writings being "Mandrágola", the first vernacular comedy in Renaissance literature).

Niccolò Machiavelli
(1469–1527)

Much better known, however, are Machiavelli's political writings. In his "Discorsi", taking his examples from Roman history, he sets out his ideas on State authority and the vicissitudes of history, and in "Príncipe" ("The Prince") he develops his doctrine of *raison d'état* as justifying anything ("The end hallows the means").

Some Notable Tuscans

Gaius Maecenas
(*c*. 70–8 B.C.)

Maecenas, a Roman noble of Etruscan origin, was a friend and adviser of Augustus. He was the patron of artists and poets, and was himself a writer. Among those who frequented his house were Horace, Virgil and Propertius. His name has now become a synonym for a generous patron of the arts.

Curzio Malaparte
(real name Kurt Erich Suckert, 1898–1957)

This journalist and writer, of German descent, was born in Prato. He wrote for various journals, was Editor of the famous Italian newspaper "Stampa" from 1928 to 1931 and founded the literary periodical "Prospettive" in the late 1930s. In 1933 he was expelled from the Fascist Party for his political views and exiled to the Lípari Islands. After the fall of Mussolini he became a liaison officer with the American Army. His novel "Kaputt", a realistic account of Europe at war, was published in 1944, his other best-seller "La Pelle" ("The Skin") in 1948. He also wrote a renowned book about Tuscany, "Maledetti Toscani" (1956).

Marino Marini
(1901–80)

The painter and sculptor Marino Marini, a native of Pistoia, ranks as one of the leading Italian artists of the 20th c. In his representational work one theme constantly recurs in numerous variants – a horse and its rider, often reminiscent of ancient, and particularly Etruscan, models.

Michelángelo Buonarroti
(1475–1564)

Michelángelo, born in Caprese (Casentino), was a universal genius – sculptor, painter, architect, poet – who carried the art of the Renaissance to its greatest heights. In 1488, at the age of 13, he became a pupil in the studio of the Florentine painter Doménico Ghirlandaio; but side by side with his painting he developed an increasing passion for sculpture, and in 1489 he was admitted to the Academy of Sculpture in the Médici Gardens. In 1494 he left Florence to work in Venice and Bologna, and from 1496 to 1501 he was in Rome, where he produced, among other works, his "Bacchus" (now in the Museo del Bargello in Florence) and the "Pietà" in St Peter's. From 1501 to 1505 he was in Florence, his principal work during this period being the colossal figure of David for the Piazza della Signoría (original now in the Galleria dell'Accadémia).

Between 1505 and 1534 his restless spirit and the commissions he received brought him an unsettled life, moving between Florence, Rome and Bologna. During these years he created, among much else, the ceiling-frescoes in the Sistine Chapel in the Vatican, the Médici Chapel in the Church of San Lorenzo, Florence, and the figure of Moses for the Tomb of Pope Julius II in the Church of San Pietro in Víncoli in Rome. From 1534 until his death in 1564, with brief interruptions, he stayed in Rome. During this period he painted the fresco the "Last Judgment" on the altar wall of the Sistine Chapel. Among his late works was a "Pietà" for the Cathedral in Florence (now in the Cathedral Museum).

During the last 20 years of his life Michelángelo was increasingly involved in architectural projects – for example the continuation of work on the Palazzo Farnese (1546 onwards), the new layout of the Piazza del Campidoglio and the dome of St Peter's (1547 onwards).

As a poet he wrote sonnets and madrigals in the tradition of Petrarch.

Michelángelo's body was taken from Rome to Florence and buried in the Church of Santa Croce.

Leonardo da Vinci

Michelángelo Buonarroti

Francesco Petrarca

Lorenzo de' Médici, known since the 19th c. as the Magnificent (il Magnífico), was the very pattern of a Renaissance prince – in his style of government, his way of life, his culture and his patronage of the arts. With his great financial resources and the support of the citizens he made Florence the leading cultural and political centre in Italy. In 1478 his brother Giuliano was assassinated in the cathedral (the Pazzi Conspiracy) and Lorenzo himself was wounded but escaped into the sacristy. He then carried through an amendment of the constitution which gave him monarchical authority. He supported the Platonic Academy which had been founded by Cosimo de' Médici and was himself a writer. He also collected antique sculpture and helped young artists.

Lorenzo de' Médici
(Lorenzo the Magnificent,
1449–92)

On the threshold of the Renaissance we encounter a figure of outstanding importance – Francesco Petrarca (known in English as Petrarch), poet and scholar, an enthusiastic student of classical antiquity and thus one of the founders of humanism.

Francesco Petrarca
(1304–74)

Born the son of a notary of Arezzo named Petracco, he later Latinised his name into Petrarca – a manifestation of his veneration for antiquity. His father's profession led the family to move to Avignon, then residence of the Pope. Francesco studied law, at first in Montpellier and then at Bologna. Returning to the Papal Curia in Avignon, he made the acquaintance in church one day of the woman to whom he dedicated a lifelong – but unfulfilled – love and whom he immortalised in his poems as Laura.

Petrarch soon became famed as a poet, and also enjoyed influence as a friend of Cardinal Colonna. He travelled widely, and one of his excursions was of key significance not only to himself but for the sensibility of a whole period: his ascent in 1336 of Mont Ventoux in southern France, the first occasion in modern times on which a mountain was climbed for its own sake.

Later Petrarch withdrew to his country property in the Vaucluse, near Avignon, and devoted himself to literary activity, writing poems himself and studying the works of Latin writers. In 1341 he was crowned in Rome as *poeta laureatus*.

19

Some Notable Tuscans

From 1363 he lived in Italy, spending some time in Venice and at Arquà, near Parma. Giovanni Boccaccio, whom he had met during his travels, was a friend of his later years.

Girólamo Savonarola
(1452–98)

The Dominican friar Girólamo Savonarola, who became Prior of the Monastery of San Marco in Florence in 1491, was a man of the strictest moral standards who believed that the time had come for a divine judgement on the world and preached repentance and spiritual and moral renewal in the spirit of the Old Testament. The end of Médici rule in Florence and the military successes of Charles VIII of France, who in 1495 gained control of the Kingdom of Naples, seemed to confirm his prophecies. He declared Christ to be King of Florence and set up a theocratic state with laws based on the Gospels. His criticisms of the Papal Court in Rome brought him into conflict with the Church, and finally he was excommunicated. In 1498 he was tortured and compelled to retract; then, declared guilty of heresy, he was hanged and his body was publicly burned.

Giácomo Puccini
(1858–1924)

Puccini was born in Lucca, the son of a family of musicians. He studied mainly in Milan, and was much influenced by Verismo, properly a literary movement but one which was also reflected in the choice of operatic themes, and by contemporary French music. He ranks as Italy's leading opera composer after Verdi, and his works including "La Bohème", "Tosca" and "Madam Butterfly" have won international renown. Puccini built a house Torre de Lago and died there in 1924.

History

The name Italia, originally Greek, applied at first only to the south-western tip of the peninsula; not until Roman Imperial times was it extended to cover the whole territory reaching north to the Alps. The names of regions of Italy still preserve the names of the peoples who once occupied them: thus the name of Tuscany is derived from the Etruscans (Latin *Tusci* or *Etrusci*) and the name of the Tyrrhenian Sea which washes its shores comes from the Greek name of the same people (*Tyrrhenoi*).
Italy was already settled by man in the Palaeolithic period.

Prehistory

Early Metal Age in Upper Italy: Remedello culture (copper daggers), named after the type site near Brescia.

1800–1600 B.C.

Bronze Age: Terramare culture (Italian *terramara*, "earth mound") in northern Italy, with fortified settlements of pile-dwellings.

1600–1200

Beginning of Indo-European migrations from the north. The Italic peoples split into the Latin group, to which the Romans belong, and the Umbro-Sabellian group, the principal branch of which includes the Oscans, the Samnites of Campania.

1200 onwards

Villanovan culture (named after the type site near Bologna), evolved by an Indo-European people.

1000–500

The Etruscans, probably coming from Asia Minor, press into Etruria (Tuscia, Tuscany), Campania and the Plain of the Po. They form a league of 12 cities on the Ionian model; lively trade with central and northern Europe; highly developed cult of the dead (cemeteries). They bring to Italy the art, culture, technology and social structures of Greek Asia Minor. Later they become the teachers of the Romans.

900–500

Establishment of naval stations in western Sicily and Sardinia by the Phoenicians (Latin *Punii*) in order to protect their trading routes in the western Mediterranean.
In the 8th c. the Etruscans become the predominant force in Italy.

From 800

The Greeks plant colonies in Lower Italy and Sicily (*Megale Hellas*; Latin *Magna Graecia*). Wars with Carthaginians and Etruscans, caused by commercial rivalries. The Latin alphabet is developed out of the Greek script.

750–550

Rome, at first merely a city-state, overcomes the resistance of the Italic peoples and extends its rule to the whole of the Italian mainland, the islands and eventually western Europe and the East. Roman generals and later the Emperors, ruling with absolute power, contrive to hold the Roman Empire (*Imperium Romanum*) together and defend it for centuries against attacks by neighbouring peoples. The spread of Christianity and of urban culture provide the basis for the development of western European culture and civilisation.

Italy under Roman rule

Tuscany in Antiquity

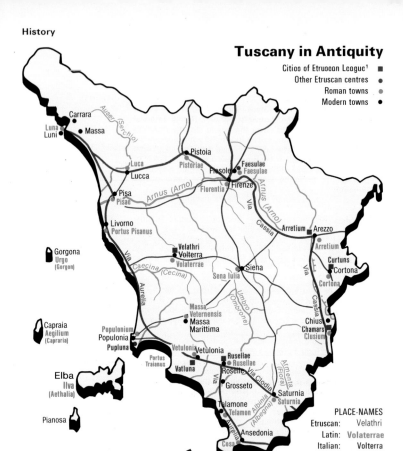

Cities of Etruscan League[1] ■
Other Etruscan centres ●
Roman towns ○
Modern towns ●

PLACE-NAMES
Etruscan: *Velathri*
Latin: *Volaterrae*
Italian: Volterra

ROMAN ROADS
Main roads ▬▬▬
Secondary roads ▬▬▬

[1] In addition to the six towns in present-day Tuscany which are shown on this map the Etruscan League of twelve cities included PERUSIA (Perugia) and VOLSINII (Orvieto) in the region of Umbria to the east and TARCHUNA (Tarquinia), CAERE (Cervéteri) and VEII (Veio) in the region of Latium (Lazio) to the south-east.

753	Legendary date of the foundation of Rome (perhaps from Etruscan *Rumlua*) by Romulus, a descendant of the Trojan Aeneas. In the 8th c. the Etruscans became the predominate force in Italy.
600–510	Rome is ruled by Etruscan kings, the Tarquins, until the establishment of the Republic in 510.
About 400	Incursion into Upper Italy by Celts; Rome defeated in the Battle of the Allia (387/386).

Rome conquers central Italy, maintaining control by building military roads and founding military colonies. Latinisation of the Italic peoples.	396–280
Extension of Roman power to Upper Italy, Lower Italy and Sicily. In the three Punic Wars Carthage is defeated and its dominant role in the western Mediterranean taken over by Rome.	About 300 to 146
Civil wars, caused by the increasing impoverishment of the rural population, and slave risings reflect grave defects in the Roman State.	133–130
Wars with Cimbri and Teutons.	113–101
Julius Caesar becomes sole ruler (murdered on 14 March 44). End of the Republic.	45
Augustus establishes the Principate and maintains peace both at home and abroad (Pax Augusta). Cultural flowering (Virgil, Ovid, Horace; fostering of the arts by men such as Maecenas); much building activity in Rome.	30 B.C.–A.D. 14
The Roman Empire reaches its greatest extent.	14–395
Arabs, Germans, Persians and other people attack the frontiers of the Empire.	From 220
Constantine the Great grants Christians religious freedom (Edict of Milan).	313
The Huns burst into Europe; beginning of the Great Migrations.	About 375
Theodosius divides the Empire into a Western Empire (capital Ravenna) and an Eastern Empire (capital Constantinople).	395
Alaric's Visigoths take Rome.	410
Devastations in the Po Plain by the Huns.	452
Rome is plundered by Genseric's Vandals.	455
The Germanic migrations have a profound influence on the development of western and southern Europe. The attempts by German Kings and Emperors to restore the unity of Italy are frustrated, mainly by the resistance of the Papacy; the Investiture conflict.	Italy in the early Middle Ages
Theodoric the Great establishes an Ostrogothic kingdom in Italy, dependent on the Eastern Empire; its capitals are Ravenna, Pavia and Verona.	493–526
Justinian makes Italy a province (exarchate) of the Eastern Empire.	535–553
Lombard kingdom in Upper Italy; Tuscia, Spoleto and Benevento become Lombard duchies.	568–774
Charlemagne conquers the Lombard Kingdom and joins it to his Frankish Empire; the duchies, except Benevento, become Frankish margraviates.	773–774

History

899	The Hungarians plunder Upper Italy.
951	Otto the Great, German Emperor, responds to an appeal for help from the Lombard King's widow, Adelheid, and gains control of Upper Italy.
951–1268	German Emperors rule in Italy. Constant conflicts with the Popes, native rulers and cities. Formation of two parties – the Ghibellines (named after the Hohenstaufen Castle of Waiblingen in Württemberg), who support the Emperor, and the Guelfs, who support the Pope.
1076–1122	In the Investiture conflict, the decisive struggle between Imperial and Papal power, the Pope establishes his freedom from Imperial influence in the appointment of bishops, and increasingly looks for support to the Italian States.
1115	Margravine Matilda of Tuscia dies. Her bequest of her possessions to the Pope gives rise to a further conflict with the Emperor, which is not settled until 1213, when the Emperor Frederick II formally renounces his claim.
1186	The Emperor Henry IV marries Constance, heiress to the Norman Kingdom of southern Italy and Sicily. The conflict between the Emperor and the Pope is aggravated by this encirclement of the Papal States by Imperial territories.
1212–1250	Frederick II, crowned Emperor at Rome in 1220, turns the Norman Kingdom into a rigidly organised absolutist state, a centre of Imperial power; conflicts with the opposing Papal and Lombard party. The Emperor fosters the arts and learning.
From the Renaissance to the periods of Spanish, Austrian and French rule	In Italy, now politically fragmented, there come into being city-states and later princely states which rise to great European intellectual, cultural and economic importance and come into conflict with the neighbouring Great Powers.
From 1250	Rise of independent individual States. In the communes the original republican constitutions give place, as a result of strife between domestic factions, to *signorie* (seigniories) ruled by a single individual. The defeat and annexation of neighbouring communes leads to the establishment of territorial States of some size. Florence, an important commercial and banking centre, gains a democratic constitution in 1282. About 1400 the Médici achieve enormous prestige and great political influence.
About 1250 to 1600	Humanism and the Renaissance. Italian humanists (Dante, Petrarch, Boccaccio, etc.) rediscover ancient literature, which provides them with models for poetry and scholarship. The Renaissance leads to great creative achievements in painting and architecture, but also in scholarship and science, which strive for independence. Increasing wealth of cities and courts; the great ecclesiastical and secular princes lead lives of great luxury and not always of high principle; in Florence and elsewhere the arts are fostered by wealthy patrons. From the 16th c. the Renaissance spreads to princely courts and great commercial cities throughout Europe.

The last campaigns by German Emperors in Italy.	1310–1452
Unsuccessful attempt by Cola di Rienzo to re-establish the Roman Republic.	1347
Girólamo Savonarola sets up a theocratic republic in Florence after the temporary expulsion of the Médici; he is executed as a heretic in 1498.	1494
France and Spain attempt, unsuccessfully, to establish predominance in Italy.	1494–1556
Four wars between the Emperor Charles V and Francis I of France, who is taken prisoner in the Battle of Pavia (1525).	1521–44
Cosimo de' Médici, Duke of Florence, becomes Grand Duke of Tuscany.	1569
Galileo is compelled by the Inquisition to retract his adherence to the Copernican picture of the Universe.	1633
Tuscany passes to the Emperor Francis I of Austria in compensation for the loss of Lorraine. He rules the Grand Duchy through a Regent. The House of Lorraine becomes the hereditary ruling family of Tuscany and remains so until the unification of Italy.	1737
A new national feeling comes into being in Italy, preparing the way for the liberation and independence movement of the 19th c.	About 1750
Genoa sells Corsica to France.	1768
Bonaparte's Italian campaign.	1796
Under the Treaty of Lunéville Tuscany passes to the House of Bourbon-Parma, which is allied with Napoleon.	1801
Napoleon becomes King of Italy. He elevates the Republic of Lucca into a Duchy for his sister Elisa, Princess of Piombino. After the union of her Duchy with Tuscany she becomes Grand Duchess.	1805
Congress of Vienna: establishment of a new order in Europe after the fall of Napoleon. The old petty States are restored.	1814–15
The Napoleonic era had strengthened national feeling in Italy, but it was some time before Cavour brought the idea of an independent national State nearer to realisation. After achieving national unification Italy, like other States, seeks to assert its imperialist interests.	From the Risorgimento to the end of the First World War
Publication in Turin of the journal "Il Risorgimento", from which the whole movement of national unification takes its name. In Tuscany a measure of liberalisation is introduced by Grand Duke Leopold II.	1847
Revolution in Italy and Sicily. Grand Duke Leopold of Tuscany grants a constitution. After his flight to the Kingdom of Naples the Republic of Tuscany is proclaimed.	1848

History

1859–60	The national unification of Italy begins with the *rapprochement* with France initiated by Count Cavour.
1860	Expulsion of the princely rulers of States in central and northern Italy. Garibaldi and his army of volunteers defeat the Bourbons and occupy the States of the Church. Popular plebiscites throughout Italy lead to union with the Kingdom of Sardinia.
1861	Victor Emmanuel II becomes King of Italy.
1865–71	Florence becomes the first capital of united Italy.
1914	Italy declares its neutrality in the First World War (3 August).
1915–18	Italy takes part in the First World War.
From the end of the First World War to the present day	After the First World War Italy pursues an expansionist policy and seeks to overcome the "crisis of democracy" by a new political ideology, Fascism. After the Second World War the Republic is rent by ideological conflict and troubled by economic and social problems. The country's domestic development is bedevilled by a proliferation of parties with their various interest groups and lobbies.
1922	The "March on Rome". Benito Mussolini is granted dictatorial powers by the Italian Parliament; Government authority is gradually taken over by the Fascists.
1937	Italy leaves the League of Nations (of which it had been a founding member in 1919).
1939–45	Second World War. Mussolini seeks, unsuccessfully, to mediate; at first Italy remains "non-belligerent".
1940	Italy declares war on Britain and France. Three-Power Pact with Germany and Japan.
1943	Fall of the Fascist system; formation of a new government under Badoglio, who concludes an armistice with the Allies and declares war on Germany.
1946	Victor Emmanuel III abdicates. A national plebiscite declares in favour of a Republic.
1948	A democratic constitution comes into force. Economic and social cleavage between the developed north and the under-developed south of Italy. After overcoming its economic difficulties with the help of Marshall Aid Italy enjoys an upswing.
1950	Partial expropriation of large properties under the Sila Law.
1966	Disastrous flooding in northern and central Italy. In Florence the Arno overflows its banks, destroying or damaging many works of art.
1985	The "Year of the Etruscans": congresses, lectures and exhibitions in Florence, Siena, Volterra, Arezzo, Orbetello and Piombino on the history and culture of the Etruscans.
1986	Florence is proclaimed European cultural capital for 1986.
1988	Regulations are gradually being introduced to ban private vehicles from the centre of large cities (Florence).

Art

The Italian Peninsula, like the rest of the Mediterranean area, has been settled by man since the earliest times; and Tuscany has preserved an extraordinary wealth of art treasures from the Etruscan and Roman periods, the period of Hohenstaufen rule, the Early Renaissance, the era of the city-states and the Grand Duchy.

Tuscan region

Remains of the Stone Age are to be found mainly in northern Italy. The museums of Florence and many smaller towns possess important archaeological material of this period (domestic implements, weapons, grave-goods, etc.).

During the Bronze Age Italy appears to have had connections with the Creto-Mycenaean culture, as has been shown by material found in settlements of this period. The Terramare culture which reached Italy from Illyria can be attributed with reasonable certainty to the early Italic peoples.

Between the 8th and 5th c. B.C. the Etruscans (Latin *Etrusci* or *Tusci*, Greek *Tyrrhenoi* or *Tyrsenoi*, in their own language *Rasenna*) achieved a predominant position in central and northern Italy: according to Cato "almost the whole of Italy was under Etruscan rule". There is still no agreement on the origin of the Etruscans, though it seems highly probable that a migration from Greek-influenced territory in Asia Minor was involved. The Etruscan art that has come down to us shows clear Greek influence, for example in painting, sculpture and mythology. The language and script of the Etruscans still pose problems. The alphabet itself, also based on Greek models, can be read; but the surviving documents, consisting almost exclusively of short formula-like inscriptions, offer little help towards an understanding of their meaning. A further difficulty is that Etruscan is not an Indo-European language, and indeed shows no similarities with any other tongues which might be used for comparative purposes.

The Etruscans

In addition to smaller local centres the Etruscan League of twelve cities included Velathri (Volterra), Arretium (Arezzo), Curtuns (Cortona), Chamars/Clevsin/Clusium (Chiusi), Rusellae (Roselle), Vatluna (Vetulonia) and other cities to the south, now in Latium. The Etruscans achieved a high standard of art and culture, as their splendid works of art, mostly recovered from tombs, bear witness. The famous bronze figure of the She-Wolf of the Capitol is Etruscan work. In architecture the Etruscans used the "true" arch (constructed of stones dressed to a wedge shape and not merely built up in overlapping courses) and knew the technique of the barrel vault. The Etruscan works of art to be seen in many museums (Archaeological Museum, Florence; museums in Chiusi, Volterra, etc.) are notable both for their number and their quality. Of the secular buildings of the Etruscans little has survived, apart from a number of necropoli (cemeteries).

The Greek colonies in Italy had little influence on the heartland of the Etruscans; but when the Romans gained control of the whole of Italy between 400 and 200 B.C. they took over the art and culture of the conquered territories, and owed a major part

The Romans

Art

Etruscan funerary casket

Adoration – School of Robbia

of their technology to the Etruscans. Rome's principal contribution to Western architecture is perhaps the further development of Etruscan vaulting techniques. Roman sculpture is mainly based on Greek models, but achieves extreme realism in the portrait sculpture of the Republican period. Roman painting shows Hellenistic influence. Mosaics were used for wall and floor decoration.

The Early Christians

In Early Christian times the Roman basilica (a law court) was developed into the Christian basilican church. The nave, which probably had a flat roof, was now divided into three or five aisles, the central aisle being higher than the others. The west end of the church faced on to the street; the east end had a semicircular apse. Externally these early basilicas were plain brick buildings, but the interiors (under Byzantine influence) were usually sumptuous. In the 7th c. they began to have a free-standing bell-tower (campanile). A small circular building served as the baptistery for adult baptism. In the reign of Justinian (527–565) a central rather than a basilican plan came into favour, the prototype for the new style of church being the Hagia Sophia in Constantinople. The main feature of this was the domed central area, with barrel-vaulted wings producing a cruciform plan. Sculpture at first continued ancient pagan traditions (sarcophagi carved with reliefs depicting Christ as a Roman youth or as the Good Shepherd).

From 400 onwards, during the great migrations, various Germanic peoples – Goths, Vandals, Lombards – came down into Italy, but left practically no traces of their passage in Tuscany.

In the 11th c. the Romanesque style, in variant forms in different regions, began to develop out of Early Christian art. At first Rome remained backward, while in Tuscany the various individual cities sought to surpass their rivals. At the beginning of this development in architecture stands the Church of San Frediano in Lucca (1112–47). About 1050 a new type of façade, in inlaid marble, came into favour (San Miniato, Florence; arcading of Pisa and Lucca cathedrals). Pisa Cathedral, with its mighty transept, is the most imposing building of this period. Secular architecture also had considerable achievements to its credit, exemplified for instance by the 13 towers and picturesque town walls of San Gimignano – 13 of the original number of more than 70 survive.

Romanesque sculpture long remained under Byzantine influence. In the 11th c. the casting of bronze doors with relief decoration reached a high standard of perfection (doors by Bonanus in Pisa Cathedral). Among the great masters of sculpture of this period in Tuscany were Guidetto and Guido Begarelli of Como (font in the Baptistery, Pisa). The appearance of Nicola Pisano (1225–78), and his son Giovanni mark the transition from Romanesque to Renaissance sculpture (marble pulpit in the Baptistery, Pisa, 1260; marble pulpit in Siena Cathedral, 1268).

Romanesque painting also shows Byzantine influence (the *maniera greca*). The leading master of the period, who sought towards the end of the 13th c. to break away from the rigidity of tradition and thereby prepared the way for Giotto, was Giovanni Cimabue (mentioned in 1272 and 1301/02; "Madonna Enthroned with Angels", Uffizi, Florence).

While in France Gothic had already passed its peak, Italian art now came fully under its influence. The heritage of antiquity, however, was never entirely forgotten: its monuments were still to be seen, and influences from the East were still finding their way into Europe by way of Italy. But at the same time a new and original artistic force was now beginning to make itself felt in Italy, later to extend its influence over the whole of Europe.

The art of the late medieval period, the Trecento (14th c.) – the *stile gótico* – was brought to Italy mainly by the Mendicant Orders. A distinctive Italian manner soon displaced the Burgundian influence (Santa Croce in Florence, possibly begun by Arnolfo di Cambio in 1295; still without a vaulted roof). But the extreme dissolution of the walls by large areas of window was contrary to Italian taste; instead the horizontals were stressed, as in Romanesque, and the façades of the cathedrals covered with decorative elements. The cathedrals erected at the expense of individual towns became increasingly sumptuous as each city sought to outdo its rivals (Siena, Florence). The Cathedral of Santa Maria del Fiore in Florence, an aisled church with a triple-apsed choir, probably begun by Arnolfo di Cambio in 1296 and later provided with its dome by Brunelleschi, is the most impressive of these cathedrals, exceeded in size and scale in Italy only by Milan Cathedral. The secular architecture of the Gothic period continued the tradition of Romanesque in severely disciplined forms; massive Gothic town halls were built (Palazzo Vecchio, Florence; Palazzo Púbblico, Siena), and the houses of patrician families became increasingly comfortable and luxurious.

Gothic sculpture established itself only towards the end of the 13th c.; its greatest master was Giovanni Pisano, son of Nicola (pulpits in Sant'Andrea, Pistoia, and Pisa Cathedral). Andrea Pisano developed still further Giovanni's rhythmically flowing style (earliest of the three bronze doors of the Baptistery in Florence). His contemporary Andrea di Cione, known as Orcagna (d. about 1368 in Florence), was a painter and architect as well as a sculptor (tabernacle in Orsanmichele, Florence, 1348–59).

In Gothic painting the artistic personality of Giotto di Bondone (c. 1266–1337) marks a great step forward. Although looking back to Cimabue and Duccio di Buoninsegna ("Maestà", a Madonna enthroned with Angels, 1308–11; now in the Cathedral Museum, Siena), in whom reminiscences of the maniera greca can still be detected, Giotto took the decisive step towards the foundation of all modern painting. The ability to represent spiritual events was now achieved in painting, as it already had been in sculpture, and, freed from the compulsions of Byzantine iconography, Giotto was able to give his Biblical scenes a new form and new meaning. His finest work in Tuscany is the frescoes in the two choir chapels in Santa Croce in Florence, now unfortunately damaged. In Florence the school of Giotto continued to flourish throughout the whole of the 14th c. (frescoes in Santa Croce, Santa Maria Novella and the Cappella degli Spágnoli by Andrea da Firenze).

The French word Renaissance (Italian Rinascimento) means rebirth (of the spirit of antiquity). Whereas the Middle Ages had seen the profound meaning of life in the conquest of things terrestrial and the preparation for the life beyond, man now began, in this rebirth of the attitudes of antiquity, to discover himself and the world as independent values and to seek his role in this world rather than the next. The metaphysically directed Gothic orientation to the life beyond could no longer satisfy him. The new conception of the beauty of the world, the joy of living and the freedom of man's spirit called for new forms of expression.

The builders and architects of the Quattrocento (15th c.) were the first to introduce the new style. Filippo Brunelleschi (1377–1446) ranks as the pioneer of the Early Renaissance. Using the new technological resources now available, he built the dome of Florence Cathedral, the churches of San Lorenzo and Santo Spírito and the Pazzi Chapel (all in Florence). In sculpture the debt owed by the new age to classical antiquity is particularly evident. The repertoire was now extended to include secular themes, and new subjects were supplied by mythology and contemporary history. The study of anatomy enabled artists to achieve a new way of representing the human body; and portrait sculpture became popular, presenting realistic likenesses of the sitters. The symbolism of medieval times gave place to representational treatment. Lorenzo Ghiberti (1378–1455), painter and sculptor, was responsible for the second and the famous third bronze door (the Porta del Paradiso) of the Baptistery in Florence, and among his other major works were the reliefs on the font of San Giovanni in Siena and some of the bronze figures on Orsanmichele in Florence. Donatello (Donato de' Bardi, 1386–1466), a pupil of Ghiberti's, ranks as the leading master of the Early Renaissance. He worked both in marble (sculpture for Florence Cathedral) and in bronze ("David", c. 1430; Bargello, Florence); other major works included "Judith and Holofernes" (Palazzo Vecchio in Florence), one of the earliest free-standing

Filippo Lippi: Madonna with Christchild

Piero della Francesca: Duke of Urbino

Sandro Botticelli: Birth of Venus

sculptured groups in modern times, and "St George" (in the Palazzo del Bargellow, Florence).

Andrea del Verrocchio (1436–88) worked mainly for the Médici ("David", 1465; bronze group, "Christ and St Thomas", for Orsanmichele in Florence).

Luca della Robbia (1399–1482) is the third of the great masters of the Early Renaissance in Florence. He applied the techniques of faience to large works of sculpture and created numerous majolica figures (Madonnas).

The painting of the Early Renaissance begins with the work of an artist who died young, Masaccio (Tommaso di Giovanni di Simone Guidi, 1401–28), who painted part of the frescoes in the Brancacci Chapel of Santa Maria del Cármine and the panel-painting "St Anne with the Virgin and Child" now in the Uffizi.

Fra Angélico (Fra Giovanni da Fiésole, 1387–1455) created works of an exclusively religious character, filled with profound piety and peopled by sublime figures of Angels (frescoes and paintings in San Marco, Florence).

Piero della Francesca (c. 1420–92) was the great master and teacher of perspective in the Quattrocento. Among his principal works are the portrait of Federigo da Montefeltre (Uffizi, Florence), the "Resurrection" (Sansepulcro Gallery, Urbino) and the "Adoration of the Child" (National Gallery, London) and frescoes in the choir of San Francesco, Arezzo.

The Florentine Sandro Botticelli (1444–1510) was active during the most brilliant period of the Médici. His gentle, pensive figures of youths and maidens are imbued with a dreamy melancholy, and even his scenes from pagan mythology seem to have a note of sorrow ("Spring" and "Birth of Venus", both in the Uffizi).

Fra Filippo Lippi (1406–69), a Carmelite friar working in Florence, transfigures Biblical scenes by giving them a secular and earthly beauty. His paintings are imbued with fresh and profound feeling and love of nature ("Coronation of the Virgin" in the Uffizi, "Annunciation" in San Lorenzo, Florence).

The High Renaissance occupies the first half of the Cinquecento (16th c.). Its leading master was Michelángelo Buonarroti (1475–1564), a universal genius and one of the greatest artistic personalities of a period rich in genius. A pupil of Ghirlandaio, he was active as an architect, a painter and a sculptor and also gained some reputation as a poet with his sonnets. Among the works he created in Florence are "David" (Gallería dell'Accadémia), his sculpture and the architecture for the Médici Chapel in San Lorenzo (Sagrestia Nuova) and the staircase hall of the Biblioteca Laurenziana. With his harmony and power – the keynotes of his work – he pointed the way beyond the High Renaissance to Baroque.

The second universal genius of the High Renaissance was Leonardo da Vinci (1452–1519), sculptor, architect, painter, scientist and constructor. Working at the Sforza Court in Milan, in Florence, in Rome and finally for Francis I of France, he displayed the universal man of the Renaissance at its richest and fullest. In Leonardo art and science merge into one, and his achievements in the field of natural science alone would entitle him to a leading place in the history of the human mind. Among his principal works are the "Virgin of the Rocks", "Madonna and Child with St Anne" and the "Gioconda" or "Mona Lisa", all in the Louvre, and the "Last Supper", a (badly damaged) wall-painting in the refectory of the Monastery of Santa Maria delle Grazie in Milan. Leonardo's drawings and studies in a great variety of fields afford a unique insight into the working of his mind.

The style known as Mannerism created in the early 16th c. delighted in the strange and unusual, in allegory and metaphor, in a distortion of its subject-matter which culminated in the grotesque. Leading representatives of this trend were the painter Parmigianino (Francesco Mazzola, 1503–40), Giuseppe Arcimboldo (1527–93), who became Court Painter to Rudolf II in Prague, and Giovanni da Bologna or Giambologna (1529–1608), the finest sculptor of the Late Mannerist period. This school claimed some of its most astonishing achievements in the field of landscape-gardening, in an extraordinary synthesis of nature, architecture and violently expressive sculpture in the antique style.

The Baroque period brought an architectural innovation in the design of churches. The basilican type now increasingly gave place to churches on a central plan topped by a dome.

Baroque

In the Settecento (18th c.) Venetian painting became predominant in Italy. The leading masters of the Rococo period were Tiépolo, Giovanni Battista Piazzetta (1682–1754) and the two Canalettos, Antonio Canale (1697–1768) and Bernardo Bellotto (1720–80).

Rococo

In the Ottocento (19th c.) Italian architecture looked backward to its great past, in variant forms of the school known as Historicism. It was only with the emergence of the group of architects who called themselves Group 7 in the year 1927 that Italian architecture broke away from its eclectic rigidity.

19th and 20th c.

The painting of the 19th c. was of exclusively local importance. Only Giovanni Segantini (1858–99) attained international reputation as a neo-Impressionist and Symbolist. The graphic artist Alberto Martini (1876–1954) also deserves mention.

At the beginning of the Novecento (20th c.) the advent of Futurism, proclaimed in 1909, marked a break with tradition. Among representatives of this school are Carlo Carrà (1881–1966), Umberto Boccioni (1882–1916), Gino Severini (1883–1966) and Luigi Rússolo (1885–1947).

Art now became increasingly international, leaving little room for regional schools. The modern school now emerging was strongly influenced by contemporary French painting. Amedeo Modigliani (1884–1920), a native of Livorno, worked mainly in Paris, where he came under the influence of Cézanne and the Cubists.

After the Second World War architectural activity was mainly concentrated in the industrial field, and industrial design rapidly increased in importance and in international recognition. Pier Luigi Nervi (1891–1979), the leading representative of the rationalist school of architecture, had a formative influence on a whole generation of architects.

After Canova Italian sculpture produced no artists of real significance until our own day, when there arose two great artistic personalities, Marino Marini (1901–80), famous for his equestrian works, and Giácomo Manzù (b. 1908), who among other work has revived an earlier form of sculpture, the bronze door with relief decoration.

After 1945 abstract painting and sculpture flourished in Italy as in other Western countries in all its varied manifestations (Taohiom, Conotruotiviom, otc.).

Note

Italian art did not acquire distinctive national characteristics until the Age of Dante, the late 13th c. This and subsequent centuries are referred to by the following terms:

Duecento	=13th century
Trecento	=14th century
Quattrocento	=15th century
Cinquecento	=16th century
Seicento	=17th century
Settecento	=18th century
Ottocento	=19th century
Novecento	=20th century

Quotations

"The City of Pisa is as much worth seeing as any in Italy; it has contended with Rome, Florence, Sardinia, Sicily, and even Carthage. The Palace and Church of St. Stephano (where the order of knighthood called by that name was instituted) drew first our curiosity, the outside thereof being altogether of polish'd marble; within it is full of tables relating to this order; over which hang divers banners and pendants, with other trophies taken by them from the Turkes, against whom they are particularly oblig'd to fight; tho' a religious order they are permitted to marry. At the front of the Palace stands a fountaine, and the statue of the greate Duke Cosmo. The Campanile, or Settezonio, built by John Venipont, a German, consists of several orders of pillars, 30 in a row, design'd to be much higher. It stands alone on the right side of the Cathedrall, strangely remarkable for this, that the beholder would expect it to fall, being built exceedingly declining, by a rare addresse of the architect; and how it is supported from falling I think would puzzle a good geometrician. The Domo, or Cathedrall, standing neere it, is a superb structure, beautified with 6 columns of greate antiquity; the gates are of brasse, of admirable workmanship. The Cemetere cal'd Campo Santo is made of divers gally ladings of earth formerly brought from Jerusalem, said to be of such a nature as to consume dead bodies in fourty houres. 'Tis cloistred with marble arches. . . . Neere this, and in the same field, is the Baptistery of San Giovanni, built of pure white marble and cover'd with so artificial a cupola that the voice uttered under it seemes to breake out of a cloud."

John Evelyn
"Diary"
1644

"To the shop of the brothers Pisani, sculptors, where for half an hour I was foolish enough to wish myself rich, that I might have bought Niobe, the gladiator, Diana, Venus, and some other casts from the antique statues. I threw away a few *pauls* instead of three or four hundred *zechins*. Before I quit Florence I must observe that besides the buildings and various objects I have mentioned there are at least a thousand more which I have not seen at all; – the famous bridge Ponta della Santa Trinita deserves, however, a word: it is the origin of that at Neuillé and so many others in France, but much more beautiful; being indeed the first in the world. The circumstance that strikes one at Florence is the antiquity of the principal buildings; everything one sees considerable is of three or four hundred years' standing; of new buildings there are next to none; all here remind one of the Medicis: there is hardly a street that has not some monument, some decoration, that bears the stamp of that splendid and magnificent family. How commerce could enrich it sufficiently to leave such prodigious remains is a question not a little curious; for I may venture, without apprehension, to assert that all the collected magnificence of the House of Bourbon governing for eight hundred years twenty millions of people is trivial when compared with what the Medicis family have left for the admiration of succeeding ages – sovereigns only of the little mountainous region of Tuscany, and with not more than one million of subjects."

Arthur Young
"Travels in France and Italy"
1792

Quotations

Joseph Forsyth
"Remarks on Antiquities,
Arts, and Letters during an
Excursion in Italy"
1802

"It would be ungrateful to leave the environs of Florence without mentioning the pleasure which I once enjoyed 'at evening from the top of Fesolé.' The weather was then Elysian, the spring in its most beautiful point, and all the world, just released from the privations of Lent, were fresh in their festivity. I sat down on the brow of the hill, and measured with my enraptured eye half the Val d'Arno. Palaces, villas, convents, towns, and farms were seated on the hills, or diffused through the vale, in the very points and combinations where a Claude would have placed them. . . .

"Fiesole stands on a hill precipitously steep. The front of it is cut into a graduation of narrow terraces, which are enclosed in a trellis of vines, and faced with loose-stone walls. Such a facing may perhaps cost less labour, and add more warmth to the plantation than turf-embankments would do; but it gives a hard, dry effect to the immediate picture, which, viewed from Florence, is the most beautiful object in this region of beauty. . . .

"Cortona, rising amidst its vineyards, on the acclivity of a steep hill with black mountains behind, struck me at a distance like a picture hung upon a wall. From Santa Marguerita it commands a magnificent prospect of the Thrasimene and Clusian lakes, the mountains of Radicofani and Santa Fiora, the wide, variegated vale of Chiana, skirted with vine-covered hills, and beautifully strewed with white cottages, white fattorias, white villas, and convents of sober grey.

"This is a favourite seat of 'Bacco in Toscana'; for good table-wine costs here but a penny the large flask. . . .

"Cortona, being considered as the capital of ancient Etruria, is the seat of the Etruscan academy, and of course swarms with antiquaries. In the museum is a portrait of the late Lord Cowper, as *Lucumone* of that academy. . . ."

Percy Bysshe Shelley
Letter
1818

"As we approached Florence, the country became cultivated to a very high degree, the plain was filled with the most beautiful villas, and, as far as the eye could reach, the mountains were covered with them; for the plains are bounded on all sides by blue and misty mountains. The vines are here trailed on low trellisses of reeds interwoven into crosses to support them, and the grapes, now almost ripe, are exceedingly abundant. You everywhere meet those teams of beautiful white oxen, which are now labouring the little vine-divided fields with their Virgilian ploughs and carts. Florence itself, that is the Lung' Arno (for I have seen no more), I think is the most beautiful city I have yet seen. It is surrounded with cultivated hills, and from the bridge which crosses the broad channel of the Arno, the view is the most animated and elegant I ever saw. You see three or four bridges, one apparently supported by Corinthian pillars, and the white sails of the boats, relieved by the deep green of the forest, which comes to the water's edge, and the sloping hills covered with bright villas on every side. Domes and steeples rise on all sides, and the cleanliness is remarkably great. On the other side there are the foldings of the Vale of Arno above; first the hills of olive and vine, then the chestnut woods, and then the blue and misty pine forests, which invest the aerial Apennines, that fade in the distance. I have seldom seen a city so lovely at first sight as Florence."

Thomas Medwin
"Conversations of Lord
Byron"

"On the occasion of Shelley's melancholy fate I revisited Pisa, and on the day of my arrival learnt that Lord Byron was gone to the sea-shore, to assist in performing the last offices to his friend. We came to a spot marked by an old and withered trunk of a fir-tree, and near it, on the beach, stood a solitary hut covered with reeds. The situation was well calculated for a poet's grave. A few weeks before I had ridden with him and Lord Byron to this very spot, which I afterwards visited more than once. In front was a magnificent extent of the blue and windless Mediterranean, with the Isles of Elba and Gorgona, – Lord Byron's yacht at anchor in the offing: on the other side an almost boundless extent of sandy wilderness, uncultivated and uninhabited, here and there interspersed in tufts with underwood curved by the sea-breeze, and stunted by the barren and dry nature of the soil in which it grew. At equal distances along the coast stood high square towers, for the double purpose of guarding the coast from smuggling, and enforcing the quarantine laws. This view was bounded by an immense extent of the Italian Alps, which are here particularly picturesque from their volcanic and manifold appearances, and which being composed of white marble, give their summits the resemblance of snow. As a foreground to this picture appeared as extraordinary a group. Lord Byron and Trelawny were seen standing over the burning pile, with some of the soldiers of the guard; and Leigh Hunt, whose feelings and nerves could not carry him through the scene of horror, lying back in the carriage, – the four post-horses ready to drop with the intensity of the noonday sun. The stillness of all around was yet more felt by the shrill scream of a solitary curlew, which, perhaps attracted by the body, wheeled in such narrow circles round the pile that it might have been struck with the hand, and was so fearless that it could not be driven away.''

(An account of Shelley's cremation on 4 July 1822)

''From Sarteano to Chianciano it is a drive of seven miles amid glorious scenery. This range of heights, indeed the whole district of Chiusi, is prodigal in charms – an earthly paradise. There are so many features of beauty, that those which are wanting are not missed. Here are hill and vale, rock and wood, towns and castles on picturesque heights, broad islet-studded lakes, and ranges of Alpine snow and sublimity; and if the ocean be wanting, it has no unapt substitute in the vast vale or plain of Chiana – a sea of fertility and luxuriance; while all is warmed and enriched by the glowing sun of Italy, and canopied by a vault of that heavenly blue, that Dolce color d'oriental zaffiro, which reflects beauty on everything beneath it. It is the sort of scenery which wins rather than imposes, whose grandeur lies in its totality, not in particular features, where sublimity takes you not by storm, but retires into an element of the beautiful. . . .

''Chianciano is only four miles from Montepulciano. The road skirts the brow of the hills, which are covered with oak-woods; about half-way it crosses the Acqua Bolgia, a sulphureous and ferruginous spring; and, on the approach to Montepulciano, passes a bare, conical hill, called Poggio Tutoni, or Tutona – a name, which from its affinity to the Tutni or Tutna, often found in Etruscan inscriptions in this district, appears to be very ancient.

''Montepulciano is a city of some three thousand inhabitants, girt by walls of the middle ages, and cresting a lofty height at the northern extremity of this range of hills. It is built on so steep a slope, that it would seem the architects of the Cathedral had leagued with the priests to impose a perpetual penance on the inhabitants by placing it at the summit of the town. The most

George Dennis
''Cities and Cemeteries of Etruria''
1848

37

interesting building is the church of San Biagio, without the walls, a modern edifice after the designs of Sangallo, which owes its existence to a miracle of a Madonna, who is recorded to have winked 'her most holy eyes' at two washerwomen, in so fascinating a manner as to bring even a herd of cattle to their knees before her image."

Maurice Hewlett
"The Road in Tuscany"
1906

"The Grand Duchy of Tuscany, speaking roughly, makes an equilateral triangle, whose base shall be the Maremma, running as the Mediterranean lies, from north to south. The angles of the base are the Magra bridge, which we have crossed, and the Orbetello isthmus, which we are to visit. The apex is La Verna, above the Casentino. Bisecting the base, more or less exactly, you have the Val d'Arno, which (with the Val di Chiana) is the only considerable plain in the country. Florence, though it is not the true, is the political middle, since it commands both road and waterway alike. A captain could hardly take his host from Milan to Rome without coming to terms with the Florentines; nor could the Aretines reach Genoa. If for no other reason, Florence was bound to get supremacy. So here you have the state of the case. Florence and the best land are in the midst; north and east of her are the Apennines – better outposts could not be. West of her are the sea and a strip of barren, inhospitable, salt-scourged coast. South of her are ridges of limestone hills, parallel as racing waves, with close valleys between them, and in every valley a grey-green languid river. But where Arno runs from east to west, and shapes the plain to her mood, these limestone hills run south to north and the rivers march with them. Among these town-crested waves of rock our course is to be. On every ridge, on every spur or fault of a ridge, you will have a town. All the massed nations of Tuscany were to be found once above the vale of Arno, or upon these southern hills. There were none worth consideration in the Apennines: the Etruscans, when they left the south for the north, kept by the sea. And there are none there now; but for a different reason. The plain has sucked in all."

D. H. Lawrence
"Etruscan Places"
1932

"But more interesting even than the symbolic scenes (on Etruscan ash-chests) are those scenes from actual life, such as boar-hunts, circus-games, processions, departures in covered wagons, ships sailing away, city gates being stormed, sacrifice being performed, girls with open scrolls, as if reading at school; many banquets with man and woman on the banqueting couch, and slaves playing music, and children around; then so many really tender farewell scenes, the dead saying good-bye to his wife, as he goes on the journey, or as the chariot bears him off, or the horse waits; then the soul alone, with the death-dealing spirits standing by with their hammers that gave the blow. It is as Dennis says, the breeze of Nature stirs one's soul. I asked the gentle old man if he knew anything about the urns. But no! no! He knew nothing at all. He had only just come. He counted for nothing. So he protested. He was one of those gentle, shy Italians too diffident even to look at the chests he was guarding. But when I told him what I thought some of the scenes meant he was fascinated like a child, full of wonder, almost breathless. And I thought again, how much more Etruscan than Roman the Italian of today is: sensitive, diffident, craving really for symbols and mysteries, able to be delighted with true delight over small things, violent in spasms, and altogether without sternness or natural will-to-power."

Suggested Itineraries

In the following suggested itineraries places which have a separate entry in the "A to Z" section of this Guide are shown in **bold** type.

The itineraries take in all the principal sights in Tuscany; but some of the places described in this Guide lie off the main routes and will involve detours of greater or lesser length. The map accompanying the Guide will facilitate the detailed planning of such trips.

All the places described, whether they are the subject of a separate entry or not, are included in the Index on p. 247.

Carrara to Pisa and Florence

From **Carrara** the Via Aurelia runs alongside the foothills of the Apennines to the provincial capital, **Massa**, and continues through the Versilia to its chief town, **Pietrasanta**.

The route then continues across the coastal plain to **Viareggio**, the principal Tuscan seaside resort, with a long sandy beach. A few miles beyond this is Torre del Lago Puccini, on the Lago di Massaciúccoli. Then through the beautiful Migliarino pine woods and across the Serchio to **Pisa**, Tuscany's greatest tourist attraction after Florence.

From Pisa take SS 67, which runs east, passing below the episcopal city of **San Miniato**, to the industrial town of **Émpoli**; then north-west to **Lucca**.

From Lucca turn east again on a road which crosses the plain and then skirts the Apennine foothills to **Pescia** and the celebrated spa of **Montecatini Terme**.

Beyond Montecatini the route continues east through the fertile and densely populated Florence Basin, passes through **Pistoia** and **Prato** and comes to **Florence**, chief town of its province and capital of the region of Tuscany.

Pisa to Ansedonia by the coast road

From **Pisa** (leaving the town on the south-west) take the Via Aurelia, which, coming from Viareggio, runs south over the coastal plain, traversed by numerous canals, to the important port town of **Livorno** and continues to San Pietro in Palazzi, where a side road branches off.

Main route

From San Pietro in Palazzi take SS 68, which follows the River Cécina upstream, passing through a district rich in minerals, and then turns away from the river and traverses hilly country to **Volterra**.

Detour

From Volterra continue east on SS 68; turn left into a side road for **San Gimignano**; return to SS 68, and via **Colle di Val d'Elsa** to Poggibonsi, linking up with the itinerary from Florence to Siena (see below).

The Via Aurelia crosses the Cécina, passes through the town of that name and continues through the **Maremma**, running at

Main route

some distance from the sea for most of the way. It then crosses the foothills, extending down to the sea, of the ore-rich Colline Metallifere to Venturina, where a road goes off on the right to the industrial and port town of **Piombino**, just to the north of which is the Etruscan site of **Populonia**. Then south to Follónica, where the Via Aurelia turns inland, and from here either on the Via Aurelia (detour from Grilli to Etruscan **Vetulonia**) or on the coast road via the seaside resort of **Castiglione della Pescaia** to **Grosseto**, provincial capital and chief town of the Maremma. North-east of Grosseto is the Etruscan site of Rusellae (Roselle).

Just beyond Grosseto the Via Aurelia crosses the River Ombrone. It then skirts the eastern slopes of the wooded Monti dell'Uccellina (nature reserve), with views of Monte Argentario to the south.

After crossing the River Albegna a rewarding detour can be made to the picturesquely situated little town of **Pitigliano**.

A few miles south a side road branches off on the right to **Orbetello**, situated in the midst of its lagoon, and the promontory of **Monte Argentario**.

The main road continues south, passing on the right the hill occupied by the commandingly situated Roman settlement of Cosa, near the little township of **Ansedonia**, and a few miles farther on enters Latium.

Florence to Siena and Monte Amiata

Main route

Leave **Florence** on the Via Cassia (SS 2), which runs south past the spa of Terme di Firenze and comes to Poggibonsi (junction with excursion described above, p. 39; also rewarding detours to **San Gimignano** and **Certaldo**); then past the walled hilltop town of Monteriggioni to **Siena**, one of Italy's great art cities.

Leaving Siena by the Porta Romana, continue south to **Buonconvento** (road on left to the **Abbazía di Monte Oliveto Maggiore**). Beyond this, at Torrenieri, a road goes off on the right to the little episcopal city of **Montalcino**, magnificently situated on its hill.

From **San Quírico d'Orcia** a detour of some length can be made to Chiusi.

Detour

SS 146 runs east from San Quírico d'Orcia along a ridge commanding extensive views to the episcopal city of **Pienza**, situated high above the Orcia Valley, and then continues along the ridge to **Montepulciano**. Then on to the well-known spa of **Chianciano Terma** and the ancient Etruscan town of **Chiusi**.

Main route

Beyond San Quírico d'Orcia the Via Cassia leads down into the Orcia Valley, with views, half left, of Pienza and Montepulciano. Some miles farther on **Monte Amiata** can be seen to the right, with the ancient little town of **Abbadia San Salvatore** situated amid chestnut forests on its eastern slopes.

Florence to Arezzo and Cortona

From **Florence** SS 69 runs south-east through the Valdarno, passes through Incisa and comes to **San Giovanni Valdarno**.

Beyond Montevarchi the road climbs slightly and then descends into the wide basin in which **Arezzo** lies.
Then along the east side of the **Valdichiana** and via **Castelfiorentino** and Camucia to **Cortona**.

Volterra to Grosseto

From **Volterra** take the Cécina road to Saline di Volterra; then on a secondary road running south through the Colline Metallífere via Pomarance (some miles beyond this, branch on left to the geothermal power station of Larderello) to **Massa Maríttima**.
Beyond Massa Maríttima the road crosses the River Pécora and continues over the wide plain at its mouth to Follónica, on the Tyrrhenian coast, from which a road runs south via the seaside resort of **Castiglione della Pescaia** to **Grosseto**.

Sights from A to Z

Within each entry the various features of interest are, so far as possible, arranged in a convenient order for sightseeing.

Abbadia San Salvatore   D 3

Province: Siena (SI)
Altitude: 812 m (2664 ft)
Population: 8500

The ancient little town of Abbadia San Salvatore, popular both with summer visitors and winter sports enthusiasts, lies some 60 km (40 miles) south-east of Siena on the eastern slopes of Monte Amiata (see entry).

Situation

Abbey

The Abbadia di San Salvatore (Abbey of the Saviour), which has given its name to the town, is one of the oldest religious houses in Tuscany and was in its day one of the wealthiest and most celebrated in Italy. Of the abbey founded in 743 by the Lombard chieftain Rachis and occupied successively by Benedictines, Camaldolese (Camáldoli – see entry) and Cistercians there survives only the church (originally 11th c.). It has a notable façade with two towers (the right-hand one unfinished), but has been much rebuilt and restored, not always entirely to good effect.

The most impressive feature is the Crypt, which was given its present form in 1036 but was probably the original pre-Romanesque church. It was originally divided into 13 aisles. The groined vaulting is borne on columns of varied form, many of them with richly decorated capitals.

*Crypt

Old Town

The centre of the little town has preserved its medieval character. A notable feature is the borgo (walled village), originally held by the Counts of Santa Fiora, which passed into the hands of Siena in 1347 and later into the possession of the Médici family.

Abbazía di Monte Oliveto Maggiore   C 3

Province: Siena (SI)
Altitude: 273 m (896 ft)

◄ *Splendours of Tuscany: Cathedral and Leaning Tower of Pisa*

Abbey of Monte Oliveto Maggiore

Situation

The Abbazía di Monte Oliveto Maggiore, seat of the Abbot-General of the Olivetans, an independent branch of the Benedictine Order, lies some 30 km (20 miles) south-east of Siena, off the road from Asciano to Buonconvento. To the north extends the lunar landscape of the Crete (see entry).

History

The abbey was founded by a teacher of law, Bernardo Tolomei, who withdrew to this remote site with two friends in 1313 to lead an ascetic life in accordance with a strict interpretation of the Rule of St Benedict, on the principle of "ora et labora" ("pray and work"). In 1319 the monks received episcopal approval and in 1344 Papal authority for the establishment of their Order. The abbey soon developed into a flourishing community, was several times enlarged and became a centre of spiritual and cultural life.

*Abbey

The abbey precincts are entered through a fortress-like gate tower built from 1393 onwards, with notable terracotta reliefs of the school of Luca della Robbia. The conventual buildings, in brick, were erected in stages between 1387 and 1514, with some later restoration. The imposing church (early 15th c.; remodelled in Baroque style) has beautiful choir-stalls.

**Frescoes

On all four sides of the great cloister are frescoes of outstanding quality. The cycle consists of 35 scenes from the life of St

Benedict of Nursia (*c.* 480–547), founder of the Benedictine Order; nine of the paintings (1479 onwards) are by Luca Signorelli, the others (1505 onwards) by Sodoma. On request a monk will explain the various scenes and the legends on which they are based.
Other features of interest in the abbey are the library, the pharmacy and the chapter-house. These rooms can be seen only in the company of a monk.

Buonconvento   C3

The little town of Buonconvento was established in the 14th c. on the site of the Roman Fort of Percanna on the Via Cassia, and is surrounded by 14th c. walls of Sienese type. It has a fine 15th c. parish church (Santi Pietro e Paolo), containing some good paintings, and an excellent picture gallery with works of the medieval Tuscan schools. The Emperor Henry VII died in the town in 1313.

Situation
9 km (6 miles) SW

Abbazía di San Galgano   C3

Province: Siena (SI)
Altitude: 301 m (988 ft)

The Abbey of San Galgano lies some 35 km (22 miles) south-west of Siena, off the road to Massa Maríttima.

Situation

San Galgano, in the hilly country at the foot of Monte Siepi, is the only religious house built by the Cistercians in Tuscany. The abbey was founded in 1218, and the building of the church began six years later. It became wealthy and influential, but the 16th c. saw the beginning of its decline, soon followed by structural decay. The roof of the church fell in towards the end of the 18th c.

General

** Abbey

The church, 69 m (226 ft) long, is a classic example of the austere Cistercian style which originated in France but never achieved full acceptance in Italy. On a Latin cross plan, with aisles, it is built partly in travertine and partly in brick. The older part of the nave has four storeys, the later part only three.
Even in its ruined state the church is still of powerful effect.
Of the conventual buildings there survive the chapter-house, refectory and part of the cloister.

San Galgano sul Monte Siepi

On nearby Monte Siepi (338 m – 1109 ft) is the little round domed Church of San Galgano sul Monte Siepi. It marks the spot on which a hermit named Galgano Guidotti is said to have died in the 12th c. The church contains notable frescoes by Ambrogio Lorenzetti.

Abbazía di Sant'Ántimo   C 3

Province: Siena (SI)
Altitude: 318 m (1043 ft)

Situation

The Abbey of Sant'Ántimo, a Benedictine foundation, lies
some 40 km (25 miles) south of Siena, from which it is reached
on SS 2 (to just south of Buonconvento) and then via
Montalcino (see entry).

**Abbey

The Abbey, which may have been founded by Charlemagne
and first appears in the records in 813, stood at the foot of a hill
covered with dense vegetation. Through various grants of land
it grew enormously wealthy, but it began to decline in the 14th
c. and was formally dissolved in 1462.
Only the church now survives. It dates from the 12th and 13th
c. and shows the uncluttered forms of Romanesque architecture. Built in travertine, it has no transept. The nave, 42 m (138
ft) long, is flanked by aisles which lead into an ambulatory with
radial chapels reminiscent of French models. On the north side
is a squat campanile, on the south side a chapel dating from the
Carolingian period. A notable feature is the richly decorated
doorway, set in the otherwise plain façade. The nave is divided
from the aisles, above which are galleries, by columns and piers
(alternately two columns and one pier). The capitals are richly

Monastic church of Sant' Antimo

Ansedonia: Etruscan cut (drainage channel)

carved with Romanesque ornament, plant and animal motifs alternating with chequer-board and interlace patterns. Note particularly Daniel in the lions' den on the second column on the right. The three-aisled crypt probably dates from the 11th c.

Ansedonia   D 3

Province: Grosseto (GR)
Altitude: 0–44 m (0–144 ft)

Ansedonia lies at the south end of the coast of Tuscany, opposite the Monte Argentario Peninsula (see entry) and some 40 km (25 miles) south of Grosseto.

Situation

The modern town

The attractive little settlement of Ansedonia with its numerous villas extends from the sea up into the coastal hills. Above it, at a height of 113 m (371 ft), are the remains of ancient Cosa.

Cosa

The Roman town of Cosa was founded in 273 B.C., on the site of an earlier settlement which was probably the port of the Etruscan city of Vulci (see below). The remains, still visible above the ground, were long thought to be Etruscan, but excavations by American archaeologists (1948 onwards) have shown that the town was a Roman foundation, designed for defence against the Etruscans.

The most impressive feature of the site is the 1·5 km (1 mile) long circuit of walls, reinforced by 18 towers, some of which are still standing (including the Porta Romana, through which the site is entered). Within the town can be seen the remains of the forum with a basilica, two temples and the walled acropolis with the capitol. There is also a small museum.

From the site a road runs down past the massive Torre San Biagio, built by the Saracens, to the so-called Tagliata Etrusca (Etruscan cut), a drainage channel cut through the tufa. The name is misleading, for the channel was cut by the Romans (though the Romans did in fact gain their knowledge of hydraulic engineering from the Etruscans). The channel was designed not only to prevent the silting-up of the ancient harbour but also to drain the low-lying hinterland and preserve the little Lago di Burano, to the south-east, from degenerating into marshland. Today, fully 2000 years after its construction, the Tagliata Etrusca still fulfils its function.

On the water's edge is a large cavity in the rock known as the Spacco of Bagno della Regina (Queen's Bath). Popularly supposed to be a rock sanctuary, it is in fact part of the drainage works.

Tarquinia   D 3

The town of Tarquinia, lying near the coast, is not in Tuscany but in Latium (province of Viterbo). It is described here on account of its important Etruscan cemetery and its museum.

Situation
45 km (28 miles) SE

In the town's main square is the Gothic Palazzo Vitelleschi (1436–39), a magnificent palace which now houses the Museo Nazionale Tarquiniense with its important collection of Etruscan material of the 4th–2nd c. B.C. (sarcophagi, vases, jewellery, glass, ivory-carvings, coins, remains of large decorative reliefs, etc.; also 15th and 16th c. paintings).

Cemetery

Around the site of the ancient city, particularly on the hill of Monterozzi (157 m – 515 ft) to the south, extends the cemetery area, discovered in 1823, one of the best preserved of Etruscan necropolises. A visit to the tombs takes between two and five hours according to programme (information and guides from the museum). The rock-cut tomb chambers with their wall-paintings give an impressive insight into the culture, religion and art of the Etruscans.

Vulci   D3

Situation
35 km (22 miles) E

The old Etruscan city of Vulci, although outside Tuscany in the province of Viterbo, is included here because of its historical importance in ancient Etruria.
Thousands of vases and bronzes were recovered by excavation in the cemeteries of Vulci in 1828 and following years. To the west, beyond the river, are remains of the ancient city, which was destroyed during the Middle Ages.

Arcipélago Toscano (Tuscan Archipelago)   C1–D2/3

Provinces: Livorno (LI) and Grosseto (GR).

Situation

The Arcipélago Toscano consists of seven islands lying off the coast of Tuscany in the Tyrrhenian Sea, which is bounded by the Italian mainland in the east and the French island of Corsica in the west.

General

The islands of the Tuscan Archipelago (in so far as they are open to the public) are becoming increasingly popular with visitors and holiday-makers, attracted by the unspoiled beauty of their hills and coasts. Most of the islands are relatively easy to reach, for example from Piombino or Livorno (see entries). The largest of the islands is Elba (see entry), with an area of 223 sq. km (86 sq. miles). After it, in order to size, come Giglio (see entry) (21·21 sq. km – 8 sq. miles), Capraia (see entry) (19·50 sq. km – 7½ sq. miles), Montecristo (see entry) (10·39 sq. km – 4 sq. miles), Pianosa (see entry) (10·25 sq. km – 4 sq. miles), Giannutri (see entry) (2·62 sq. km – 1 sq. mile) and Gorgona (see entry) (2·23 sq. km – 550 acres).

Arezzo   C3

Province: Arezzo (AR)
Altitude: 296 m (971 ft)
Population: 92,000

Situation

Arezzo, chief town of its province, lies in north-eastern Tuscany near the left bank of the Arno, some 80 km (50 miles) south-

east of Florence. To the south extends the wide basin of the
Valdichiana (see entry).

History

The hills on which the town stands, rising above the fertile
surrounding countryside, were occupied by the Umbrians and
Etruscans. The Roman road from Rome to Florence, the Via
Cassia, ran past the site, and here in 294 was built the military
station of Arretium, which later acquired a forum, a theatre and
public baths. This was the birthplace of Gaius Maecenas (*c.*
70–8 B.C.), a member of an Etruscan noble family who became
a friend of the Emperor Augustus and as the patron of the poets
who frequented his palace (particularly Horace, Propertius and
Virgil) made his name synonymous with a munificent patron of
the arts.

In Etruscan times Arezzo was a noted centre of craft production
(mainly pottery and metalworking). It grew in size and
importance after it became the see of a bishop about the year
270. In 1098 it became a municipal republic governed by
elected consuls, able to assert its independance even against
Florence and Siena. In the Battle of Campaldino in 1289,
however, Arezzo, then a Ghibelline city supporting the Emperor
against the Pope, suffered a defeat at the hands of the
Florentines. It was able to stave off final submission for another
100 years, but in 1384 it finally became subject to the mighty
city-state of Florence. Arezzo was the birthplace of Guido
Mónaco (*c.* 990–1050), who invented musical notation, the
humanist poet Petrarch (Francesco Petrarca. 1304–74), the
painter and architect Giorgio Vasari (1511–74) and the writer
Pietro Aretino (1492–1556).

*Piazza Grande

The Piazza Grande, the most charming square in the old town,
lies to the west of the Fortezza, the castle built by the Médici.
Facing the square is the apse of the Romanesque Church of
Santa Maria, to the right of which are the Renaissance façade
of the Palazzo del Tribunale and the elegant Palazzo della
Fraternità dei Laici. The north side of the square is bounded by
the loggias of the Palazzo delle Logge.

*Santa Maria

The Pieve di Santa Maria (Parish Church of St Mary), known
simply as the Pieve, is the town's oldest surviving church and
its most important Romanesque monument. It was already in
existence in the 12th c., was destroyed and then rebuilt in the
13th c. and was subsequently reconstructed, altered and
restored in the 15th, 16th and 17th c. and in 1863.

The church is the finest example of Pisan Romanesque in
eastern Tuscany. The four-storey façade on the Corso d'Italia,
set in front of an earlier façade in the 13th c. The lowest storey,
relieved by five blind arcades, has three doorways. The dwarf
galleries above this have 12 columns on the second level, 24 on
the third and 32 on the fourth, creating the effect of a tapered
structure. In the topmost storey the columns bear a continuous
architrave in place of the arches on the lower levels. Thus, in
contrast to other comparable churches, the façade does not
reflect the structure of the tall nave with its lower aisles. To the

right of the façade is the 60 m (200 ft) high Romanesque campanile, with five rows of double geminate windows.

In the architrave and lunette of the central doorway are two early 13th c. figures of the Virgin; on the archivolt, in four compartments, are bas-reliefs of the Months. The right-hand doorway has a Baptism of Christ, the left-hand one vine branches. The columns and fine capitals are notable for their variety of form.

The interior is simple and severe. Over the crossing is a timber dome. Below the raised presbytery, the oldest part of the church, is the crypt. The baptistery chapel, to the right, has a beautiful font with three reliefs by Agostino di Giovanni (before 1345) of scenes from the life of John the Baptist.

Palazzo del Tribunale

A flight of steps, narrowing towards the top, leads up to the Palazzo del Tribunale (Law Courts), built in the 17th–18th c.

Palazzo della Fraternità dei Laici

Immediately adjoining the Palazzo del Tribunale is the Palazzo della Fraternità dei Laici, an elegant building erected in the 14th and 15th c. by the lay Fraternity of Santa Maria della Misericordia, a charitable body established by the Dominicans in 1262. The striking façade was begun in Gothic style by Baldino di Cino in 1375, continued in Renaissance style by Bernardo Rossellino in 1433 and completed in 1460. The bell-cote was added by Giorgio Vasari in the 16th c.

Palazzo delle Logge

The Palazzo delle Logge (Palace of the Loggias) closes the north-east side of the Piazza Grande. Built between 1573 and 1581 to the design of Giorgio Vasari, it takes its name from the wide loggias opening on to the square. In front of the palazzo is a reproduction of the Petrone, a pillory in which delinquents were exposed to public infamy.

Palazzo Pretorio

The Palazzo Pretorio (formerly Palazzo Albergotti) stands just north of the Church of Santa Maria. Originally built in 1322, it was much altered in the 17th c. The façade, with two orders of windows, bears numerous coats of arms belonging to *podestà* and *commissari* (Florentine governors) from the 15th c. onwards. From 1404 to 1926 the palazzo also served as a prison; it now houses the municipal library.

Casa del Petrarca (Petrarch's House)

In the same block, in Via dell'Orto, is the Casa del Petrarca, said to be the birthplace of the poet (1304–74). In fact the building dates only from the 17th c. The building, largely destroyed

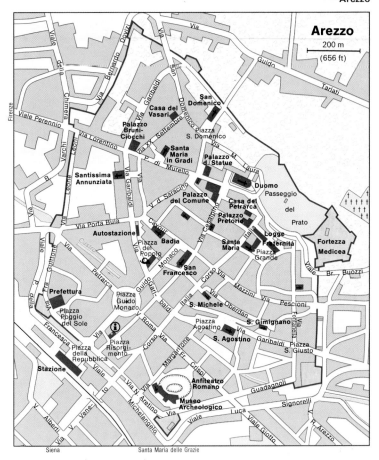

Arezzo
200 m
(656 ft)

Siena · Santa Maria delle Grazie

during the Second World War but rebuilt in 1948, is now the headquarters of the celebrated Accadémia Petrarca di Léttere, Arti e Scienze.

* Cathedral (Duomo)

On the highest point of the hill stands the cathedral, occupying the site of an earlier Benedictine church, San Pietro Maggiore. It was begun in 1277, continued in 1313 and 1510 but not completed until the beginning of the 20th c. The campanile was built in 1857–60, the façade with its three doorways and large rose-window added between 1900 and 1914.

Interior

The interior (aisled, without transept) is in the severe architectural style of the Mendicant Orders (Franciscans, Dominicans). It contains a number of notable works of art.

In the right-hand aisle are stained-glass windows by Guillaume de Marcillat (1477–1529), a Frenchman who worked almost exclusively in Italy: "The Calling of Matthew", "The Woman taken in Adultery", "The Cleansing of the Temple", "The Raising of Lazarus". Here, too, are the Tomb (after 1320) of Pope Gregory X (d. 1276) and the Burial Chapel of Ciuccio Tarlati (1334), with marble ornament and a fresco.

In the presbytery is the high altar, with the Late Gothic tomb and relics of St Donatus, Bishop of Arezzo, martyred in the time of Diocletian. The tomb has marble reliefs of scenes from the Saint's life. The chapel to the left of the presbytery has a stained-glass window by Marcillat ("SS. Lucia and Silvester"); the sacristy has fine frescoes and terracottas. In the left-hand aisle are a fresco, "The Magdalene" by Piero della Francesca (1459), the Tomb of Bishop Guido Tarlati (c. 1330), with 16 fine bas-reliefs, and the organ gallery by Giorgio Vasari (1535). Opening off this aisle are the Chapel of the Madonna del Conforto (18th–19th c.), partly in neo-Gothic and partly in classical style, and the baptistery.

Outside the west doorway of the cathedral is a monument to Grand Duke Ferdinando I de' Médici by Giovanni da Bologna, (1595).

Passeggio del Prato

To the east of the cathedral is the beautiful park known as the Passeggio del Prato, with monument to Petrarch (1928). It extends south-east to the Fortezza (rebuilt in the 16th c. on 13th c. foundations), from which there are extensive views.

Palazzo del Comune

Facing the cathedral, to the west, is the Palazzo del Comune (formerly also known as the Palazzo dei Priori), now the Town Hall. It was built in 1333 as the official residence of the Governor of the municipal guilds. From 1384 it was the seat of the Florentine *commissari*, who adorned the façade lavishly with their coats of arms.

San Doménico

North of the cathedral, in Piazza San Doménico, is the Church of San Doménico, a plain aisleless structure which is one of the most impressive of the 13th c. churches of the Mendicant Orders. It was founded in 1275 by the Tarlati family, and according to Vasari was designed by Nicola Pisano. It is notable for its sober unornamented façade. The bell-cote of the original campanile contains two 14th c. bells.

The church has fine 14th and 15th c. frescoes by Aretine painters ("The Virgin with SS. John, Dominic and Nicholas" by Parri di Spinello; "SS. Philip and James" by Spinello Aretino). On the right-hand side of the nave is a Gothic tabernacle known as the Altare Dragondelli (c. 1350), by Giovanni di Francesco. On the high altar is a "Crucifixion" by Cimabue (between 1260 and 1270).

*Crucifixion

Casa del Vasari

This two-storey house in Via XX Settembre was acquired by the painter and architect Giorgio Vasari (1511–74) in 1540, and between that year and 1548 he decorated it with a series of fine frescoes; the so-called Cámera d'Apollo is particularly notable. The house is now occupied by the Museo e Archivio Vasariano (admission by appointment).

Palazzo Bruni-Ciocchi (Palazzo della Dogana)

The Palazzo Bruni-Ciocchi is an elegant building of the Early Renaissance (c. 1450), thought to have been designed by Bernardo Rossellino.

The palazzo now houses the Galleria e Museo Medioevale e Moderno, which contains works by Margaritone d'Arezzo ("St Francis"), Parri di Spinello ("Angels and Saints"), Bartolomeo della Gatta ("St Roch"), Luca Signorelli ("Adoration"), Andrea della Robbia ("Madonna and Saints") and Rosso Fiorentino ("Madonna"), as well as majolica, sculpture and other works of art of the Middle Ages, the Renaissance and the Baroque period (but, in spite of the name of the gallery, no modern work).

Santa Maria in Gradi

The Church of Santa Maria in Gradi is approached by a flight of steps: hence its name. The present building was erected on the site of an earlier Romanesque church (13th c.) by the Florentine architect and sculptor Bartolommeo Ammannati (1511–92). Notable features are the campanile (1631) and, in the interior, a terracotta group ("Madonna del Soccorso") by Andrea della Robbia, a number of pictures and the crypt of the original church.

Santissima Annunziata

The Church of the Santissima Annunziata (the Virgin Annunciate) occupies the site of an earlier oratory (14th c.). It was designed by the Renaissance architects Bartolomeo della Gata and Antonio da Sangallo.

The façade, which was left unfinished, has three doorways; the right-hand one, together with the fresco depicting the Annunciation by Spinello Aretino (1370) above it, is a relic of the original oratory. The aisled interior is of considerable effect, with elaborately carved capitals on the columns and stained glass by Guillaume de Marcillat.

Chiesa di Badía

A long flight of steps leads up to the Chiesa di Badía (abbey church), originally founded in the 14th c. by Benedictines from Monte Cassino. Its present form is the result of a major reconstruction by Giorgio Vasari in the 16th c.

Arezzo: Via delle Torre Rossa . . .   *. . . and Church of San Francesco*

The church, dedicated to SS. Flora and Lucilla, has lateral aisles separated from the nave by pillars. The nave is roofed by two shallow domes, the second of which has a highly effective architectural painting in *trompe-l'œil* perspective by Andrea Pozzo (1703).

San Francesco

In the centre of the old town is the Church of San Francesco, dedicated to St Francis of Assisi. It was begun in 1290, but various rebuildings and extensions continued down to the present century (campanile *c.* 1600; most recent renovation work 1900–20).

The façade overlooking the square is completely without ornament, articulated only by narrow string-courses projecting from the brickwork. The interior (53 m – 174 ft long, 17 m – 56 ft wide), is aisleless, as is normal in the churches of the Mendicant Orders. The chapels entered from the left-hand side of the church were added in the 15th c. At the far end are one large and two small choir chapels.

Above the doorway is a circular window by Guillaume de Marcillat ("Pope Honorius III approving the Rule of St Francis"). The church is mainly celebrated, however, for its frescoes, brought to light again only at the beginning of the 20th c. To the right are two pictures of Saints by Andrea del Castagno and an "Annunication" by Spinello Aretino; in the lateral chapel on the right (Cappella Guasconi) are pictures of

Saints by Spinello; and in the chapel on the left (Cappella Tarlati) are a "Crucifixion" by Spinello and an "Annunciation" which is believed to be by Luca Signorelli.

The church's principal attraction is the main choir chapel, with frescoes by Piero della Francesca telling the story of the Cross – a theme particularly dear to the Franciscans. Following the account given in the "Golden Legend", Piero – the leading master of the Early Renaissance in Italy – painted this cycle in the 15th c. creating the greatest series of paintings in Arezzo; they rank among the most expressive works in the whole of Italian painting. The solemn figures, aware of the importance of the events in which they are involved and set against a background of landscapes, flowers and stately apartments, in compositions of consummate skill, radiate an air of extra-ordinary sublimity.

*Frescoes

The first scenes depict the death of Adam and the life-giving tree growing from his tomb; then the Queen of Sheba kneels before the wood of the tree, which, being found unsuitable for the building of a temple, was used as a bridge; the Queen appears before Solomon; the Jews take the wood out of the water and use it to make Christ's Cross; the Roman Emperor Constantine has a dream in which the Cross appears as a symbol of victory; he conquers his rival Maxentius; a Jew named Judas tells the Emperor's mother, Helena, where the Cross is buried; three crosses are found; the True Cross brings a dead man back to life; King Chosroes of Persia, having carried off the Cross, causes himself to be worshipped as a god, but is defeated and killed by the Byzantine Emperor Heraclius; Heraclius brings the Cross back to Jerusalem. The cycle is completed by two figures of Prophets and an Annunciation. The late 13th c. painted Crucifix which formerly hung in this chapel is now in a lateral chapel on the left.

Roman Amphitheatre

The Roman Amphitheatre (Anfiteatro Romano), built in the 2nd c. A.D., bears witness to the importance of Arezzo in Roman times. In later centuries it suffered much dilapidation, being used as a convenient source of building stone for the town walls, the Church of San Bernardo, the seminary and other buildings. The amphitheatre (121 m – 397 ft long by 68 m – 223 ft across), could accommodate between 8000 and 10,000 spectators.

*Museo Archeológico Mecenate

The former Monastery of San Bernardo, built by Olivetan monks in 1547 in the ruins of the amphitheatre seating and badly damaged during the Second World War, has since 1934 housed the Museo Archeológico Mecenate. It contains material of the Stone and Bronze Ages and the Etruscan and Roman periods, largely from Arezzo and the surrounding area. Of particular interest are the Etruscan vases and bronzes and the so-called Arretine ware of *terra sigillata*, the fine decorated pottery which was widely exported from Arezzo during the

Imperial period. Other notable items include Etruscan terracotta reliefs, urns, sarcophagi, mirrors, craters (wine-mixing
jars), amphorae and Roman mosaics.

Santa Maria delle Grazie

The Church of Santa Maria delle Grazie lies outside the town to
the south. In pagan times this had been the site of a sacred
spring. Then in 1428 San Bernardino of Siena came here and
caused all traces of heathen worship to be destroyed and a
chapel to be built on the spot. In 1449 the building of the
present church, dedicated to the Madonna delle Grazie (altar-
painting by Parri de Spinello), was begun, and a graceful
portico was added in 1478.

The altar by Andrea della Robbia, of marble and terracotta, was
installed at the end of the 15th c. To the right of the church is
an oratory dedicated to San Bernardino.

Asciano   C3

Province: Siena (SI)
Altitude: 200 m (655 ft)
Population: 6000

Situation

The little town of Asciano lies in the foothills of the Crete (see
entry), in the Upper Valley of the Ombrone, 25 km (15 miles)
south-east of Siena.

The town

Asciano, once held by the Counts of Sinalunga, was acquired
by Siena in 1285 and defended against Florentine attack until
1554. Notable features of the town are a Romanesque church,
the Collegiata (Sant'Agata), built of travertine; the Museum of
Religious Art (Museo di Arte Sacra), with some fine pictures by
medieval painters; the Etruscan Museum (Museo Etrusco),
housed in a small Romanesque church, with finds from five
Etruscan chamber tombs discovered in 1957 on the Poggio
Pinci, to the east of the town, as well as gold jewellery, bronze
fibulas and funerary urns; and the abandoned and dilapidated
Romanesque and Gothic Church of San Francesco.

Bagni di Luca   B2

Province: Lucca (LU)
Altitude: 150 m (490 ft)
Population: 8000

Situation

The spaciously laid out spa of Bagni di Lucca, now frequented
mainly by Italians, but in the 19th c. highly popular with British,
French and German visitors, lies in northern Tuscany, 22 km
(15 miles) north of the provincial capital, Lucca. The little River
Lima flows through the town and into the Serchio a short
distance to the west.

The spa

The history of the spa goes back to the High Middle Ages: it is recorded that in 1101 Margrave Matilda caused a stone bridge (the present-day Ponte della Maddalena) to be built over the Serchio at Borgo a Mozzano (see entry). Bagni di Lucca enjoyed a great upsurge of prosperity in the 19th c., when it became a very popular and fashionable resort. The town then acquired the aspect which it still largely preserves.

Of the 19 hot springs which come to the surface here, with temperatures of between 38 °C (100 °F) and 54 °C (129 °F), four – the Doccione, Bagno San Giovanni, Bagni Bernabò and Bagni alla Villa – are used for therapeutic purposes. The principal spa installations are in the district of Bagni Caldi (Hot Baths); in a cave in this part of the town is the spring known as the Doccione (54 °C – 129 °F). The waters of Bagni di Lucca are recommended for the treatment of metabolic disturbances, gynaecological conditions, etc.

Barberino Val d'Elsa   C3

Province: Firenze/Florence (FI)
Altitude: 373 m (1224 ft)
Population: 3500

Barberino Val d'Elsa lies on the old Roman road known as the   Situation
Via Cassia, some 40 km (25 miles) south of Florence.

The town

Barberino Val d'Elsa is still surrounded by the walls which served to defend this Florentine town during the conflict with Siena. The only gate in the circuit of walls, the Porta Senese, dates from the 14th c., as does the old hospice for pilgrims at the other end of Via Francesco da Barberino, which leads through the town from the gate.

The Palazzo Pretorio, in the town's central square, the Piazza Barberini, is decorated with numerous coats of arms, mostly of the 15th c. Close by stands the Parish Church of San Bartolomeo (much restored in the 19th and 20th c.), which contains the remains of frescoes of the 14th and 15th c. (Annunciation).

Barga   B2

Province: Lucca (LU)
Altitude: 410 m (1345 ft)
Population: 11,000

The little industrial town of Barga lies in the extreme north of   Situation
Tuscany on the River Serchio, on the slopes of the Apennines,
some 35 km (22 miles) north of Lucca.

The town

During the Middle Ages the nearby towns of Lucca, Pisa and Florence contended for the possession of Barga, a fortress which controlled the narrow Serchio Valley. It also served as a defence against the rulers of Módena (the Este family), who had an outpost farther up the valley at Castelnuovo di Garfagnana (see entry).

The medieval centre of the town is a maze of steep and narrow lanes. On the highest point stands the cathedral (San Cristofano), which was begun in the 9th c. and completed in the 15th. It was thoroughly restored and rebuilt after suffering earthquake damage in 1920. The rather blank and forbidding façade of this aisled church shows the characteristic features of Lombard Romanesque. Above the entrance doorway is a relief of a vintage scene. The church has a beautiful marble pulpit, one of the best preserved of the second half of the 13th c. It is borne on four marble columns, two of them supported by lions and one by the crouching figure of a bearded man, and is decorated with finely carved reliefs depicting the Adoration of the Kings, the Nativity, the Annunciation, the Prophet Isaiah.

Bibbiena   C 3

Province: Arezzo (AR)
Altitude: 425 m (1394 ft)
Population: 11,000

Situation

The lively market town of Bibbiena, the chief place in the fertile Casentino area, lies at the junction of the Archiano with the Arno, some 30 km (20 miles) north of Arezzo.

The town

The town may originally have been an Etruscan foundation. On account of its excellent strategic situation its possession was hotly contested during the Middle Ages and down to the 15th c.

Bibbiena's principal historical monument is the Palazzo Dovizi, a Renaissance palace built for Cardinal Bernardo Dovizi in 1498. Like most of the other town mansions in Bibbiena, it is privately owned and is not open to the public. Facing it is the Church of San Lorenzo (originally built 1474), with terracottas by the della Robbias.

The Parish Church of San Ippolito, higher up, dates from the 12th c. but was remodelled in the Baroque period. Notable features are stained-glass windows by Ruggiero Biggeri and frescoes of the 14th and 15th c.

Santa Maria del Sasso   C 3

Situation
1·5 km (1 mile) N

The Church of Santa Maria del Sasso is a Renaissance structure of 1495, replacing earlier churches on the same site. The original church was built on the spot where there was an apparition of the Virgin in 1347. Above the altar is a fresco,

"Madonna del Sasso", probably by the Florentine painter Bicci di Lorenzo (1350–1427); on the rear face of the central tabernacle is a representation of the miraculous apparition of the Virgin.

Borgo a Mozzano   C 2

Province: Lucca (LU)
Altitude: 97 m (318 ft)
Population: 8000

The little town of Borgo a Mozzano lies in the Valley of the Serchio some 20 km (12½ miles) north of Lucca.

Situation

The town

The most striking feature of the town is the Ponte della Maddalena or Ponte del Diávolo (Devil's Bridge). It takes its name from a statue of the Magdalene which formerly stood here and is now in the parish church. The bridge, which spans the Serchio in a wide arch (37 m – 121 ft), was built in the 11th c. by Margravine Matilda (Bagni di Lucca – see entry); it is one of the great engineering achievements of the Middle Ages.
In addition to the statue of the Magdalene the parish church (San Iácopo) contains a number of 16th c. works of art, including terracottas of the school of Andrea della Robbia.

* Ponte della Maddalena

Borgo San Lorenzo   C 3

Province: Firenze/Florence (FI)
Altitude: 193 m (633 ft)
Population: 15,000

Borgo San Lorenzo, the chief market centre of the Mugello region, lies 30 km (20 miles) north of Florence near the left bank of Sieve.

Situation

San Lorenzo

The Church of San Lorenzo is dedicated to the town's Patron Saint, St Lawrence. It is an aisled church, built in the 13th c. and partly rebuilt in the 17th. Damage caused by an earthquake in 1919 was made good in 1922. The church contains panel-paintings and terracottas of the 15th to 17th c. The brick-built campanile (mid 13th c.) is in a style transistional between Romanesque and Gothic.

Scarpería   B/C 3

The little industrial and agricultural town of Scarpería lies in a basin opening off the Sieve Valley. In the main square stands the massive Palazzo Pretorio (early 14th c.), once the seat of the Vicars of the Mugello. There are numerous coats of arms on

Situation
10 km (6 miles) NW

the façade and in the courtyard. Opposite the palazzo is the Prepositurale (Provostry Church), which contains a marble tondo of the Madonna and Child by Benedetto da Maiano.

Autodromo del Mugello

Just outside the town is the Autodromo del Mugello, a car-racing circuit 5·245 m (3¼ miles) long, with 15 bends, where various international car and motor-cycle races take place, including qualifying races for the European Formula 2 championship and the world motor-cycling championship.

Buonconvento

See under Abbazía di Monte Oliveto Maggiore

Camáldoli   C3

Province: Arezzo (AR)
Altitude: 816 m (2677 ft)

Situation

The Abbey of Camáldoli, still the centre of the Camaldolese Order, lies in the densely wooded hills of the Casentino in the extreme north-east of Tuscany, some 50 km (30 miles) north of Arezzo.

History

About the year 1000 a Benedictine monk named Romuald, a member of a noble Lombard family and a trusted adviser of the Emperors Henry II and Otto III, set out to renew monastic life, as part of the great movement for Church reform then in progress in the West. With this in mind cells were built in remote spots so that the individual monk might devote himself to contemplation. The Rule thus established attracted many adherents, and in 1012 the mother house of the new Order was built here, in the little town of Camáldoli, at an altitude of 800 m (2625 ft). Soon afterwards some monks moved still higher up to find solitude at a height of 1100 m (3600 ft) on the Campo Amabile, in what is now the Éremo di Camáldoli. During the 12th c. the Camaldolese Order flourished, but in later centuries it was torn by dissensions and splits and never developed into a great and powerful Order.

Monastero di Camáldoli

The monastery founded by St Romuald in 1012 is in the little town of Camáldoli. In addition to the conventual buildings the complex includes the church and a hospice for pilgrims.
The church (Santi Donato e Ilariano) was rebuilt at the beginning of the 16th c. and was given its present Baroque form (including the large ceiling-fresco) in the late 18th c. Giorgio Vasari (1511–74) painted a number of pictures for the church, among them "Descent from the Cross", "Virgin and Child with Saints" and "SS. Donatus and Hilarianus".
The charming cloister was built in 1543, as was the pharmacy at the entrance to the monastery, still containing its original furnishings.

Hermitage of Camaldoli: monks' cells

*Éremo di Camáldoli

Soon after the foundation of the monastery a number of monks moved up to the solitude of the Campo Amabile, where, surrounded by forest, they established the Éremo di Camáldoli, a hermitage consisting of a group of monks' cells and a church. The area was enclosed by walls in the late 17th c.

The Chiesa del Salvatore (Church of the Saviour) was founded in 1027 but was given its present Baroque aspect by rebuildings and remodellings carried out in 1658, 1708 and 1714. On the façade are figures of the Saviour and of SS. Romuald and Benedict. The interior (aisleless) has carved Baroque choir-screens and 17th c. frescoes of scenes in the life of St Romuald. The plain choir-stalls date from the 15th c. On either side of the altar is a marble tabernacle (16th c.).

Beyond an iron screen are the monks' cells: 20 of them, in five rows, each with its tiny garden. Five of them (including No. 5, the Cella di San Francesco; No. 10, the Cella della Croce; and No. 15, the Cella di San Martino) are traditionally said to have been built by the founder of the Order, St Romuald.

Capraia (Ísola di Capraia)   C1

Province: Livorno (LI)
Area: 19·5 sq. km (7½ sq. miles)
Population: 400

The island of Capraia, in the Arcipélago Toscana (see entry) (Tuscan Archipelago), lies some 50 km (30 miles) west of Populonia in the Tyrrhenian Sea.   Situation

Access

There are boat services from Livorno and from Elba (Portoferraio); the crossing takes from two to three hours. Cars are not carried.

The island

Capraia, known to the Romans as Capraria (Goat Island), is of volcanic origin. Its highest point is Monte Castello (447 m – 1467 ft). Capraia was already populated in ancient times, and during the Middle Ages its possession was contested by Saracens, the Pisans and the Genoese. The most notable building on the island is a Genoese stronghold, the Fortezza di San Giorgio (15th c.). The coasts are predominantly rocky, with a number of sea-caves, offering great attractions for subaqua enthusiasts. A motor-boat trip round the island of about 30 km (20 miles) is a very rewarding experience.

Caprese Michelángelo   C 3

Province: Arezzo (AR)
Altitude: 653 m (2142 ft)
Population: 1800

Situation

Caprese Michelángelo is a small township near the north-eastern border of Tuscany, about 25 km (15 miles) north-east of Arezzo as the crow flies.

Caprese: Michelángelo's birthplace

Caprese would be unknown to fame but for the fact that it was the birthplace of one of the world's greatest artists, Michelángelo Buonarroti (1475–1564). This was established only in 1875, when a copy of his birth certificate, prepared by his father Lodovico, then Mayor of the town, was found. The finding of the certificate settled a long-standing dispute between Caprese and the little town of Chiusi della Verna, which had also claimed to be Michelángelo's birthplace.

The town

The Casa Comunale (14th c.; formerly the seat of the Podestà) is believed to be the house in which Michelángelo was born on 6 March 1475. The trim little building now houses a Michelángelo Museum (casts of sculpture, etc.).
Above the town is a partly ruined medieval castle, which also contains a small museum with copies of Michelángelo's works and examples of modern art.

Carrara   B 2

Province: Massa-Carrara (MS)
Altitude: 80 m (260 ft)
Population: 70,000

Carrara lies in an enclosed valley on the western slopes of the   Situation
Apuan Alps (nature reserve), near the northern Tuscan coast.

* Marble quarries

Carrara, with Massa (see entry), is one of the largest marble-quarrying and marble-working centres in the world. This much-sought-after fine-grained stone was formed in the course of millions of years by the crystallisation of calcium (calcium carbonate). Various types of marble are distinguished, differing in colour and structure. The most highly prized is the pure white Statuario; but where traces of metallic salts were present in the rock during the process of formation this has given rise to colourings in red, green, orange (Paonazzo, Bardiglio, Venato), etc. The marble of Carrara was already in great demand in Roman times, being shipped from the Roman port of Luni; but it was not until the Renaissance that it achieved world-wide fame. Of all the sculptors who used Carrara marble the greatest was Michelángelo.
In earlier times the difficulties involved in quarrying the huge blocks of marble and still more in transporting them to the sea must have been immense; and not infrequently lives were lost when a heavy block broke loose and crushed the workmen. Nowadays the marble is worked with the most modern equipment – wire saws, compressed air drills, gang saws, etc. In 1876 a railway was built from sea-level to a height of 450 m (1475 ft), with a "main line" 20 km (12½ miles) long and 11 km (7 miles) of branch lines, passing over 16 bridges and through 15 tunnels; but some years ago the railway system, an outstanding technical achievement for its day, was closed

down when transport by lorries proved more economic. The marble of Carrara is shipped all over the world from the ports of Marina di Carrara, Marina di Massa, Forte dei Marmi and Marina di Pietrasanta.

The huge marble quarries (*cave di marmo*) lie north-east of the town in the Colonnata, Fantiscritti and Ravaccione valleys, which are served by good roads. The quarries can be visited without any special permit; but care should be exercised in driving to the quarries and looking round them.

The town

Although Carrara has traditions going back to pre-Roman times it is predominantly a modern town. In Via Roma is the Accadémia di Belle Arti (Academy of Fine Art), founded by Maria Teresa Cybo in 1769; visitors are admitted with the Director's permission.

Cathedral

To the north, on the little River Carrione, stands the marble-faced cathedral, begun in the 12th c. and completed in the 15th. The façade, in Pisan style, has an arcade of seven round-headed arches along the base; within the higher central arch is the doorway, with figural decoration. In the upper part is an elaborate rose-window flanked by columns. In the simply decorated interior a marble "Annunciation" of the 14th c. can be seen.

Museo Cívico del Marmo

South-west of the town centre, in Viala XX Settembre, is the Museo Cívico del Marmo (Marble Museum). It has five sections, illustrating the history of marble-quarrying since ancient times, the geology of marble and the artistic and technological use of marble down to modern times.

Castelfiorentino   C2

Province: Firenze/Florence (FI)
Altitude: 50 m (165 ft)
Population: 18,000

Situation

The little town of Castelfiorentino lies in the valley of the River Elsa, some 40 km (25 miles) south-west of Florence.

The town

Castelfiorentino was founded as a stronghold directed against the Sienese, but has preserved few remains of those earlier warlike times.

Working in the marble quarry ▶

Carrara with the Apuan Alps in the background

The Church of San Francesco (begun in 1213) has a façade decorated with coats of arms. Behind it is the Church of Santa Verdiana, built in the 18th c. on the site of the earlier Parish Church of Sant'Antonio; it has a lively Baroque façade (designed by Bernardo Fallani) and an interior (aisled) in Baroque style. Adjoining it is the small municipal gallery (Pinacoteca), with some good pictures, mainly by medieval artists, notable for their deep sincerity and piety as well as their beauty.

A short distance away at Via Benozzo Gozzoli 35 is the Cappella della Visitazione (mid 15th c.), with a cycle of frescoes on the life of the Virgin by Benozzo Gozzoli (1420–97) and his pupils.

Castelnuovo di Garfagnana   B2

Province: Lucca (LU)
Altitude: 277 m (909 ft)
Population: 6000

Situation

The township of Castelnuovo di Garfagnana lies in the Serchio Valley, some 45 km (28 miles) north of Lucca and 30 km (20 miles) east of Massa.

The town

Throughout its history Castelnuovo was more closely associated with Módena and Ferrara – that is with the House of Este
– than with the municipal republics of Florence and Lucca
which were geographically closer. Evidence of the warlike
activities in which the town was involved is provided by the
rocca (castle), the oldest part of which dates from the 13th c.;
it was later enlarged, and was restored in 1946–48.

The cathedral was rebuilt in 1504. The interior (aisled) contains
a beautiful 14th c. Crucifix, a terracotta group ("St Joseph with
two Angels") of the school of the della Robbias and a number
of other works of art.

To the north of the town are the ruins of the old Castello San
Nicolao.

Castiglione della Pescaia   D2

Province: Grosseto (GR)
Altitude: 0–51 m (0–167 ft)
Population: 8000

The popular seaside resort of Castiglione della Pescaia lies on   Situation
the Tyrrhenian coast at the foot of Poggio Petricchio (342 m –
1122 ft), 20 km (12½ miles) west of Grosseto.

The town

The medieval part of the town, also known as Castiglione
Castello, occupies a spur of hill above the sea, enclosed within
a circuit of walls and massive towers. The formidable rocca
(castle) looms over the town and its picturesque little harbour,
in which fishing-boats and yachts are moored. Outside the
town is a shady pine wood, the Pineta.

Punta Ala   D2

Punta Ala, another and more sophisticated seaside resort, is   **Situation**
situated on a headland north-west of Castiglione, 12 km (7½   20 km (12½ miles) NW
miles) as the crow flies. The road to Punta Ala (20 km – 12½
miles) skirts the foot of the Poggio Peroni, which rises above
the resort. Off the coast, due west, can be seen the island of Elba
(see entry).

Castiglion Fiorentino   C3

Province: Arezzo (AR)
Altitude: 345 m (1132 ft)
Population: 11,000

Castiglion Fiorentino lies in eastern Tuscany, roughly half-way   Situation
between Arezzo and Cortona. To the west the land falls away
to the Valdichiana (see entry).

The town

Castiglion Fiorentino, still surrounded by its medieval walls, is commandingly situated on a hill. In the town's main square, the Piazza del Municipio, the 16th c. Loggia del Vasari has a fresco of the Annunciation and old coats of arms. Close by is the Palazzo Comunale (early 16th c.; restored 1935), with the Pinacoteca Comunale, which has a fine collection of pictures, reliquaries and sculpture by Tuscan artists.

The Church of San Francesco, built in the second half of the 13th c. in the period of transition from Romanesque to Gothic, has a beautiful façade and contains a number of good pictures and frescoes in its side chapels. The cloister was added in the 15th c.

Near the Porta Fiorentina, a 14th c. town gate, stands the Collegiate Church of San Giuliano, rebuilt in neo-classical style in 1840–53.

At the Porta San Michele is the Church of the Madonna della Consolazione (1607), a Late Renaissance building on an octagonal plan. It has an elegant interior, with a fresco ("The Madonna") attributed to Luca Signorelli.

Castello di Montecchio Vesponi

This massive 12th c. castle stands in the fertile countryside 3 km (2 miles) south of the town, its 30 m (100 ft) high central keep visible from afar. It has an imposing circuit (263 m – 863 ft) of battlemented walls and square towers.

Certaldo   C3

Province: Firenze/Florence (FI)
Altitude: 130 m (425 ft)
Population: 16,000

Situation

Certaldo lies in hilly country on the River Elsa, 15 km (9 miles) north-west of Poggibonsi and 30 km (20 miles) south-west of Florence.

History

Once the seat of the Counts Alberti, Certaldo became Florentine in 1293. Thereafter it was the headquarters of the "Vicars" who governed the area on behalf of Florence. The writer Giovanni Boccaccio (born in 1313 in either Florence or Certaldo) died here in 1375.

The town

The town, situated on a hill covered with wheatfields, cypresses and olive groves, consists of a medieval part known as the Castello and a modern district. The narrow streets of the old town are lined with restored medieval houses and palazzos. In the Casa del Boccaccio, in which the great writer is said to have spent his last years, is a Boccaccio Museum.

Close by is the Palazzo Pretorio or Palazzo del Vicariato, originally the residence of the Counts Alberti and later the seat of the Florentine Vicars. It is a handsome building, richly decorated with terracotta coats of arms and frescoes; from the loggia in front of it judgements were pronounced. The interior is also of interest. From the tower there are fine views of the hilly country around the town.

San Lázzaro   C3

San Lázzaro has a parish church originally built in the 10th–11th c. and radically rebuilt in the 16th–17th c. It contains charming 15th c. frescoes.

Situation
5 km (3 miles) NE

Chianciano Terme   C3

Province: Siena (SI)
Altitude: 550 m (1805 ft)
Population: 7500

Chianciano Terme, a leading spa, lies 10 km (6 miles) north-west of Chiusi in a region of gentle hills in south-eastern Tuscany which is bounded on the west by the Valdichiana (see entry).

Situation

There was a settlement here in Etruscan times, and it is likely that the healing powers of the springs were already known in these early days. Horace mentions them by name, and objects of the Roman period have been found in the basin of the spring now known as the Acqua di Sillene. During the Middle Ages the waters of Chianciano were so highly prized that Orvieto, Siena and Montepulciano contended for possession of the town. It was only at the beginning of the 20th c. that the development of Chianciano into a major spa began.

History

*The spa

The elegant spa area occupies the southern part of the commune. In the Parco delle Fonti is the Stabilimento dell'Acqua Santa (spa establishment). To the east, beyond the Viale delle Terme, is the much larger Parco di Fucoli. The Bagni di Sillene spa establishment is some distance away to the west. The waters of Chianciano's three springs (Acqua Santa, Acqua di Sillene, Sorgente Sant'Élena) are mainly used (in the form of both drinking and bathing cures) for the treatment of diseases of the liver and gall bladder.

Old town

To the north of the spa area is the old medieval town, still partly surrounded by walls. Features of interest are the Museo d'Arte Sacra (Museum of Sacred Art; mainly works of the 14th and 15th c.), housed in the old Palazzo dell'Arcipretura, and the Palazzo del Podestà (13th c.), the façade of which is decorated with 15th and 16th c. coats of arms.

Chianti C3

Provinces: Firenze/Florence (FI) and Siena (SI)

Situation

The hilly Chianti region lies between Florence in the north and Siena in the south, between the valleys of the Arno and the Ombrone. The principal road through the area is SS 222, the Via Chiantigiana. A drive through the Chianti hills with their vineyards, olive groves and forests of holm-oak, oak and chestnut is a delightful experience at any time, but particularly when the foliage has taken on its autumn tints.

The wines of Chianti

Outside Italy the name Chianti has almost become a synonym for any Italian red wine. This is misleading, though it is true that the Chianti wine drunk in many countries of the world now comes from an area extending on both sides of the Via Chiantigiana well beyond the original Chianti region.

Chianti Classico, the classic red wine of the Chianti region, is identified by the black cockerel which appears in the coat of arms on the label. It comes from the communes of Castellina, Gaiole, Radda and Greve and in parts of the communes of Barberino Val d'Elsa, Castelnuovo Berardenga, San Casciano, Tavernelle and Poggibonsi.

Chianti which is not from the Classico region has a *putto* (cherub) on the label instead of the black cockerel. The best Chianti Putto is in no way inferior to Chianti Classico. It comes from the Colli Fiorentini, around Montalbano, the Colli Senesi, the Colli Aretini and the Colline Pisane.

Chianti: Vineyard

The soil of the Chianti Classico area is particularly suited to the growing of vines; and the altitude of between 250 and 600 m (820 and 1970 ft) and the sunny exposure also make their contribution. Unfortunately the drive to achieve increased production and higher sales at low prices has sometimes led to a deterioration in the quality of the wine sold in the familiar wicker-protected flasks. The quality wines are sold in standard Bordeaux-type bottles.

Chiusi   C3

Province: Siena (SI)
Altitude: 375 m (1230 ft)
Population: 10,000

The town of Chiusi lies in eastern Tuscany at the south end of the Valdichiana (see entry), some 20 km ($12\frac{1}{2}$ miles) south-east of Montepulciano.

Situation

Chiusi is believed to have originally been an Umbrian settlement, but in the 6th c. B.C., under the name of Chamars, it became a considerable Etruscan city, a member of the Etruscan League of twelve cities and equal in status to such major centres as Tarquinia, Populonia and Vetulonia. A King of Chiusi named Porsenna (Macaulay's "Lars Porsena of Clusium"), in alliance with Tarquinius Superbus, was strong enough to attack even Rome, which made great efforts to shake off Etruscan dominance. After its defeat by Rome it became known as Clusium. In the 5th c. A.D. it became the see of a bishop, and after being held by the Goths and the Lombards it passed into the hands of Orvieto, Siena and finally Florence during the later Middle Ages.

History

*Museo Nazionale Etrusco

On the east side of the town, in a building modelled on an ancient temple, is the Museo Nazionale Etrusco (National Etruscan Museum), which has a rich collection of Etruscan material and Greek pottery recovered from excavations in the Chiusi area. Notable items include ash-urns, sarcophagi, bronze and pottery masks, tombstones, amphorae and other vessels. Of particular interest are the Canopic jars, with lids modelled in the form of a portrait of the dead person, and the *cippi* (gravestones with relief ornament). The museum offers an excellent insight into the life of the Etruscans, their cult of the dead, their craftsmanship and their artistic sensibility.

Cathedral

Opposite the museum, to the south, stands the cathedral (San Secondiano), the origins of which date back to the 7th c. It owes its present form to rebuilding in the 13th c. and restoration work carried out between 1887 and 1895. The campanile (altered in the 16th c.) is built over a Roman cistern hewn from the tufa and roofed with two domes. The nave of the church is separated from the aisles by 18 columns of different forms taken from Roman buildings in the area. The wall-paintings in the interior, imitating mosaics, date from the late 19th c.; of greater artistic interest are the font and the carving on the columns. In the chapter-house, which is reached from the sacristy, are 22 choir-books illustrated with miniatures from the Abbazía di Monte Oliveto Maggiore (see entry).

*Etruscan tombs

There are about 400 Etruscan tombs in the area around Chiusi. Some of them can be visited: information can be obtained from the National Etruscan Museum (above).

Close to the town on the east is the Tomba del Colle (Tomb on the Hill), which is also known as the Tomba Casuccini after its discoverer, and which dates from the early 5th c. B.C. It has retained the original door, a stone slab, and contains fine wall-paintings (some restored, others copies).

On the road to the Lago di Chiusi is the Tomba della Scimmia (Tomb of the Monkey, after a monkey depicted in one of the wall-paintings), which also dates from the early 5th c. It has notable wall-paintings of funerary ceremonies.

Near by is the more recent Tomba della Pellegrina, approached by a *dromos* (passage). It contains a number of urns and sarcophagi, some of them with relief decoration.

Farther north is the Tomba del Granduca (Tomb of the Grand Duke), which contains several urns of the 2nd c. B.C. with figural ornament.

Monte Cetona   D3

Situation
20 km (12½ miles) S

Monte Cetona (1148 m – 3767 ft), at the foot of which is the source of the River Orcia, is a limestone hill, mostly bare and devoid of vegetation. From the summit, to which a number of footpaths lead, panoramic views can be enjoyed. There are remains of buildings (at present in course of restoration) belonging to the Camaldolese Order. Recently traces of prehistoric occupation have been discovered on the slopes of the hill, in which there are numerous caves.

Colle di Val d'Elsa   C3

Province: Siena (SI)
Altitude: 137–223 m (449–732 ft)
Population: 16,000

Situation

The town of Colle di Val d'Elsa lies almost in the centre of Tuscany, some 45 km (28 miles) south of Florence.

The town

Colle di Val d'Elsa consists of a modern lower town, the Colle Basso or Piano, in the plain and the old upper town or Colle Alta.

The upper town has preserved its medieval aspect and remains of its 13th c. walls. In the Piazza del Duomo stands the

Monteriggioni: 13th c. circuit of walls

cathedral, built in 1619, which contains a Crucifix attributed to the sculptor Giambologna (Giovanni di Bologna, 1529–1608). Adjoining the cathedral is the Palazzo Pretorio (originally 13th c.), with the Museo Archeológico (material from a nearby Etruscan cemetery).
The Palazzo Vescovile (Bishop's Palace) contains a small collection of religious art. The Museo Civico (Municipal Museum; pictures, etc.) is housed in the Palazzo dei Priori.

*Monteriggioni   C3

The little town of Monteriggioni is impressively situated on a hill above the Elsa Valley. It is surrounded by a complete circuit of 13th c. walls, perfectly preserved, with 14 square towers which can be seen from a considerable distance away.

Situation
10 km (6 miles) SE

Collodi

See under Pescia

Cortona   C3/4

Province: Arezzo (AR)
Altitude: 500–650 m (1640–2135 ft)
Population: 23,000

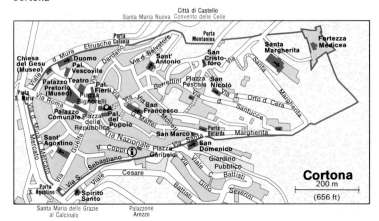

Situation

The town of Cortona lies near the eastern borders of Tuscany in the Veldichiana, just north of Lake Trasimene (which is in Umbria) and 30 km (20 miles) south of Arezzo.

History

Cortona is one of the oldest towns in Italy; as Curtuns it was a member of the Etruscan League of twelve cities. Later it became a Roman colony. During the Middle Ages, after much fighting, it passed into the possession of Florence in 1411. It was the birthplace about 1441 or 1450 of the painter Luca Signorelli and in 1596 of the painter and architect Pietro Berrettini, known as Pietro da Cortona.

Piazza della Repúbblica

In the centre of the old town, built on the slopes of the hill and still surrounded by well-preserved walls, lies the Piazza della Repúbblica, on the east side of which is the Palazzo del Pópolo (14th c., rebuilt 1514 onwards).

Palazzo Comunale

The west side of the square is dominated by the imposing Palazzo Comunale, which was already in existence in 1241; it was rebuilt in 1275, enlarged in the 16th c. and rather clumsily restored in 1896. The front of the palazzo is given its characteristic aspect by the battlemented clock-tower (1509) and the flight of steps (also 16th c.) leading up to it.

Palazzo Pretorio

A narrow lane beside the steps in front of the Palazzo Comunale leads into Piazza Signorelli, just to the north. In this square is the Palazzo Pretorio or Palazzo Casali, built in the 13th c. and remodelled in Renaissance style. On the façade are many coats of arms belonging to former *podestàs* (governors of the town).

The Palazzo Pretorio houses the Accadémia Etrusca, which was founded in 1726. The museum contains Roman and Egyptian antiquities as well as Etruscan material. Its greatest treasure is a famous Etruscan bronze lamp of the 5th c. B.C. Notable among the Etruscan bronze statues are a figure of Jupiter hurling a thunderbolt ("Giove Tonante") and a winged goddess (both 7th–6th c. B.C.).

* * Museo dell'Accadémia Etrusca

The Egyptian section of the museum displays a rare funerary boat of painted wood (12th Dynasty, *c.* 2000 B.C.), sarcophagi, etc. Also of interest are the collection of coins and medals, ceramics and paintings by Italian masters, mainly of the 13th–17th c.

On the east side of Piazza Signorelli is the rear of the 15th c. Palazzo Fierli (main front on Via Benedetti).

Cathedral

A short distance north of Piazza Signorelli, in the Piazza del Duomo, stands the cathedral (Santa Maria), a Renaissance structure built over an earlier Romanesque church. In its present form it is predominantly the work of Giuliano da Sangallo (1445–1516) or of his followers. The interior is divided into three aisles by slender columns, with fine carved altars (1644) by Francesco Mazzuoli. The choir contains a number of good paintings, including some by pupils of Luca Signorelli.

Adjoining the cathedral is the Bishop's Palace (Palazzo Vescovile), the present aspect of which dates mainly from the late 19th c.

*Museo Diocesano

Opposite the cathedral, to the west, is the Chiesa del Gesù, a Jesuit church now deconsecrated. It has an unusual structure, consisting of two churches, one on top of the other. Originally built between 1498 and 1505, it was altered in the 16th c. by Giorgio Vasari.

The upper church and its adjoining rooms now house the Museo Diocesano (Diocesan Museum). Among the most

Cortona: Diocesan Museum (L. Signorelli: Scourging)

notable items are works by Fra Angélico ("Annunciation", triptych with Virgin and Child; scenes from the life of St Doménic), Pietro Lorenzetti ("Crucifixion", "Madonna") and the school of Duccio di Buoninsegna, altar-pieces by Luca Signorelli and Sassetta, a Roman sarcophagus of the 2nd c. A.D. and the Vagnucci Reliquary (1457), of gilded bronze, silver and precious stones.

The lower church has rich fresco decoration painted or designed by Giorgio Vasari (16th c.) and a painted terracotta "Descent from the Cross" (*c.* 1500).

San Francesco

To the east of the Palazzo Comunale is the Church of San Francesco, the building of which began in 1245, making it one of the earliest Franciscan churches. The exterior of this aisleless Gothic church is plain and undecorated; the interior was, rather unhappily, remodelled in the Baroque period. Its greatest treasure (not always visible) is a Reliquary of the True Cross, consisting of a Byzantine ivory tablet in a 16th c. frame.

In the choir can be seen the tomb of the church's founder, Fra Elia da Cortona. The painter Luca Signorelli (d. 1523) is also believed to have been buried here.

San Doménico

The Church of San Doménico, outside the town walls to the south, was originally the church of a Dominican friary to which the famous painter Fra Angélico (Giovanni di Pietro, *c.* 1400–1455) belonged for a time. This aisleless Gothic church was built in the early 15th c., in the plain architectural style favoured by the Mendicant Orders, and altered later in the century. The altar has a triptych by Lorenzo Gherini (14th/15th c.); in the chapel on the right is a "Madonna with Angels and Saints" by Luca Signorelli (15th c.) and on the wall of the presbytery an "Assumption" by Bartolomeo della Gatta (15th c.).

To the east of San Doménico extend the Giardino Púbblico (Public Garden).

San Nicolò

Above the centre of the old town, half-way up to the Fortezza (see below), is the little 15th c. Church of San Nicolò which has a small porch with slender columns. The interior (remodelled in Baroque style) has paintings by Luca Signorelli (two-sided panel-painting, "Descent from the Cross" and "Madonna Enthroned"; fresco, "Madonna with Saints").

Santuario di Santa Margherita

Just below the Fortezza, on the flank of the hill, is the Santuario di Santa Margherita, with a pilgrimage church dedicated to St Margaret of Cortona (1247–97). The present church, in neo-Byzantine style, was built between 1856 and 1897. The Saint's tomb dates from 1362; her relics are in a silver shrine (1646) on the high altar.

From the square in front of the church there is a magnificent view into the Valdichiana (see entry).

Fortezza Medicea

High above the old town, at the north-east corner of the walls, looms the Fortezza Medicea. This Médici stronghold was built in 1556 on earlier foundations. It now houses an agricultural college and research institute. Fine panoramic views.

Santa Maria Nuova

Outside the town walls (Porta Colonia), to the north, is the Church of Santa Maria Nuova, a Renaissance structure on a square plan with a high dome. Designed by Giovanni Battista Infregliati, it was completely remodelled by Giorgio Vasari. Of the paintings in the interior the most notable is a "Birth of the Virgin" by Alessandro Allori (16th c.).

Santa Maria delle Grazie al Calcinaio

From the Porta Sant'Agostino, the south-western town gate, the road to Camucia runs south-east to the Renaissance Church of Santa Maria delle Grazie al Calcinaio or of the Madonna del Calcinaio (1485–1513). This is one of the most architecturally important Renaissance churches of Tuscany, was designed by Francesco di Giorgio Martini, it is a finely proportioned aisleless domed church on a Latin cross plan. It was built to house a miraculous image of the Virgin, originally on the wall of a limestone quarry (*calcinaio*) belonging to the local Tanners' Guild and now on the high altar of the church.

Tanella di Pitagora (Cave of Pythagoras)

To the south of the town (also reached by the road from the Porta Sant'Agostino) is the so-called Cave of Pythagoras, an Etruscan tomb of the 4th c. B.C. on a cruciform plan. The tomb chamber, measuring 2·05 m by 2·53 m (6 ft 9 in by 8 ft 4 in), was enclosed by large wedge-shaped blocks. The tomb has no connection with Pythagoras; the name seems to come from a confusion between Cortona and the Greek city of Kroton (now Crotone) in Calabria.
There are other Etruscan tombs at Camucia and Il Sodo, in the plain below the town.

Palazzone Passerini

Outside the town to the east is the Palazzone Passerini, built by Giovanni Battista Caporali for Cardinal Passerini. Dominated by a massive battlemented tower, it has a charming garden with arcades. The rooms of the palace are decorated with frescoes; those in the chapel are attributed to Luca Signorelli, and the story goes that while working on them in 1532 he fell from the scaffolding and died from his injuries. The palace now houses an educational establishment.

Convento delle Celle C4

Situation
3·5 km (2 miles) NE

The Convento delle Celle, on the slopes of Monte Sant'Egidio, is a charming complex of monks' cells, the first of which were founded by St Francis of Assisi between 1211 and 1221. Visitors can see the little church (1573) and a number of cells. From the convent there is a very fine view of Cortona.

Crete C3

Province: Siena (SI)
Altitude: up to 350 m (1150 ft)

Situation

The barren rolling hills known as the Crete, which form one of the most impressive and most unusual landscapes in Tuscany, lie south-east of Siena between Taverne d'Arbia and Asciano.

Topography

Much indented by valleys and continually threatened by erosion, the Crete are quite unsuitable for cultivation. A scanty growth of grass offers only meagre pasture for sheep. There could hardly be a greater contrast to the gentle green hills found elsewhere in Tuscany.

Geologically the Crete belong to the Cretaceous system, making them between 65 and 135 million years old; and the *creta* (Latin "chalk") after which the Cretaceous is named has also given its name to this lunar landscape.

Elba (Ísola d'Elba) D2

Province: Livorno (LI)
Area: 223 sq. km (86 sq. miles)
Population: 30,000

Situation

Elba, the largest island in the Arcipélago Toscano (Tuscan Archipelago – see entry), lies in the Tyrrhenian Sea 10 km (6 miles) south-west of the mainland port of Piombino. In the Canale di Piombino, the channel between Elba and the mainland, are the small islands of Topi, Palmaiola and Cérboli.

Access

There are jet-foil (passengers only) and car ferry services from Piombino to the island's port and capital Portoferraio. Advance booking is advisable, at least during the main season (in Piombino: Toremar, tel. 0565/3 25 08 and 3 11 00; Navarma, tel. 0565/3 30 31–32; in Portoferraio: Toremar, tel. 0565/9 20 22; Navarma, tel. 0565/91 67 43). There is also a service from Livorno to Portoferraio.
There is a daily flight from Pisa Airport to the little airfield of Marina di Campo.

General

Elba is 27 km (17 miles) long from east to west and 18 km (11 miles) across from north to south. Its highest point is Monte Capanne (1019 m – 3343 ft), in the west of the island. The coast, with a total length of 147 km (91 miles), is partly rugged and rocky, partly flat and sandy.

Elba: Harbour of Portoferraio

The island, known to be rich in minerals, was settled in early times by Ligurians. They were followed by the Etruscans who began to work the iron ore. The Romans, who knew the island as Ilva, established a number of settlements (*coloniae*); and Virgil (70–19 B.C.) celebrated the island's inexhaustible mineral wealth. During the Middle Ages Elba changed hands several times: from 962 it was held by the Pisans, from 1290 by Genoa, later by Lucca and from 1736 by Spain. Then at the Treaty of Amiens in 1802 it came under French rule. In 1814 possession of the island, with full sovereign rights, was granted to Napoleon after his dethronement, and he lived here from 4 May 1814 to 26 February 1815. At the Congress of Vienna Elba was re-incorporated in the Grand Duchy of Tuscany.

History

Etruscan predominance in Italy was made possible by their possession of the iron-mines of Elba, which were later worked by the Romans. The working of iron ore still ranks as a major element in the island's economy, together with fishing (tunny, anchovies) and agriculture (fruit, wine). Thanks to its mild and equable climate and its scenic attractions Elba is also attracting steadily increasing numbers of visitors and holiday-makers, with whom the beaches and rocky inlets along its 147 km (91 miles) of coast are particularly popular.

Economy

Portoferraio

The chief place on the island, Portoferraio (iron port), lies on a tongue of land on the west side of the entrance to a wide bay on the north coast. In Via Garibaldi, the main street, is the Town

Hall; and a short distance away to the north-east, in Via Napoleone, stands the Church of the Misericordia, in which a Mass is said for Napoleon's soul on 5 May every year, the church contains a replica of his sarcophagus and a bronze cast of his death-mask. Farther up the hill, on the highest point in the town, one comes to the Piazza Napoleone (view). To the west is the Forte Falcone (79 m – 259 ft), to the east, above the lighthouse, the Forte Stella (48 m – 157 ft), both originally built in 1548 and renovated by Napoleon. On the seaward side of the square is the modest Palazzina dei Mulini, which was Napoleon's official residence; it contains his library and other mementoes.

Villa Napoleone

Some 6 km (4 miles) south-west of Portoferraio, set amid luxuriant vegetation on the slopes of the wooded Monte San Martino (370 m – 1214 ft), is the Villa Napoleone, the ex-Emperor's summer residence (terrace affording fine views; collection of pictures).

*Round the island

From Portoferraio a road runs 18 km (11 miles) west by way of the seaside resort of Procchio, in the Golfo di Procchio, to the popular resort of Marciana Marina. Some 4 km (2½ miles) inland is the village of Marciana with its ruined castle, amid beautiful chestnut forests, another popular holiday resort. From here a cableway ascends Monte Capanne (1019 m – 3343 ft), the highest point on the island (view). From the village of Poggio there is a rewarding climb (one hour) up Monte Perone (630 m – 2067 ft) to the south-east.

On the east coast are Rio Marina (large opencast iron-mine) and, picturesquely situated in a bay, the little fishing town of Porto Azzurro, which was fortified by the Spaniards in the 17th c.

Charmingly situated in the Golfo di Campo on the lonelier south coast is the popular resort of Marina di Campo.

Émpoli   C2

Province: Firenze/Florence (FI)
Altitude: 28 m (92 ft)
Population: 44,000

Situation

The prosperous modern industrial town of Émpoli lies in the Arno Valley in northern Tuscany, some 35 km (22 miles) west of Florence on the road to Pisa.

The town

In the centre of the town, in the arcaded Piazza Farinata degli Uberti with its Naiad Fountain, is the Collegiate Church of Sant'Andrea, which was originally founded in the 5th c. but owes its present aspect to rebuilding in the 11th c. (lower part) and the 17th and 18th c. (upper part and campanile). It has a very beautiful façade with alternating bands of white and green marble.

Adjoining is the Museo della Collegiata, with a fine collection of pictures and sculpture. It is particularly rich in Tuscan paintings of the 14th–17th c.

The Church of Santo Stéfano, in the same street, was badly damaged during the Second World War but was completely restored after the war. It has some notable frescoes, including work by Masolino da Panicale (15th c.).

Vinci   C2

The township of Vinci, in fertile countryside on the southern slopes of Monte Albano, was the birthplace of the great artist, engineer and scientist Leonardo da Vinci (born 1452, died at Amboise, in France, 1519).

Situation
11 km (7 miles) N

The old 13th c. castle (Castello) contains a library and a small museum, the Museo Vinciano, with models based on Leonardo's drawings.

The house in which Leonardo is said to have been born is 3 km (2 miles) outside the town at Archiano.

Fiésole   C3

Province: Firenze/Florence (FI)
Altitude: 295 m (968 ft)
Population: 15,000

The ancient little town of Fiésole, beautifully situated on a hill overlooking Florence (see entry) from the north-east, attracts large numbers of visitors for the sake of its magnificent view of the Tuscan capital in the Arno Valley below, as well as for the sights within the town itself.

Situation

* View

Fiésole was founded by the Etruscans in the 7th/6th c. B.C.; it first appears in the records in the year 225 B.C. Towards the end of the 1st c. B.C. it became the Roman town of Faesulae, complete with capitol, forum, temple, theatre and public baths. In the period of the great migrations, however, it declined and was completely overshadowed by the nearby town of Florence. It became the see of a bishop in 492.

History

Piazza Mino da Fiésole

In the centre of the town is the spacious Piazza Mino da Fiésole, named after the sculptor of that name (c. 1430–1484), which occupies the position of the ancient forum. On the north side of the square stands the cathedral (San Rómolo), begun in 1028, enlarged in the 13th and 14th c. and altered in the 19th. It became an episcopal church in the 11th c. (replacing an earlier church on the site of the Badía Fiesolana). The battlemented campanile, 42 m (138 ft) high, was erected in 1213. The cathedral contains fine frescoes and sculpture, particularly in the Cappella Salutati.

* Cathedral

Adjoining the cathedral on the north is the Museo Bandini which owes its existence to a former Librarian of the Biblioteca Medíceo-Laurenziana in Florence, Canon Ángiolo Maria Bandini. The collection includes terracottas by Della Robbia, a statue by Pisano, and 14th and 15th c. paintings.

Museo Bandini
(closed Sun.)

Fiésole

Vinci: Castle

Fiésole: Archaeological site

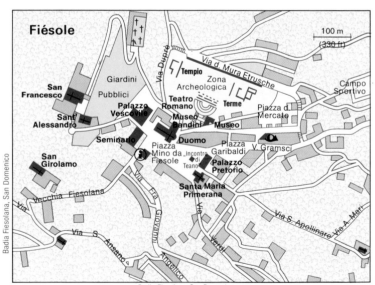

Badia Fiesolana, San Domenico
Firenze

The north-west end of the Piazza Mino da Fiésole is occupied by the imposing building (1697) which houses the seminary and, beside it, the Bishop's Palace (Palazzo Vescovile), originally dating from the 11th c.

Seminary
Bishop's Palace

On the south-west side of the square are the Palazzo Pretorio (14th and 15th c.), decorated with coats of arms, and the medieval Oratory of Santa Maria Primerana, with a 16th c. portico.

Palazzo Pretorio

Santa Maria Primerana

The monument in the square (1906) represents the "Incontro di Teano", the meeting between King Victor Emmanuel II and Garibaldi at Teano in 1860.

Monument

*Zona Archeológica (Excavations)

Beyond the cathedral, to the north-east, is a large excavation site, the Zona Archeológica. The most prominent feature is the Roman theatre, which was discovered only in the early 19th c. Originally constructed at the beginning of the Imperial period (1st c. A.D.), it was enlarged in the reigns of Claudius and Septimius Severus. It is semicircular in form, with a diameter of 34 m (112 ft), and its 24 rows of seating could accommodate some 3000 spectators; the stage measures 26·40 by 6·40 m (87 by 21 ft).

Theatre

Near the theatre are the remains of Roman baths, also built at the beginning of the Imperial period and enlarged in the time of Hadrian. Although the arches, borne on massive piers, had remained above ground, the structure was not identified as a bathing establishment until the end of the 19th c. The whole complex was excavated in 1891–92.

Baths

At the north-west corner of the site are the remains of a Roman temple of the 1st c. B.C. and an Etruscan temple of the 3rd c. B.C.

Temples

The north side of the site is bounded by a section of the massive Etruscan town walls.

Etruscan walls

On the south side of the site, above the theatre, is a small archaeological museum containing Etruscan and Roman material.

Museum
(closed Mon.)

San Francesco

To the north-west of the Piazza Mino da Fiésole are the Giardini Púbblici (Public Gardens), which afford extensive views.

Giardini Púbblici

On the west side of the gardens, at a height of 345 m (1132 ft), is the Church of San Francesco, built in the 14th c. and made over to the Franciscans in 1407. Apart from the interior of the church the main features of interest are the Missionary Museum and the cloisters.

Missionary Museum

Fiésole

Sant'Alessandro

To the south of San Francesco the Church of Sant'Alessandro (originally San Pietro in Gerusalemme), dedicated to Bishop Alexander of Fiésole, occupies the site of an Etruscan temple, later replaced by a Roman Temple of Bacchus, which is believed to have been converted into a Christian church by Theodoric the Great at the beginning of the 6th c. Thereafter the church was much altered and rebuilt. From the terrace there is a superb view of Florence lying in the valley below.

Villa Médici

On the Strada Vecchia Fiesolana, which runs down from Fiésole to the south-west, is the Villa Médici (also known as Belcanto or the Palagio di Fiésole), probably built by Michelozzo in 1458–61 for Cosimo the Elder, in which Lorenzo the Magnificent entertained his literary friends.

San Doménico di Fiésole

1 km ($\frac{3}{4}$ mile) south-west of Fiésole, on the Florence city boundary (panoramic view), is the hamlet of San Doménico di Fiésole (alt. 148 m – 486 ft). The Church of San Doménico (1406–35; rebuilt in 17th c.) has a richly decorated interior; in the first chapel on the left is a beautiful altar-piece by Fra Angélico (c. 1430) and Lorenzo di Credi.

▼ *Florence: Panorama of the city from the south-west*

Badía Fiesolana

Below San Doménico to the north-west (alt. 123 m – 404 ft) is
the Badía Fiesolana, where the episcopal church of Fiésole
stood until 1023, when it gave place to the present cathedral.
A new church and abbey (Badía) were built by the Camaldo-
lese Order but later passed to the Benedictines. At the Renais-
sance both the church and the abbey were again remodelled.
The façade of the church still preserves some 12th c.
Romanesque work.
Since 1976 the Badía Fiesolana has housed the European
University (Università Europea).

Florence (Firenze)   C3

Province: Firenze/Florence (FI)
Altitude: 50 m (165 ft)
Population: 450,000

Since there is a separate volume on Florence in the series
of Baedeker's pocket guides the account in this guide is
deliberately abbreviated.

Florence (in Italian Firenze), known as Firenze la Bella   Situation
(Florence the Fair), the ancient capital of Tuscany and now the
chief town of its province, the seat of a university and the see
of an archbishop, lies in northern Tuscany, beautifully situated

on both sides of the Arno and surrounded by the foothills of the Apennines.

Culture, art and learning

While in antiquity the life of Italy was centred on Rome, from medieval to modern times the main focal point of the country's intellectual development has been Florence. Here the Italian literary language and Italian literature came into being, here Italian art came to its full flowering. Its extraordinary wealth of art treasures, its great historical associations and the beauty of its surroundings make Florence one of the world's great tourist magnets, one of its most interesting and most fascinating cities. Since the Renaissance Florence has maintained its importance as a centre of art and culture, and has also preserved the setting in which that role developed. The churches, palaces, squares and bridges, the frescoes and pictures created in the period of its great cultural flowering are still there, and in consequence Florence attracts not only tourists but artists, students of art and historians. Universities and scholarly institutions, theatres and orchestras, art galleries, museums and libraries all bear witness to the lively artistic and cultural life of the city.

Commerce and industry

As skilled craftsmen, shrewd merchants and efficient administrators the Florentines have maintained the prosperity of their city down the centuries from the Middle Ages to the present day. For a time Florentine banks dominated the money-markets of Europe and Florentine bankers influenced European policy. But since Florence was unable to achieve political power comparable with that of other Italian states – the Republic of Venice, the Papal States and the Kingdom of Naples and Sicily – it lost its economic predominance and now no longer ranks as an international commercial and banking centre. In the late Middle Ages Florence became wealthy through its textile industry (weaving, dyeing, tailoring, the silk trade), which is still, as the modern clothing industry, an important source of income; and the highly developed craft industries of Florence (ceramics, porcelain, embroidery, leather-working, basket-work) have maintained its artistic traditions. The major sources of employment, however, are now the chemical and pharmaceutical industries, the trade in art and antiques, and printing and publishing. Much of the agricultural produce of Tuscany is also processed in Florence.

Commerce also plays a major part in the city's economy. Many banks have their headquarters in Florence; Florentine fashion shows, in this home of *alta moda*, are world-famed; and the trade fairs held here (furs, antiques, books) attract an international clientele. Associated with these activities, too, is the tourist trade: the stream of visitors continues throughout the year without intermission, and at special times such as Church festivals Florence is always overcrowded. The service industries in general make an important contribution to the city's prosperity.

History

The Roman city of Florentia was a place of little consequence in the history of antiquity. At the beginning of the 13th c. A.D., however, the town developed into the leading state in central Italy, thanks to the fortunes of war and the industry of its craftsmen and merchants (wool, silk). The noble families which ruled the city were weakened by continual intestine strife between Guelfs (supporters of the Pope) and Ghibellines (supporters of the Emperor), and the municipal guilds grew

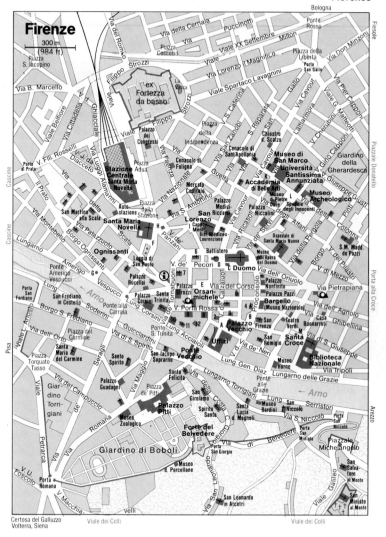

Florence

Firenze

300 m
(984 ft)

A Piazza della Signoria
B Piazza San Firenze
C Piazza del Duomo
D Piazza San Giovanni
E Piazza della Repubblica
F Piazza Santa Maria Novella

G Piazza Ognissanti
H Piazza dell' Unità Italiana
I Piazza Madonna degli Aldobrandini
K Piazza San Marco
L Piazza della Santissima Annunziata
M Piazza Santa Croce

1 Loggia dei Lanzi
2 Palazzo Fenzi
3 Palazzo Uguccione
4 Badia Fiorentina
5 Casa di Dante
6 Santa Maria Maggiore

7 San Gaetano
8 Mercato Nuovo
9 Palazzo Davanzati
10 Palazzo Spini-Ferroni
11 Santi Apostoli
12 Palazzo di Parte Guelfa

steadily in importance until in 1282 they gained control of the government, their *priori* (presidents) forming the Signoría which henceforth ruled the city.

In literature Florence's principal glories were Dante Alighieri (1265–1321), author of the "Divine Comedy" and creator of the Italian literary language, and Giovanni Boccaccio (1313–75), whose "Decamerone" created a model for Italian prose style. Petrarch (Francesco Petrarca, 1304–74), the third great Florentine of the 14th c., played a major part in preparing the way for humanism.

In 1434 the wealthy merchant family of the Médici came to power in Florence. Its most notable members were Cosimo (1434–64), "Father of his Country" (*pater patriae*), and Lorenzo the Magnificent (1469–92), who brought the Republic to its peak of prosperity and made it a brilliant centre of art and learning. In 1494 the Médici were driven out; then in 1498 their great opponent, the Dominican monk and preacher Girólamo Savonarola, died at the stake. In 1512 the Médici were restored to power by Spanish troops; in 1527 they were again expelled; but only three years later, in 1530, after the capture of the city by the Emperor Charles V, Alessandro de' Médici was installed as Hereditary Duke of Florence (murdered in 1537). In 1569 his successor Cosimo I became Grand Duke of Tuscany.

After the Médici line became extinct in 1737 the Duchy passed to Francis III of Lorraine and continued to be ruled by the House of Lorraine until 1860, with the exception of the Napoleonic Interregnum (1801–14). Tuscany then became part of the new Kingdom of Italy, and as its temporary capital (1865–70) enjoyed a period of developing prosperity.

The city survived the Second World War almost unscathed, apart from the blowing up of the Arno bridges by German forces at the end of 1944; fortunately the oldest of them, the Ponte Vecchio, was not destroyed, and the others were restored after the war, so far as possible in their original form. In November 1966, after heavy rain, the Arno overflowed its banks and caused great damage to the city's historic buildings and the loss of many lives.

* * Piazza della Signoría

The ancient centre of the city's life is the Piazza della Signoría, once the forum of the Republic, which was given its present form in 1386, with the Palazzo Vecchio and the Loggia dei Lanzi as the dominant features on the south side of the square.

* Palazzo Vecchio
(closed Sat.)

The Palazzo Vecchio (Old Palace), Florence's town hall, a massive fortress-like structure with a 94m (308 ft) high tower, was built in 1298–1314 as the Palazzo dei Priori, the seat of the Signoría. The architect is believed to have been Arnolfo di Cambio. The building was extended to the rear in the 16th c.

To the left of the entrance is a replica of Michelángelo's "David" (original in the Galleria dell'Accadémia), and in the picturesque front courtyard (redesigned 1454) a copy of Verrocchio's charming "Boy with a Dolphin" (original on second floor).

Florence: Palazzo Vecchio, City Hall ▶

Florence: Loggia dei Lanzi

On the first floor is the large Hall of the Five Hundred (Salone dei Cinquecento, 1495), with a marble group by Michelángelo, "Victory of Virtue over Vice" (*c.* 1520) On the first and second floors are the state apartments (Quartieri Monumentali). From the wall-walk and the tower there are superb panoramic views.

Fontana del Nettuno

At the north-west corner of the Palazzo Vecchio is the large Fountain of Neptune (Fontana del Nettuno, 1563–75), in front of which a stone slab marks the spot where Savonarola was burned at the stake.

*Loggia dei Lanzi

Adjoining the Palazzo Vecchio is the Loggia dei Lanzi (originally Loggia dei Signori, 1376–82), an open vaulted hall used for official ceremonies and proclamations. It takes its name from the German mercenaries (*landsknechte*) of Cosimo I. In the loggia are a number of important works of sculpture, including a marble "Rape of the Sabines" by Giovanni da Bologna (1583) and Cellini's bronze "Perseus with the Head of Medusa" (1553).

Palazzi

On the east side of the Piazza della Signoría stands the Mercanzia (Chamber of Commerce, 1359); on the north side the Palazzo Uguccioni (16th c.); on the west side the Palazzo Fenzi (1871), in the style of the old Florentine palazzi.
Palazzo degli Uffizi: see Uffizi Palace and Gallery

*Orsanmichele

From the Piazza della Signoría the busy Via dei Calzaiuoli (Street of the Stocking-Makers) runs north to the Piazza del Duomo. Just beyond the intersection with Via del Lamberti, on the left, is the Church of Orsanmichele, a massive three-storey structure originally built in 1284–91 as a corn exchange and rebuilt between 1337 and 1404. Round the outside a series of statues of Saints, of notable artistic quality, includes figures by Verrocchio, Ghiberti and Donatello.

A short distance north-east of the Piazza della Signoría, in Piazza San Firenze, is the fortress-like Palazzo del Podestà, usually known as the Bargello. It was begun in 1254 and from 1574 was the headquarters of the city's Chief of Police (Bargello) and a prison. Since 1865 it has housed the Museo Nazionale del Bargello, a museum devoted to the history of Italian culture and art from the Middle Ages to modern times, with an outstanding collection of Florentine Renaissance sculpture. The courtyard with its sturdy arcades, handsome staircase and walls covered with coats of arms gives an excellent impression of a medieval castle ward.

**Museo Nazionale del Bargello (closed Mon.)

Opposite the Bargello, to the west, stands the Badía Fiorentina, an old Benedictine abbey (founded 978) with an elegant pointed campanile (1310–30).

Badía Fiorentina

On the south-east side of Piazza San Firenze is the Baroque Church of San Firenze (1633–48).

San Firenze

Florence
Galleria degli Uffizi

Piazza della Signoria

Loggia dei Lanzi

Palazzo Vecchio

Via della Ninna

SECOND FLOOR: Picture Gallery

1 Ancient sculpture
2 13th c. Tuscan painters: Cimabue, Giotto, etc.
3 14th c. Sienese painters
4 14th c. Florentine painters
5 Gothic painting
6 Gothic painting
7 Tuscan painters (Early Renaissance)
8 Lippi, Pollaiuolo
9 Botticelli, etc.
10 Botticelli
11 Botticelli, Lippi
12 Memling and Flemish painters (15th c.)
13 Lippi, Botticelli
14 Lippi, van der Goes, Ghirlandaio
15 Credi, Perugino, da Vinci, Verrocchio, etc.
16 Maps of Tuscany; da Vinci
17 Umbrian painters
18 Tribuna: Médici Venus and Greek sculpture; pictures by Vasari, Bronzino Pontormo Raphael and Rosso Fiorentino

19 Perugino, Francia
20 Dürer, Cranach, Mantegna
21 Dürer, Bellini, Carpaccio, etc.
22 Holbein, David, Altdorfer
23 Correggio, Metsys
24 Miniatures of 15th–18th c.
25 Michelangelo, Raphael, Bronzino
26 Sarto, Pontormo
27 Pontormo
28 Titian
29 Parmigianino
30 Parmigianino, Dossi
31 Dossi
32 Piombo, Bordone
33 Various 16th c. painters
34 Veronese
35 Tintoretto, Bassano, Baroccio
36–40 Vestibule: sculpture
41 Rubens, Van Dyck
42 Sala della Niobe: Roman marble copies of Niobe group (originals lost)
43 Flemish and Dutch paintings
44 Caravaggio, Rembrandt
45–49 In course of re-arrangement

N

20 m
(65 ft)

West Gallery

East Gallery

Piazzale degli Uffizi

Entrance

Bar

Servizi

Vasari Staircase

Stairs to Vasari Corridor

Lungarno

South Gallery

Casa di Dante
(closed Wed.)

North-west of the Bargello in Via Dante Alighieri are the Houses of the Alighieri (Case degli Alghieri), in one of which Dante is erroneously said to have been born. Number 1 is known as the Casa di Dante and contains a Dante Museum.

**Uffizi Palace and Gallery (Palazzo e Galleria degli Uffizi)

Palazzo

**Galleria
(closed Mon.)

To the south of the Palazzo Vecchio and the Loggia dei Lanzi, extending to the banks of the Arno, is the Palazzo degli Uffizi, built by Vasari in 1560–74 as offices (*uffizi*) for the city's administration. They now house the world-famous Galleria degli Uffizi (the Uffizi for short), one of the world's leading art collections, which offers an almost complete survey of the Florentine schools of painting and also displays important works by northern Italian painters, particularly the Venetians, excellent examples of Dutch and German art and numbers of pieces of ancient sculpture.

Vasari Corridor

From the Uffizi the Vasari Corridor (Corridor del Vasari or Vasariano) extends over the Ponte Vecchio to the Palazzo Pitti. It contains an interesting collection of self-portraits by Italian and foreign artists.

**Piazza del Duomo/Piazza San Giovanni

Piazze

At the far end of Via dei Calzaiuoli, which runs north from the Piazza della Signoría, are (on the right) the Piazza del Duomo, with the cathedral and campanile, and (on the left) the Piazza San Giovanni, with the baptistery.

Piazza del Duomo   **Florence**

BAPTISTERY
1 East Doorway
   (Porta del Paradiso)
2 North Doorway
3 South Doorway (entrance)

CATHEDRAL
A Portale Maggiore
B Porta della Balla
C Porta della Mandorla
D Porta del Campanile

E Porta dei Canónici
F Santa Reparata (Crypt)
G Dome
H New Sacristy
I Old Sacristy

Florence: 'The Gate of Paradise' in the baptistery

On the left, at the corner of the Piazza San Giovanni, can be seen the beautiful Gothic Loggia del Bigallo, built in 1352–58, which was later used for displaying foundling children for adoption.

Loggia del Bigallo
(closed Sun.)

In the centre of Piazza San Giovanni stands the Baptistery (Battistero San Giovanni), a domed structure on an octagonal plan. Probably founded in Early Christian times on the site of a Roman building, between the 11th and 13th c. it was rebuilt and faced externally and internally with marble of different colours. The Baptistery's three doors are decorated with magnificent bronze reliefs, each divided into 28 square panels. Those on the south door (1330–36), illustrating the life of John the Baptist, are the work of Andrea Pisano while the scenes from the life of Christ which adorn the north door (1403–24) and from the Old Testament on the east door (1425–52) are by Lorenzo Ghiberti. Each relief represents an extraordinary achievement. The east door, facing the cathedral, is known as the Porta del Paradiso (the Door of Paradise) so superb is its execution.

* * Baptistery

* * Bronze doors

Of special note in the interior are the magnificent mosaics by 13th and 14th c. Florentine artists which embellish the dome (diameter 25.6 m (84 ft)).

The Cathedral (Cattedrale di Santa Maria del Fiore – so called after the lily which is Florence's heraldic emblem) is a massive Gothic structure, begun in 1296 by Arnolfo di Cambio, continued by Francesco Talenti from 1357 and consecrated in 1436. The great octagonal dome was the master work of Filippo Brunelleschi (1420–34). Faced externally with marble

* * Cathedral

of different colours, the Cathedral is 169 m (554 ft) long, 104 m (341 ft) across the transept and 91 m (299 ft) high to the top of the dome, or including the lantern (completed 1461) 107 m (351 ft). The façade dates only from 1875-87.

Santa Reparata

The spacious interior, severely Gothic in style, is impressive in its restraint. Steps lead down to the earlier Cathedral of Santa Reparata (4th–5th c.), excavated from 1965 onwards.

*Dome
(not on Sun.)

It is well worth climbing up to the dome, which affords more extensive views than the campanile.

**Campanile

The square campanile, 82 m (269 ft) high, was begun in 1334 by Giotto, continued by Pisano and Talenti and completed in 1387. With its multicoloured marble facing, it is one of the finest of its kind in Italy. The sculpture (originals in Cathedral Museum) is by Donatello and his assistant Rosso (1420), Andrea Pisano and Luca della Robbia (1437).

*Cathedral Museum

Opposite the choir of the cathedral, in the courtyard of the building at No. 9 (on the left), is the entrance to the Cathedral Museum (Museo dell'Ôpera del Duomo), which is mainly devoted to works of art from the cathedral (including the famous singing galleries with reliefs of children by Luca della Robbia and Donatello) and the baptistery.

A little way south-east of the Piazza del Duomo, in Via del Procónsolo, are two fine palaces: at No. 12 the imposing Palazzo Nonfinito (Unfinished Palace, 1592), which since

Florence: Dome and campanile of the cathedral

1869 has housed the National Museum of Anthropology and Ethnology (Museo Nazionale di Antropologia ed Etnologia), and No. 10 Palazzo Pazzi (1470) designed by Brunelleschi.

Museum of Anthropology and Ethnology (1st & 3rd Sun. 9 a.m. –1 p.m.)

Town centre

The area to the south-west of the cathedral, known as the Centro, was modernised in the late 19th c. Its focal point is the large Piazza della Repúbblicas, which is particularly busy in the evening.

Piazza della Repúbblica

From the south-east corner of the Piazza della Repúbblica Via Calimala runs south to the Mercato Nuovo (New Market), an open loggia built in 1547–51 which now houses stalls selling craft goods.

Mercato Nuovo

In Piazza Davanzati is the massive Palazzo Davanzati (14th c.), with the Museo della Casa Fiorentina Antica (Museum of the Old Florentine House), which gives an excellent picture of Florentine domestic life from the 14th to the 17th c.

Museo della Casa Fiorentina Antica
(closed Mon.)

In the western part of the old town is the busy Via dei Tornabuoni, lined with handsome palazzi and quality shops. A particularly notable feature of this street is the Palazzo Strozzi, the most splendid example of the Florentine Palace style (1489–1538), with a beautiful courtyard (by Crónaca). Note the elaborate wrought-iron lamps at the corners, the torch-holders and the rings on the façade with its faceted stones. The palace is used for periodic art exhibitions.

*Palazzo Strozzi

Near the south end of Via dei Tornabuoni is the Church of Santa Trínita (pronounced, unusually, with the stress on the first syllable rather than the last), originally one of the oldest Gothic churches in Italy but rebuilt between the 13th and 15th c. and given a Baroque façade in 1593.

Santa Trínita

Opposite Santa Trínita to the south-east, on the banks of the Arno, is the Palazzo Spini-Ferroni, the largest of Florence's medieval palazzi, a fortress-like structure built in 1289 and restored in 1874.

Palazzo Spini-Ferroni

North-west of Santa Trínita, between Via del Parione and the Arno (Lungarno Corsini), we come to the 17th c. Palazzo Corsini, which contains the largest private art collection in Florence.

Palazzo Corsini

From the Palazzo Strozzi Via della Vigna Nuova runs west to the Palazzo Rucellai (1446–51), one of the finest Renaissance palazzi in Florence.

Palazzo Rucellai

*Santa Maria Novella

On the north-western edge of the central area extends the large Piazza di Santa Maria Novella, with the Loggia di San Paolo (1489–96) and two obelisks set up in the 17th c. to mark the finishing line of a race.

On the north side of the square is the Dominican Church of Santa Maria Novella, built in Gothic style between 1246 and 1360.

*Church

The Renaissance façade by Alberti is of outstanding importance and beauty. In the choir and the apse can be seen oustanding frescoes by Ghirlandaio and Massacio.

Cloisters
(closed Fri.)

To the left of the church is the entrance to the Green Cloister, a treasure-house of superb frescoes by Uccello (and his pupils). Separating the Green Cloister from the Little Cloister of the Dead is the Cappellone degli Spagnoli (Spanish Chapel). The frescoes in this former chapter-house were inspired by St Thomas Aquinas.

Railway station

North-west of Santa Maria Novella lies the Piazza della Stazione, with Florence's principal railway station, the Stazione Centrale di Santa Maria Novella (1935).

Ognissanti

South-west of Santa Maria Novella in the Piazza Ognissanti, which opens on to the Arno (Lungarno Amerigo Vespucci), stands the Church of Ognissanti (All Saints), one of the earliest Baroque churches in Florence (originally 13th c.; rebuilt in 16th and 17th c.). Frescoes by Botticelli ("St Augustine") and Ghirlandaio ("St Jerome") can be seen in the refectory museum.

*San Lorenzo

* Church

From the Piazza dell'Unità Italiana, on the east side of Santa Maria Novella, Via del Melarancio runs a short distance east of the Church of San Lorenzo, Florence's first cathedral, consecrated by St Ambrose in 393, rebuilt in Romanesque style in the 11th c. and again rebuilt by Brunelleschi and his successors from 1421 onwards in the form of an Early Christian columned basilica. The interior wall of the façade was the work of Michelángelo.

* Old Sacristy

At the end of the left-hand transept is the Old Sacristy (Sagrestia Vecchia; by Brunelleschi, 1420–29), one of the early achievements of Renaissance architecture, with sculptural decoration by Donatello.
On the left an attractive cloister with an upper loggia adjoins the church.

* Biblioteca Mediceo-
Laurenziana
(closed Sun.)

From the north-west corner of the cloister a staircase leads up to the Biblioteca Mediceo-Laurenziana, begun in 1524–26 to the design of Michelángelo. The library, originally founded in 1444 by Cosimo the Elder, possesses some thousands of manuscripts of Greek and Latin classics assembled by the Médici family.

* Médici Chapels
(closed Mon.)

* New Sacristy

Beyond the Church of San Lorenzo, in the Piazza Madonna degli Aldobrandini, is the entrance to the Médici Chapels (Cappelle Medicee). From the crypt a flight of steps leads up to the Princes' Chapel (Cappella dei Príncipi), built in 1604–10 to house the sarcophagi of the Grand Dukes of Tuscany and which is faced with fine stone mosaics. From here a passage continues left to the New Sacristy (Sagrestia Nuova), built by Michelángelo in 1520–24 as the burial chapel of the House of Médici. This square domed chamber contains the tombs by Michelángelo of a son and grandson of Lorenzo the Magnificent.

At the north-east corner of Piazza San Lorenzo is the imposing Palazzo Médici-Riccardi, built in 1444–52 for Cosimo the Elder and enlarged in the 17th–18th c.

In the courtyard is the entrance to the palace chapel, with important frescoes by Benozzo Gozzoli (c. 1460), and the Médici Museum, with mementoes of the Médici family, who occupied the palace until 1537.

Médici Museum

*San Marco

From the east side of the Palazzo Médici-Riccardi Via Camillo Cavour runs north-east to Piazza San Marco, in which are the church (much rebuilt) and Convent of San Marco, now the Museo di San Marco. The convent was rebuilt for the Dominicans in the 15th c. and decorated with frescoes by Fra Angélico.

*Museum
(closed Mon.)

To the south of San Marco, at Via Ricasoli 52, is the Accadémia di Belle Arti (Academy of Fine Art), with the Gallería dell'Accadémia, a study collection which supplements the Uffizi and the Pitti Gallery (Tuscan painting of the 13th–16th c.). The most notable exhibit is the famous "David" ("il Gigante") which the young Michelangelo carved in 1501–03 from a single huge block of stone. (There are copies in the Piazza della Signoría and the Piazzale Michelángiolo.)

Gallería dell'Accadémia

*Santíssima Annunziata

From Piazza San Marco Via Cesare Battisti runs past the University to the magnificent Church of the Santíssima Annunziata (the Virgin Annunciate), founded in 1250 and remodelled in 1444–60; porch rebuilt 1601. The atrium has frescoes by Andrea del Sarto (1505–14).
The interior is partly decorated in Baroque style. Above the outside of the doorway leading from the left transept into the cloister (Chiostro dei Morti) is a fresco by Andrea del Sarto ("Madonna del Sacco", 1525).

Opposite the church to the south is the Spedale degli Innocenti (begun by Brunelleschi in 1419), an early example of Renaissance architecture. Between the arches of the portico are coloured medallions of infants in swaddling clothes by Andrea della Robbia (c. 1463).

Spedale degli Innocenti
(Foundling Hospice; closed Mon.)

South-east of Santíssima Annunziata stands the Palazzo della Crocetta (1620), housing the Museo Archeológico Centrale dell'Etruria, founded in 1870 (entrance at Via della Colonna 38). The museum has excellent collections of Etruscan and Graeco-Roman material as well as a considerable Egyptian collection.

Archaeological Museum
(closed Mon.)

*Santa Croce

On the south-eastern edge of the old town, near the Arno, is the Gothic hall-church of Santa Croce (Holy Cross), begun in 1295 for the Franciscans but not completed until 1442 (façade 1857–63). In the majestically spacious interior are the tombs of many famous Italians, including Michelángelo, Alfieri, Machiavelli, Rossini, Cherubini and Galileo. Other major features of interest are the remains of frescoes (those in the choir chapels by Giotto and pupils) and the splendid marble pulpit by Benedetto da Maiano (1472–76). On the far side of the First Cloister (Primo Chiostro) is the Pazzi Chapel (Cappella de'Pazzi; by Brunelleschi, 1430), one of the earliest examples of Renaissance architecture. Note on the façade, to the left, the mark showing the height reached by the floodwaters of the Arno on 4 November 1966 – no less than 4·90 m (16 ft). The Second Cloister (Secondo Chiostro), in the manner of Brunelleschi, is a fine creation of the Early Renaissance.

Cloisters
* Pazzi Chapel

Museum
(closed Wed.)

In the former refectory, on the south side of the first cloister, is the richly stocked Museo dell'Ópera di Santa Croce. Among its many remarkable works of art is a "Crucifixion" by Cimabue, now restored following the floods.

National Central Library

Adjoining Santa Croce on the south is the huge complex (1911–35) of the National Central Library (Biblioteca Nazionale Centrale), the largest library in Italy, with more than 4 million titles, including valuable manuscripts, incunabula, music, atlases and maps.

Casa Buonarroti
(closed Tue.)
Michelángelo Museum

A little way north of Santa Croce, at Via Ghibellina 70, is the Casa Buonarroti, which Michelángelo acquired for his nephew Leonardo di Buonarroto. In 1620 Leonardo established a memorial to his uncle in the house, which is now a Michelángelo Museum (early works of the master, copies of other works, drawings, manuscripts, portraits and other mementoes).

Horne Museum
(closed Sun.)

Some 200 m (220 yd) west of the National Central Library, at the end of Corso dei Tintori (Via dei Benci 6), is the Museo della Fondazione Horne, with a valuable collection of pictures, drawings, sculpture, furniture, jewellery and everyday objects of the 14th–16th c. The collection was presented to the Italian State by the English art critic Herbert Percy Horne (1864–1916).

Ponte alle Grazie

A few paces south of the Horne Museum the Ponte alle Grazie (fine view) crosses to the left bank of the Arno.

**Ponte Vecchio

Some 250 m (275 yd) south-west of the Piazza della Signoría the famous Ponte Vecchio (Old Bridge), the oldest of Florence's bridges (first appearance in the records in 996; after repeated destruction rebuilt in 1345; the only one of the bridges not blown up during the Second World War), crosses to the south bank of the Arno at the river's narrowest point. The bridge was so wide that arcades were built along both sides and soon occupied by houses and shop (including butchers, who threw their offal into the river). At the end of the 16th c., however, Grand Duke Ferdinand I decreed, "for the benefit of strangers to the town", that henceforth only goldsmiths should be allowed to have shops on the bridge – a regulation which is still observed today.

Florence: The Ponte Vecchio across the Arno

**Palazzo Pitti

South-west of the Ponte Vecchio, on the slopes of the Colle di Bóboli, is the Palazzo Pitti, a massive fortress-like palace 36 m (118 ft) high, built about 1458 for Luca Pitti and altered and enlarged in the 16th–18th c.

In the left-hand half of the first floor is the famous Pitti Gallery (Gallería Palatina), founded by the Médici in the 16th–17th c., which now contains many hundreds of pictures, including a wealth of masterpieces by Raphael, Fra Bartolommeo, Andrea del Sarto, Titian and other artists. Within the gallery are ten of the former Royal Apartments (Appartamenti Reali, 18th–19th c.).

**Gallería Palatina
(closed Mon.)

On the ground floor is the Museo degli Argenti (Silver Museum), originally the royal collection of silver, with treasures which belonged to the Médici. Also on the ground floor is the Coach Museum (Museo delle Carrozze).

Silver Museum
(closed Mon.)
Coach Museum

On the second floor is the Gallery of Modern Art (Gallería d'Arte Moderna), with 19th c. pictures, mainly by Tuscan artists.

Gallery of Modern Art
(closed Mon.)

There is an interesting collection of costume in the Palazzina della Meridiana.

Gallery of Costume
(Tue., Thu., Sat. 9 a.m.–
2 p.m.)

To the south of the Palazzo Pitti are the Bóboli Gardens (Giardino di Bóboli; area 45,000 sq. m (11 acres)). Laid out in 1560, with fountains and statuary, the gardens extend up the hill, offering beautiful views of Florence from the terraces.

*Bóboli Gardens

Palazzo Pitti

Florence

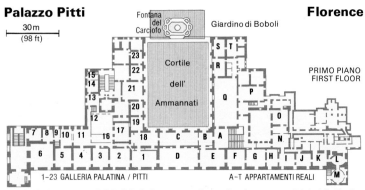

Fontana
del
Carciofo

Giardino di Boboli

30m
(98 ft)

Cortile
dell'
Ammannati

PRIMO PIANO
FIRST FLOOR

1–23 GALLERIA PALATINA / PITTI   A–T APPARTAMENTI REALI

1 Sala di Vénere:
  Titian, Tintoretto
2 Sala di Apollo:
  Van Dyck, Rubens,
  Reni, del Sarto,
  Titian, Tintoretto
3 Sala di Marte:
  Tintoretto, Reni,
  Titian, Rubens,
  Murillo, Veronese
4 Sala di Giove:
  Raphael, Bordone,
  Rubens, del Sarto,
  Perugino, Guercino
5 Sala di Saturno:
  Raphael
  ("Madonna della
  Seggiola")
6 Sala dell'Iliade:
  Velázquez, Titian,
  Raphael

7 Sala della Stufa:
  frescoes by
  Rosselli and Pietro
  da Cortona
8 Sala
  dell'Educazione di
  Giove:
  Caravaggio, Allori
9 Saletta da Bagno
10 Sala di Ulisse:
  Raphael, Reni,
  Lippi
11 Sala di Prometeo:
  Signorelli, Lippi
12 Corridoio delle
  Colonne
13 Sala della
  Giustizia:
  Veronese, Titian
14 Sala di Flora:

Canova, Bronzino
15 Sala dei Putti:
  Jordaens, Rubens
16 Gallería Poccetti:
  Pontormo, Rubens,
  Ribera, Dughet
17 Sala della Música
18 Sala Castagnoli
19 Sala delle
  Allegorie
20 Sala delle Belle
  Arti
21 Salone d'Ércole
22 Sala dell'Aurora
23 Sala di Berenice

A Vestíbolo
B Sala degli Staffieri
C Gallería delle
  Statue

D Sala delle Nicchie
E Sala Verde
F Sala del Trono
G Sala Celeste
H Cappella
I Sala dei Pappagalli
J Sala Gialla
K Camera da Letto
L Gabinetto da
  Toletta
M Sala da Música e
  da Lavoro
N Camera da Letto
O Salotto di
  Ricevimento
P Sala di Bona
Q Sala da Ballo
R Sala della Fede
S Sala della Carità
T Sala della Giustizia

Porcelain Museum (Tue., Thu., Sat. 9 a.m.– 2 p.m.)	In the Casino del Cavaliere is an interesting Porcelain Museum (Museo delle Porcellane).
Forte del Belvedere	Above the gardens, to the south-east (entrance on south side), is the commanding Forte del Belvedere or Forte di San Giorgio, built in 1590–95 by Bernardo Buontalenti. From the bastions there are superb views.
Santo Spírito	To the north-east of the Palazzo Pitti is the Church of Santo Spírito (Holy Ghost), begun in 1436 to the design of Brunelleschi and completed in 1487, with a campanile of 1543. Notable features are the sacristy (1489–92), the numerous altar-pieces and two 16th c. cloisters.
Santa Maria del Cármine	Farther west stands the former Carmelite Church of Santa Maria del Cármine, almost completely rebuilt in 1782 after a fire. The Brancacci Chapel contains celebrated frescoes by Masolino and Masaccio on the legends of the Apostles (1424–27), pioneering works of Renaissance painting.

Florence: Palazzo Pitti, Apollo Room

*Viale dei Colli

The Viale dei Colli (Avenue of the Hills), constructed from 1868 onwards, which runs for a distance of 6 km (4 miles) from the Porta Romana to the Piazzo Francesco Ferrucci, is one of the finest panoramic roads in Italy, affording magnificent views.

The first part of the road, here named Viale Niccolò Machiavelli, winds its way up to the circular Piazzale Galilei; then, as the Viale Galileo Galilei, it continues along the hillside, where stands the Church of San Miniato (below) and comes to another large square, the Piazzale Michelángiolo (alt. 104 m – 341 ft). On the terrace is a bronze copy of Michelángelo's "David" (original in the Galleria dell'Accadémia), with representations of the Four Seasons round the base. From here there are splendid views of Florence and the Arno Valley, with Fiésole (see entry) on its hill to the north-east.

Viale Machiavelli

Piazzale Galilei

Viale Galileo Galilei

**Piazzale Michelángiolo

From Piazzale Michelángiolo the road, now named Viale Michelángiolo, runs down in a great bend to the Piazzo Francesco Ferrucci, from which the Ponte San Niccolò crosses the Arno.

Viale Michelángiolo

Above Piazzale Michelángiolo, to the south, is the Franciscan Friary of San Salvatore al Monte, with a church completed in 1504.

San Salvatore al Monte

Still higher up is the Monastic Church of San Miniato al Monte, prominently visible with its façade of inlaid marble. One of the

San Miniato al Monte

finest examples of Tuscan Romanesque, it was built in the 11th–12th c.; the campanile was rebuilt in 1524–27. Notable features of the picturesque interior are a chapel built by Michelozzo (1448) at the far end of the nave, and a fine mosaic of 1297 in the apse; the crypt has frescoes by Taddeo Gaddi. Near the church is a fort built by Michelángelo in 1529. The fort itself is now an Olivetan convent, and the walls enclose a cemetery, established here in 1839.

From the terrace there are magnificent views.

Cascine

2 km (1½ miles) west of the Ponte Vecchio, in Piazza Vittorio Véneto, is the municipal park (area 118 hectares – 290 acres) known as Le Cascine (Dairy-farms: originally country estates belonging to the Médici and Lorraine families), which extends for more than 3 km (2 miles) along the north bank of the Arno (swimming-pool, cycle and horse-racing tracks).

Certosa del Galluzzo   C3

Location
5 km (3 miles) S

From the Porta Romana SS 2 (the Siena road) runs south to the Certosa del Galluzzo. In 2 km (1¼ miles), on the right, is a Protestant cemetery, the Cimitero degli Allori, where the grave of the Swiss painter Arnold Böcklin (1827–1901) is situated. 2 km (1¼ miles) farther on, beyond the village of Galluzzo, the fortress-like Certosa del Galluzzo or Certosa di Firenze can be seen on the hill to the right. As its name (Charterhouse) indicates, this was originally a Carthusian house (construction begun 1341), but since 1958 it has been occupied by Cistercians. In the picture gallery note the frescoes by Pontormo (after Dürer) in the lunettes.

Fiésole

See p. 81.

Forte dei Marmi   C2

Province: Lucca (LU)
Altitude: 0–2 m (0–6½ ft)
Population: 10,000

Situation

The fashionable seaside resort of Forte dei Marmi lies on the Ligurian Sea at the northern end of the Tuscan coast. Above the town rise the Versilia hills.

The town

Forte dei Marmi owes its name (Fort of Marble) to the marble-quarries in the Apuan Alps (Carrara – see entry) and within the town itself and to the fort which was built here by Grand Duke Leopold I in 1788.

The coast road (Viale Itálico; in the broader central section Viale della Repúbblica) runs past the town's long sandy beach. The landing-stage, 300 m (330 yd) long, from which the marble was once shipped is now used by the boats sailing to the islands of the Arcipélago Toscano (see entry) (Tuscan Archipelago).
The long beach of fine sand and the shallow water which extends far out to sea make Forte dei Marmi particularly suitable for families.

Giannutri (Ísola di Giannutri)   D3

Province: Grosseto (GR)
Area: 2·62 km (1 sq. mile)

The island of Giannutri lies 10 km (6 miles) south of Monte Argentario in the Tyrrhenian Sea.   Situation

Boat services from Porto Santo Stéfano (Monte Argentario – see entry).   Access

The island

Giannutri is the most southerly island in the Arcipélago Toscano (see entry) (Tuscan Archipelago). It reaches its highest point in Capel Rosso (88 m – 289 ft). The coast is mainly rocky, with short stretches of sandy beach only in the

Giannutri: Roman villa

north-west and north-east; it will appeal more, therefore, to skin-divers than to bathers. There are remains of a Roman villa of the 1st c. A.D. on the island.

Giglio (Ísola del Giglio)   D2

Province: Grosseto (GR)
Area: 21·21 sq. km (8 sq. miles)
Population: 1800

Situation

The island of Giglio (island of the Lily) lies 15km (9 miles) west of Monte Argentario in the Tyrrhenian Sea.

Access

Car ferry service from Porto Santo Stéfano (Monte Argentario – see entry).

The island

The hilly island of Giglio is the largest in the Arcipélago Toscano (Tuscan Archipelago – see entry) after Elba. Its highest point is the Poggio della Pagana (498 m – 1634 ft). The coasts are mainly steep and rocky, inaccessible from the landward side; only in the east and north-west are there a few sandy beaches. There are three villages on the island, which is mainly agricultural (vines, olives): Giglio Porto (with the ferry harbour), Giglio Castello (the administrative centre) and Giglio Campese.

Giglio: Harbour of Giglio Porto

Giglio Porto lies in a bay on the east coast. Higher up, the holiday village of La Ginestra has been developed. To the south are the beaches of Cala delle Canelle and Cala degli Álberi.
The chief place of the island, Giglio Castello, lies inland at a height of some 400 m (1300 ft). It has largely preserved its picturesque old-world aspect, with its circuit of walls and winding lanes. Over it looms a medieval castle, the Rocca.
Giglio Campese, on the north-west coast, looks out on to a beautiful bay with the longest sandy beach on the island. It has some facilities for visitors (holiday village, camping site).

Gorgona (Ísola di Gorgona)   C1

Province: Livorno (LI)
Area: 2·23 sq. km (550 acres)

The little island of Gorgona lies in the Ligurian Sea 35 km (22   Situation
miles) from the port of Livorno in northern Tuscany.

Boat services from Livorno and from Elba (see entries).   Access

The island

The sparsely populated island of Gorgona is the most northerly in the Arcipélago Toscano (see entry) (Tuscan Archipelago). There is a penal establishment on the island, and it can, therefore, be visited only with the permission of the Italian Ministry of Justice.

Grópina   C3

Province: Arezzo (AR)
Altitude: 381 m (1250 ft)
Population: 1000

The little village of Grópina lies half-way between Florence and   Situation
Arezzo above the right (east) bank of the Arno, near the A1
motorway (Valdarno exit).

The village

The Romanesque Parish Church of St Peter (Pieve di San Pietro) was built in the 12th c. on Etruscan and Roman foundations. The façade, apse and campanile (1232) and the aisled interior are of rare harmony and striking beauty. Particular features of interest are the monolithic columns (with one pair of pillars interrupting the series), with curious, finely carved capitals (a pig with piglets; battle between Virtue and Vice; fighting animals; vines; Samson, etc.), and the fine pulpit with bas-reliefs (symbols of the Evangelists) and rich ornament. The history of the church can be traced back to the time of Charlemagne, who presented an earlier church on this site to the Benedictine Abbey of Nonántola near Módena.

Grosseto D3

Province: Grosseto (GR)
Altitude: 10 m (60 ft)
Population: 70,000

Situation

The provincial capital of Grosseto lies in the alluvial plain of the Ombrone in southern Tuscany, 12 km (7½ miles) from the sea.

History

Grosseto, now chief town of the province of the same name and the principal centre in the Maremma (see entry), grew up in the Middle Ages around a small fort guarding the Via Aurelia, the old Roman road from Rome to Pisa. When the drainage system of the Maremma fell into decay and the Etruscan town of Rusellae was destroyed by the Saracens the episcopal see was transferred from there to Grosseto in 935. During the Middle Ages the walled town of Grosseto, like other towns in Tuscany, frequently changed hands. Only under the Grand Duchy of Tuscany did the town achieve a modest growth in prosperity; but this was always dependent on the state of the drainage system and subject to the hazards of malaria. The town's development into a thriving agricultural centre with some industry made little progress until after 1930, when the Maremma was completely drained. During the Second World War Grosseto suffered severe damage from Allied air raids.

The old town

The Centro Stórico, the historic town centre, is surrounded by an irregular hexagon of walls, with six bastions, begun by Grand Duke Francesco I in 1574 and completed by

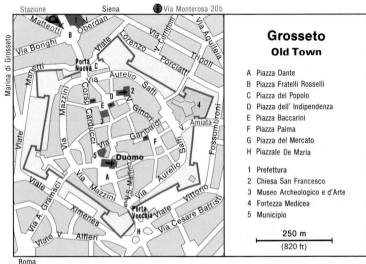

Grosseto
Old Town

A Piazza Dante
B Piazza Fratelli Rosselli
C Piazza del Popolo
D Piazza dell' Indipendenza
E Piazza Baccarini
F Piazza Palma
G Piazza del Mercato
H Piazzale De Maria

1 Prefettura
2 Chiesa San Francesco
3 Museo Archeologico e d'Arte
4 Fortezza Medicea
5 Municipio

250 m
(820 ft)

Grosseto: Piazza Dante

Ferdinand I in 1593. They are reminiscent of the walls of Lucca (see entry), and accordingly Grosseto is sometimes referred to as a "little Lucca".

Cathedral

The main square of the old town is the Piazza Dante, on the north side of which is the cathedral (San Lorenzo). It was built between 1294 and 1302 on the foundations of an earlier church and several times rebuilt or altered in later centuries (campanile originally 1402, rebuilt 1611; façade rebuilt 1840–45). The interior was restored in the 19th c. In the left transept is an "Assumption" by Matteo di Giovanni (known as Matteo da Siena; *c.* 1433–1495).

Museo Archeológico e d'Arte della Maremma

A short distance north of the cathedral, in Piazza Baccarini, is the Museo Archeológico e d'Arte della Maremma (Museum of Archaeology and Art), with prehistoric as well as Etruscan and Roman material and collection of religious art.

San Francesco

The Church of San Francesco, a little way north of the museum in the Piazza dell'Indipendenza, was built by Benedictines in the 13th c. and later taken over by Franciscans. It contains remains of 14th c. frescoes.

Roselle: Remains of the walls of ancient Rusellae

* Roselle (Rusellae)   D3

Situation
6 km (4 miles) NE

On the edge of the hilly country, a few miles north of Grosseto near the village of Roselle, are the remains of the Etruscan city of Rusellae, once a member of the Etruscan League of twelve cities. After it was taken by Rome its importance declined, and during the great migrations it was largely destroyed. There are remains of the town's rectangular circuit of walls, an amphitheatre of the Roman period and a few Etruscan houses.

Talamone   D3

Situation
25 km (15 miles) S

The little fishing village and seaside resort of Talamone is charmingly situated on a spur of land which forms the west side of a bay. Above the village are the ruins of a castle.

· Parco Naturale della Maremma

To the north of Talamone the Parco Naturale della Maremma, a nature reserve, takes in a strip of land along the coast and the parallel chain of the Monti dell'Uccellina and extends to beyond the mouth of the River Ombrone.
The reserve is open to visitors only at week-ends, public holidays and on Wednesdays from 9 a.m. until an hour before sunset. Cars are not admitted.
The reserve shows a variety of landscape forms. The area around the mouth of the Ombrone is flat and marshy; the hills are covered with *macchia* (scrub) and coniferous woodland,

and on bluffs near the coast there are numbers of old watch-towers. Herds of half-wild white Maremma cattle are frequently encountered, and in winter this is the haunt of various migrant birds.

Ísola di . . .

See under the name of the island.

La Verna

Province: Arezzo (AR)
Altitude: 1129 m (3704 ft)

The pilgrimage centre of La Verna lies in the hills of the Casentino in north-eastern Tuscany, some 60 km (37 miles) north of Arezzo.

Situation

After giving up the direction of the Order which he had founded Francis of Assisi withdrew about 1222 to the solitude of the hills. Here on 17 September 1224 tradition has it that he received the stigmata, the marks of Christ's wounds: an event described by Dante in the "Divine Comedy" ("Paradiso" 11, 106 ff.). Since then La Verna, beautifully situated amid pine forests, has been a hallowed place, and the Franciscan friary is

History

La Verna: Sanctuary . . .   *. . . and entombment (workshop of della Robbia)*

109

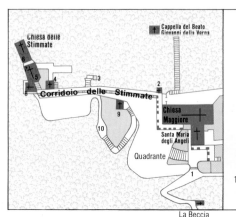

La Beccia

La Verna
Franciscan Friary

1 Entrance (arch)
2 Cappella della Pietà
3 Grotto
4 Cappella Loddi
5 St Francis's second cell
6 Chapel of St Bonaventure
7 Chapel of St Antony of Padua
8 Chapel of St Sebastian
9 St Francis's first cell
10 Sasso Spicco (Detached Stone)

the goal of countless pilgrims. Days of high festival are 14 September, commemorating the stigmatisation, and 4 October, St Francis's Day.

*Franciscan friary

Near the entrance to the precincts of the friary stands the little Church of Santa Maria degli Àngeli, the foundation-stone of which was laid by St Francis; the building was altered in later times. There are a number of coats of arms on the façade, and the church contains terracottas from the workshop of the della Robbias and the Tomb of Count Orlando Cattani, who presented the site of the friary to St Francis. Immediately adjoining is the Chiesa Maggiore, an aisleless church in Renaissance style which was begun in 1348 and completed in the 16th c. It contains terracottas by Andrea della Robbia ("Adoration of the Child", "Virgin in Prayer", "Annunciation", "Assumption").

The Corridor of the Stigmata (Corridoio delle Stimmate), with frescoes of 1670 (restored) on the life of St Francis, leads to the Cappella della Stimmate, an oratory built in 1263 which also contains terracottas by Andrea and Luca della Robbia. A memorial stone set here in the 14th c. marks the spot on which St Francis received the stigmata.

Livorno (Leghorn)   C2

Province: Livorno (LI)
Altitude: 0–3 m (0–10 ft)
Population: 177,000

Situation

Livorno (traditionally known in English as Leghorn), chief town of its province and Tuscany's principal port, lies 20 km (12½ miles) south of Pisa on the edge of the alluvial cone deposited by the Arno.

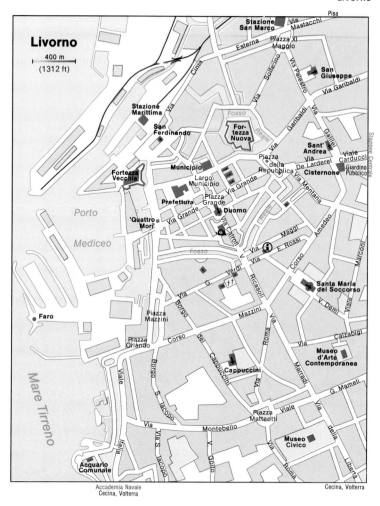

Livorno

400 m
(1312 ft)

Pisa

Stazione
San Marco

Via Mastacchi

Piazza XI
Magglo

Esterna

Via Palestro

Solferino

San
Giuseppe

Via Garibaldi

Stazione
Marittima

Via

Fosso

Regio

Garibaldi

Via

Galilei

Sant'
Andrea

Stazione Centrale

San
Ferdinando

For-
tezza
Nuova

Via

Piazza
della
Repubblica

Via
De Larderel

Viale
Carducci

Giardino
Pubblico

Municipio

Cisternone

Fortezza
Vecchia

Largo
Municipio

Via Grande

Via Mentana

Prefettura

Piazza
Grande

Duomo

Via Amedeo

Via Marcon

Porto

'Quattro
Mori

Via Grande

Via Cairoli

Fosso

Maggl

E. Rossi

Corso

Mediceo

G. Verdi

Ricasoli

Santa Maria
del Soccorso

Faro

Piazza
Mazzini

Borgo

Mazzini

Via

V. Deml

Via
Roma

Calzabigi

Piazza
Orlando

Corso dei

Borgo

S. Jacopo

Cappuccini

Via
Marrad

Via

Museo
d'Arte
Contemporanea

G. Mameli

Mare Tirreno

Viale

Italia

Via S. Jacopo

V.
Golo

Montebello

Piazza
Matteotti

Viale

Museo
Civico

Via della

Via
Roma

Liberta

Acquario
Comunale

Accademia Navale
Cecina, Volterra

Cecina, Volterra

Faced with the present-day city of Livorno, with its industrial installations and modern buildings, it is easy to forget that this is a town with a long history. First mentioned in the records in 904, it was for long the port for Pisa, but after the Pisans' defeat in 1405 it passed into the hands of the Genoese, who sold it to Florence in 1421 for 100,000 gold florins. The Médici then fortified the town and in 1571 constructed a new harbour and at the same time laid out a new town. Livorno thereafter enjoyed a rapid upsurge of prosperity, and by the end of the 18th c. had become the largest town in Tuscany after Florence.

History

111

During the Second World War the town suffered heavy damage, particularly to its historic buildings, and now preserves only a few buildings of any age.
Livorno was the birthplace of the painter Amedeo Modigliani (1884–1920) and the composer Pietro Mascagni (1863–1945).

Old town

The old town – the town founded by the Médici – has the form of a pentagon, surrounded by the Fosso Reale (the old moat, still filled with water) and is traversed by streets laid out on a rectangular grid.

Cathedral

In the centre of the old town, at the intersection of Via Grande and Via Cairoli, is the Piazza Grande, in which stands the cathedral (San Francesco d'Assisi), built between 1594 and 1606 to the design of Bernardo Buontalenti and Alessandro Pieroni. After its destruction during the Second World War (1943) it was rebuilt in its original form. The interior (aisleless) contains a number of tombs and ceiling-frescoes by Iácopo Ligozzi, Passignano and Iácopo da Émpoli (all 16th–17th c.). Via Cairoli leads south-east from the cathedral in a straight line and passes the Fosso Reale.

Piazza della Repúbblica

At the east end of Via Grande is the Piazza della Repúbblica, a large square laid out over part of the Fosso Reale. In the square are 19th c. statues of Ferdinand III (by Francesco Pozzi) and Leopold II (by Emilio Santarelli).

Fortezza Nuova

Opposite the north end of the Piazza della Repúbblica rises the Fortezza Nuova, a moated stronghold built in 1590.

Port

The port, at the west end of the old town, is one of the largest in the Mediterranean. There are boat services from here (some carrying cars) to Elba (see entry) and other islands in the Arcipélago Toscano (see entry) (Tuscan Archipelago), as well as to Sardinia and the French island of Corsica. The old part of the port is known, after its founders, as the Porto Mediceo.

*Monument to Ferdinand I

In Piazza Micheli, which opens on to the harbour, can be seen a monument to Grand Duke Ferdinand I (1587–1609), popularly known as the Monumento dei Quattro Mori (Monument of the Four Moors) after the bronze figures on the base. The monument, with its marble statue of the Grand Duke, was originally erected in 1599; the vigorously depicted figures of slaves were added, after long-drawn-out preliminary trials, in 1623.

Livorno: Fosso Reale and Fortezza Vecchia

Livorno: Monument of the Four Moors

Lucca: Façade of cathedral

113

Fortezza Vecchia

At the north end of the old port area is the Fortezza Vecchia (Old Fortress), built by Antonio da Sangallo for Cardinal Giulio de' Médici between 1521 and 1534. It is dominated by a squat tower known as the Mástio di Matilde, part of an earlier 11th c. castle.

San Ferdinando

The little Church of San Ferdinando, also known as the Chiesa della Crocetta, stands outside the old town to the north-west. A Baroque structure (1707–14) by Giovanni Battista Foggini, it was largely rebuilt after the Second World War, like many other churches in Livorno. It contains sculpture by Giovanni Baratta (1670–1747), including figures of St Louis of France and St Henry the Pious of Germany and allegorical representations of the Christian virtues.

Cisternone

To the east of the Piazza della Repúbblica, reached by way of Via de Larderel, is the Cisternone (1829–32), a neo-classical building fronted by a Doric portico and a large vaulted niche. It is a water-tower, supplied by an aqueduct. Beyond it lies the Giardino Púbblico (Public Garden).

Viale Italia

From the south end of the port area the Viale Italia skirts the seafront, flanked by gardens and beaches.

Aquarium

On the Terrazza Mascagni is the Acquario Comunale (Municipal Aquarium to which is attached an institute of marine biology. Beyond this the seafront promenade passes the Accadémia Navale (Naval Academy).

Museo d'Arte Contemporanea

In a park to the south-east of the old town is the Museo d'Arte Contemporanea (Museum of Contemporary Art), mainly devoted to work by Italian artists. Special exhibitions on particular themes are put on from time to time.

Museo Cívico

The Museo Cívico (Municipal Museum), in the Villa Fabbricotti Park to the south of the modern town, is notable particularly for its collection of works by the group known as the Macchiaioli, formed in the mid 19th c., whose main aim was to get away from the academic school of art. The museum also contains pictures by Italian masters of the 15th–17th c. and a number of icons.

Lucca   C2

Province: Lucca (LU)
Altitude: 19 m (62 ft)
Population: 92,500

Lucca, chief town of its province, lies on the left bank of the
Serchio in north-western Tuscany, some 25 km (15 miles)
inland from Viareggio.

Situation

The town's name is probably of Etruscan origin, from the word
luk meaning a marsh, such as extended in ancient times
between the arms of the River Serchio. The area was inhabited
by Ligurians, but it was the Etruscans, their successors, who
began to drain the area and thus brought about a great
improvement in the conditions of human occupation. The
Romans preserved the old name when they established a
settlement here, strategically situated both from the military
and economic points of view at the intersection of the extended
Via Cassia and a branch of the Via Aurelia. in 60 B.C. Julius
Caesar, Pompey and Marcus Licinius Crassus met here to
establish their triumvirate.
During the troubled period of the Great Migrations the
Lombards, who had pushed into Italy from Pannonia, made
Lucca the capital of a Duchy. From Carolingian times onwards
the Holy Roman Emperors showed special favour to the town,
which before the rise of Florence and Pisa became the largest
and most important commune in Tuscany in the High Middle

History

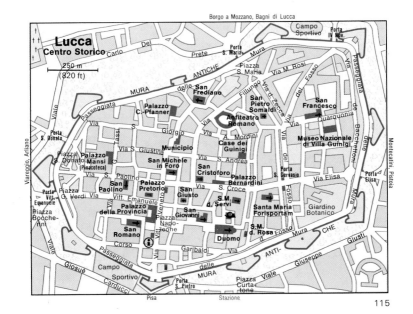

Ages. Its crafts (production of silks and brocades, manufacture of gold-leaf), its commerce and its banks brought prosperity to the town and developed the civic pride of its citizens, who as early as about 1080 established their independence of the Counts of Tuscany and were henceforth ruled by elected consuls. The city now enjoyed a heyday of prosperity, to which its Romanesque churches (in particular San Michele in Foro, dedicated to the Archangel Michael) and its works of sculpture and painting bear witness. This prosperity led to an increase in population; and the town, having outgrown its old Roman walls, was surrounded by a new circuit of fortifications.

Lucca's increasing economic power, however, brought it rivals and enemies. Although the city was victorious in its long-continued conflict with Pisa – helped by the Genoese defeat of the Pisans in 1284 – it then had to reckon with the increasing strength of Florence; and it was also weakened by internal strife, in particular continuing feuds between Guelfs and Ghibellines. After a period of rule by *condottieri* (commanders of bands of mercenaries) Lucca recovered its freedom at the hands of the Emperor Charles IV in 1369. A period of peace under the protection of the Emperor and the rule of Paolo Guinigi (1400–30), a noble, led to a revival of prosperity. The circuit of walls which still survives was built between the early 16th c. and 1645; and although the walls never had to withstand a siege they protected the town from the floodwaters of the Serchio in 1812.

The shrewd policies pursued by Lucca in its dealings with the Great Powers of the day enabled the Republic to survive until 1799, when Napoleon elevated it into a Principality which he presented to his sister Elisa Baciocchi. In 1815 this became a Duchy, which was finally incorporated into Tuscany in 1847.

Piazza Napoleone

The Piazza Napoleone, Lucca's principal square, lies in the south-west of the old town within the walls. It was laid out in the time of Elisa Baciocchi.

Palazzo della Provincia

The whole of the west side of the square is occupied by the handsome façade of the Palazzo della Provincia, formerly known as the Palazzo della Signoría or Palazzo Ducale. Designed by Bartolomeo Ammannati, it was built from 1578 onwards on the site of the earlier Palazzo degli Anziani (seat of the Council of Elders). The large main courtyard and the Cortile degli Svízzeri (named after the Swiss Guard formerly maintained by the city) remained unfinished.

San Romano

Location
Piazza San Romano

To the south-west of the Palazzo della Provincia is the Church of San Romano, built by the Dominicans in 1280 (apse added in 1373); the façade is unfinished. The lower part of the campanile is of stone, the upper part of brick. The church contains the Tomb of St Romanus (1490).

San Giusto

Near the north-east corner of the Piazza Napoleone is the little
12th c. Church of San Giusto, with a severe façade of
sandstone and bands of marble relieved by blind arcades and a
richly decorated main doorway. The interior was remodelled in
Baroque style in the mid 17th c.

Location
Piazza San Giusto

San Giovanni

Passing between the Piazza Napoleone and the cathedral (see
below) to the east, we come to the Church of San Giovanni,
which was rebuilt in the 12th c. Its predecessor, dedicated to St
Reparata (first Patron Saint of Florence), had been the seat of
the Bishop since the 8th c. Following the complete reconstruction of San Giovanni in 1622 only the central doorway and part
of the south front of the Romanesque church survive.
The interior of the church is divided into three aisles by columns
(with one Roman and other Romanesque capitals). A door in
the left transept leads into the large Baptistery of San Giovanni
(rebuilt in the 14th c., with a dome borne on pointed arches).

Location
Piazza San Giovanni

*Cathedral

The original church, which became the seat of the Bishop in the
8th c., is believed to have been founded by St Fredianus in the
6th c. The church, dedicated to St Martin, was rebuilt by Bishop
Anselmo da Baggio, later Pope Alexander II (1061–73), and
was again completely rebuilt in the 13th c. As a result it is
predominantly Romanesque, with some Gothic features.
The richly decorated Romanesque façade was the work of the
Lombard architect Guidetto da Como (1204, according to an
inscription in the first dwarf gallery). It consists of a lower
storey, with three arches opening into a portico, and three tiers
of dwarf galleries; it was presumably intended to top the façade
with a pediment, but this was never constructed. To allow for
the campanile the right-hand part of the façade is two arches
narrower than the left-hand side. The lower part of the massive
campanile, 69 m (226 ft) high, is of light-coloured travertine,
the upper part of brick. The windows in the campanile are
single-arched on the lowest level, rising to five arches in the
highest.
The portico was decorated in the mid 13th c. with fine sculpture
by Lombard sculptors (among them Guido da Como). In the
main doorway are four scenes from the life of St Martin, to
whom the church is dedicated; in the tympanum of the right-
hand doorway is the "Beheading of St Regulus"; on the lintel
of the left-hand doorway the "Annunciation", the "Nativity"
and the "Adoration of the Kings"; and in the tympanum the
"Entombment" – all work of the highest quality by Nicola
Pisano dating from about 1260–70.
The interior consists of a nave flanked by aisles and a two-
aisled transept, with a semicircular apse at the east end. Round-
headed arches borne on piers support galleries with two
tripartite windows. The interior received its present form in the

Location
Piazza San Martino

14th–15th c. (restored in the 19th c.). Just inside the entrance, on the right, is the famous group depicting St Martin and the beggar (early 13th c.), one of the finest examples of Romanesque sculpture in Lucca, formerly on the outside of the façade. On the fifth pier on the right is the pulpit by Matteo Civitali (1494–98). In the sacristy are a "Pietà", believed to be by Bartolomeo di Giovanni, and pictures by Doménico Ghirlandaio or his school.

In the right-hand transept are the Tomb of Pietro da Noceto, Secretary to Pope Nicholas V (1447–55), and, facing it, the Tomb of Doménico Bertini. Both are notable examples (by Matteo Civitali) of Florentine funerary sculpture of the 15th c. To the right of the apse is the large Altar of St Regulus, and in the adjoining Chapel of the Sacrament are two Angels; both of these works are by Civitali. The stained glass in the apse, by Pandolfo di Ugolino, dates from about 1485. To the left of the sanctuary is a statue of St John the Evangelist by Iácopo della Quercia; and in the adjoining Cappella del Santuario is a beautiful "Madonna" (1509) by Fra Bartolommeo.

In the left transept is the impressive Tomb of Ilaria del Carretto (d. 1405), Paolo Guinigi's second wife, who died young. It is a master work by Iácopo della Quercia. The dead woman is depicted lying on a sarcophagus, with an expression of great repose; her dress is disposed in elaborate folds; and at her feet is a dog, the symbol of fidelity. The sarcophagus is decorated with reliefs of *putti* (cherubs), representing spirits of death.

`Volto Santo

The cathedral's greatest treasure, from the religious artistic point of view, is the Volto Santo or Holy Face, an effigy of Christ on the Cross, housed in a *tempietto* (little temple) made for it by Matteo Civitali. Legend has it that it was carved by Nicodemus from the wood of a cedar of Lebanon and brought by mysterious ways to Lucca, where it was highly venerated. Every year on 13 September the Volto Santo is carried through the streets of the town in solemn procession. The date of the Crucifix, which is honoured as miracle-working, is uncertain, but is probably 11th to 12th c. The present Volto Santo is undoubtedly based on a much earlier prototype.

Santa Maria della Rosa

Location
Via della Rosa

A short distance east of the cathedral is a small low church dedicated to Santa Maria della Rosa, built against the Roman town walls in 1309 by the Università dei Mercanti. On the side wall are Gothic arcades enclosing elegant windows. On the left-hand wall of the interior are large dressed blocks of stone from the Roman walls.

Santa Maria Forisportam

Location
Piazza Santa Maria
Forisportam

This church is called Santa Maria Forisportam (Outside the gate) because when it was built in the 13th c. it stood outside the gate in the Roman town walls. The façade, in Pisan Romanesque style, is unfinished. The interior is aisled. It contains an Early Christian sarcophagus (with representations of the Good Shepherd and Daniel in the lions' den) converted for use as a font. In the right transept is a Baroque ciborium by

Giovanni Vambrè, in the left transept is a picture, the "Death and Assumption of the Virgin", painted on a gold ground by Ángelo Puccinelli (1386).

A few paces north-east of the church in Via del Fosso (with the old town moat) is the Porta Santi Gervasio e Protasio, a massive gate protected by two round towers which formed part of the 12th c. circuit of town walls, now largely destroyed.

Porta Santi Gervasio e
Protasio

San Cristóforo

To the north-east of the Piazza Napoleone, at the near end of the busy Via Fillungo, stands the Church of San Cristóforo, which dates from the 12th–13th c. There are three doorways in the façade, the central one having a richly ornamented architrave. Set in the wall to the right are two iron standard measures marking the width of a bolt of cloth as fixed by the Università dei Mercanti. In the upper part of the façade is a large rose-window (14th c.).

Location
Via Fillungo

Palazzo Bernardini

A little way east of San Cristóforo can be seen the long three-storeyed façade of the Palazzo Bernardini, built by Matteo Civitali in the early 16th c. It has a beautiful doorway and an elegant courtyard.

Location
Via Santa Croce

Case dei Guinigi (Houses of the Guinigi)

In Via dei Guinigi, almost exactly in the centre of the walled old town, the visitor's eye is caught by a massive tower with holm-oaks growing on the top. It belongs to the Case dei Guinigi, a complex consisting of two mansions belonging to the noble family under whose rule Lucca enjoyed a period of peace and prosperity at the beginning of the 15th c. The two palaces, standing opposite one another, were built in the 14th–15th c. and altered in later centuries. On the ground floor are porticoes, now walled up; the windows of the upper storeys are separated by columns and surmounted by round-headed arches.
In Via Sant'Andrea is the Loggia dei Guinigi (now walled up), in which family weddings and other occasions were once celebrated.

Location
Via dei Guinigi

Anfiteatro Romano

The present Piazza del Mercato (market-place) follows the ground-plan of a Roman amphitheatre of the 2nd c. B.C. In ancient times it lay outside the town walls to the north; during the Great Migrations it was largely destroyed, and the remains now lie several feet below street-level. During the Middle Ages houses were built on the walls of the superstructure (scanty remains of which can still be seen); their siting still reveals the oval form of the arena. The square in its present form, in which the market is still held, was laid out by Lorenzo Nottolini in 1830–39.

Location
Piazza del Mercato

Lucca: Market Place on site of old Roman amphitheatre

San Pietro Somaldi

Location
Piazza San Pietro Somaldi

San Pietro Somaldi: Central doorway

A little way east of the Piazza del Mercato, in a triangular piazza, is the Church of San Pietro Somaldi, an aisled basilica of the 12th c. occupying the site of an earlier church which is believed to have been built by the Lombards in the 8th c. The façade, with its banding of white and grey marble and its two tiers of delicately articulated loggias, dates from 1248. On the lintel of the central doorway is a representation of St Peter receiving the keys by Guido da Como (1203). On the north side of the church is a plain brick campanile. The vaulting (partly recently renewed) which spans the three-aisled interior of the basilica, rests on massive square columns; on the left-hand side the third column bears the date 1199. In the south aisle is a 12th c. fresco of the Madonna.

San Francesco

Location
Piazza San Francesco

At the east end of the old town, not far from San Pietro Somaldi, is the Piazza San Francesco, from which the picturesque Via del Fosso (with a canal which marked the boundary of the medieval town) runs north and south. The square is dominated by the Church of San Francesco, begun in 1228 (only two years after St Francis's death), rebuilt in the 14th c. and again restored in the 17th c. The façade, much restored, has three tiers of arcading, a Gothic doorway and a rose-window. Flanking the doorway are two medieval tombs.

The church (aisleless) has choir-stalls with intarsia decoration, frescoes of the 15th c. Florentine school, tombs (including the Cenotaph of the *condottiere* Castruccio Castracani) and a memorial to the composer Luigi Boccherini. Adjoining the church is a small cloister.

*Museo Nazionale di Villa Guinigi

The Villa Guinigi, beyond the Church of San Francesco at the extreme east end of the old town, was built for Paolo Guinigi, who ruled Lucca from 1400 to 1430. It now houses the Museo Nazionale (National Museum), with its rich art collection. Of particular interest are the Etruscan and Roman sculpture, sculpture from Lucca's medieval churches (San Michele and the cathedral) and numbers of panel-paintings (including a famous 13th c. "Crucifixion" by Berlinghiero Berlinghieri and works by Francesco di Giorgio Martini, Doménico Beccafumi and Jácopo da Pontormo).

Location
Via della Quarquonia

Palazzo Pretorio

In Via Vittorio Véneto, which runs north from the Piazza Napoleone, is the Palazzo Pretorio, begun in 1492 to the design of Matteo Civitali and completed in Renaissance style in 1589. On the ground floor is a portico with a statue of Matteo Civitali (1893). The palazzo is now occupied by the Pretura, a law court.

Location
Via Vittorio Véneto

*San Michele in Foro

The Church of San Michele, an aisled basilica, stands on the site of the Roman forum. The building of the present church was begun in the 12th c. but dragged on into the 14th c.; a planned enlargement, however, was never carried out.
The imposing five-storey west front was designed for the enlarged church, and accordingly reflects the planned section of the nave, which was to be much larger than the present church. In the lowest storey, which is broken up by arches borne on columns, are three doorways; on the pillar at the right-hand end is a "Madonna and Child" by Matteo Civitali (1476–80), set here in thanksgiving for the city's deliverance from plague. The upper storeys have dwarf galleries, the columns of which are inlaid with coloured stone and topped by capitals of varying form. Some of the columns are carved with inlaid figures of animals and monsters. On the highest point of the façade is an over-life-size figure of the Archangel Michael, flanked by two smaller figures of Angels.
The dwarf galleries and arcading on the two lower tiers of the façade are carried round the south side and, in part, round the north side of the church. Built against the right transept is the campanile, with a flat 19th c. roof replacing the original battlemented top.
Until the 16th c. the nave had a flat roof, which was then replaced by the present vaulting; in other respects, however, the Romanesque character of the interior has been preserved. On the central pier is a terracotta "Madonna and Child" by

Location
Piazza San Michele

121

Lucca: San Michele in Foro

Andrea della Robbia. In the left transept is a panel-picture (*c.* 1480–1500) depicting SS. Roch, Sebastian, Jerome and Helen, one of Filippo Lippi's finest works.

San Paolino

Location
Via San Paolino

San Paolino, Lucca's only Renaissance church, stands to the west of the Piazza San Michele. This aisleless church was built between 1522 and 1539 by Baccio da Montelupo and his successor Bastiano Bertolani, probably on a site once occupied by a Roman temple. In the presbytery is an Early Christian sarcophagus with a representation of the Good Shepherd in which St Paulinus, the church's patron, was buried.

Palazzo Mansi

Location
Via Galli Tassi

The 17th c. Palazzo Mansi, at the west end of the old town, has a plain exterior and a sumptuous 18th c. interior. It is now occupied by the Pinacoteca Nazionale (National Gallery), with a fine collection of pictures of the medieval period and, more particularly, the period from the Renaissance to the 19th c.

Most of the pictures were presented to Lucca by Grand Duke Leopold II when the town was incorporated in Tuscany in 1847. Among the most notable items are works by Fra Bartolommeo ("God the Father with the Magdalene and St Catherine"), Doménico Beccafumi, Tintoretto, Veronese and Andrea del Sarto.

Palazzo Controni-Pfanner

The Palazzo Controni-Pfanner, just inside the walls on the north side of the old town, was built in 1667. It is noted for its opon two storey loggia with staircase, a harmonious Renaissance creation. The garden, laid out in the 17th c., has a number of fine statues.

Location
Via degli Asili 33

* San Frediano

The Church of San Frediano, dedicated to the 6th c. Bishop of Lucca of that name, was built between 1112 and 1147 on the site of an earlier 8th c. church (some remains of which were brought to light in 1950). Originally the church had the usual orientation, with the chancel at the east end. In the 13th c., however, it was heightened and the façade was given another storey; the baptistery and the Cappella della Santa Croce, to the right and left of the present entrance, were incorporated in the church; the apse, containing the altar, was built on to the west end so that the entrance front should not face the town walls which had by then been erected.

The lower part of the façade is plain, vertically articulated by pilasters and columns. The upper part is dominated by a huge mosaic depicting Christ in a mandorla (pointed aureole) flanked by two Angels, with the Twelve Apostles below. In the Italo-Byzantine style (much restored in the 19th c.), it is attributed to Berlinghiero Berlinghieri.

Location
Piazza San Frediano

Lucca: Façade of San Frediano . . .   *. . . and Rampart Gardens*

123

The nave is separated by columns (with Romanesque capitals or capitals imitating ancient models) from the aisles, off which open Renaissance chapels. It is much higher than the aisles – twice as high as it is wide. In the first chapel on the right is a very beautiful font of the mid 12th c. which was broken up in the 18th c. and put together again only in 1952. Round the outside of the lower basin are reliefs depicting scenes from the life of Moses (by one Master Robertus) and Christ as the Good Shepherd with Apostles or Prophets. The upper basin is in the form of a *tempietto* (little temple) with allegorical representations of the Months.

The fourth chapel on the left, the Cappella Trenta (1413), has a richly decorated Gothic marble polyptych with bas-reliefs by Iácopo della Quercia depicting the Madonna and Child with Saints, accompanied by the legends of the Saints (1422). Here, too, are the much-worn tomb-slabs of a merchant named Lorenzo Trenta and his wife.

* * Town walls

The old town is enclosed within a circuit of walls 4·195 km (2½ miles) long with eleven bastions (*baluardi*) and six gates. The walls, 12 m (39 ft) high and 30 m (98 ft) thick at the base, were built by Flemish engineers between 1504 and 1645 to protect the rectangular area of the town (1500 m – 1640 yd long by 900 m – 985 yd across). Between 1823 and 1832 Maria Luigia of Bourbon, Duchess of Parma, had the old fortifications converted into a public garden.

A walk round the tree-shaded ramparts affords superb views of the old town with its palazzi and churches. The old town gates are also of interest, in particular the Porta San Pietro on the south side of the circuit, the Porta Santa Maria on the north side and the Porta San Donato at the west end.

Arliano   C2

Situation
8 km (5 miles) W

The village of Arliano has a fine Romanesque parish church whose origins go back to the 8th c., making it one of the oldest surviving churches in the region. It contains a number of works of art of the 14th–16th c.

Segromigno Monte   C2

Situation
10 km (6 miles) N

The Mansi, a patrician family of Lucca, acquired in the early 18th c., the 15th c. villa at Segromigno Monte which bears their name and set about enlarging it on the most sumptuous scale. The façade, to which a flight of steps leads up, is decorated with statues of classical divinities. In the course of the 18th c. the house was given its present Baroque appearance and the gardens were laid out in the English fashion.

A few kilometres to the east is the Villa Torrigiani, another sumptous country house, originally dating from the 16th c. but remodelled in Baroque style. It has a beautiful park.

Bagni di Lucca

See entry.

Maremma

The Maremma is a large expanse of low-lying country traversed by drainage canals and broken up by various hills and promontories (former islands); it extends along the coast from the mouth of the River Cécina (south of Livorno) to near the town of Civitavecchia in the region of Latium (Lazio). The name Maremma is a form of the adjective *maríttima*; in prehistoric times the sea reached into this area, leaving a residue in the form of coastal lagoons.

The Etruscans were the first to drain the marshes of the Maremma by constructing a carefully contrived system of drainage channels.

In this area they established the towns of Rusellae (Roselle, see Grossetto) and Vetulonia (see entry) and worked the deposits of minerals in the Colline Metallífere, south of the River Cécina. In Roman times the fertile land of the Maremma was distributed to veterans of the legions; but after the collapse of Roman power the drainage system fell into decay, the land reverted to marsh and malaria became rife. The inhabitants fled from the fever-ridden marshland to the hills, where new centres of spiritual and secular authority were established. During the Middle Ages various religious houses sought to restore the drainage system; but their success was short-lived, since the area was frequently raided and plundered by the Saracens. From this period date the many ruined watch-towers and defensive works to be seen in the Maremma.

The Maremma was not finally drained until the years between 1930 and 1960; and only then was malaria finally eradicated. This meant, of course, a radical change in the pattern of vegetation and animal life, and the buffaloes and half-wild horses formerly so numerous in this area have now almost completely disappeared.

See under Grosseto.

Parco Naturale della Maremma

Massa

Province: Massa-Carrara (MS)
Altitude: 65 m (213 ft)
Population: 66,000

Massa (not to be confused with Massa Maríttima – see entry) lies near the coast at the northern extremity of Tuscany.
To the east extends the chain of the Apuan Alps (part of which is now a nature reserve), famous for their marble. On the coast is a separate part of the town, Marina di Massa, a popular seaside resort.

Situation

Massa first appears in the records in 882. During the Middle Ages it frequently changed hands, passing successively under

History

Massa: Resort of Marina di Massa

the control of Lucca, Pisa, Milan and Florence. In the 15th c. it was held by the Margraves Malaspina and later by the Cybo Malaspina family (1533–1790), who began a complete rebuilding of the town.

Piazza Aranci

The central feature of the old town is the Piazza Aranci. On the south side of the square stands the Palazzo Cybo Malaspina (now occupied by the Prefecture), a large and sumptuous mansion converted from an earlier villa by the Margraves (by Giovanni Francesco Bergamini, 1665; façade by Alessandro Bergamini, 1701).

Cathedral

A short distance north-east of the Piazza Aranci by way of Via Dante we come to the cathedral, built at the behest of Giácomo Malaspina in the 15th c. but altered in later centuries. The modern façade (1936) is faced with Carrara marble. The interior is notable for the sunken funerary chapel of the Cybo-Malaspina family.

Rocca

On the hill to the south-east of the town is the rocca (castle), originally dating from the Middle Ages but enlarged in palatial

style by the Malaspinas in the 15th and 16th c. From the rocca
there is a magnificent view over the town, extending to the sea. *Views

Marina di Massa

Marina di Massa lies some 5 km (3 miles) south-west of Massa.
With its long beach of fine sand, it is a popular resort. Inland
extends a shady pine wood, the Pineta.

Massa Maríttima   C2

Province: Grosseto (GR)
Altitude: 65 m (213 ft)
Population: 10,000

The name of the town is misleading: Massa Maríttima does not   Situation
lie on the sea, but some 20 km (12½ miles) inland, north-east of
Piombino. The adjective Maríttima refers to the Maremma (see
entry).

The area around Massa, on the southern slopes of the Colline   History
Metallífere, the "ore-bearing hills", was already settled in
ancient times, and both Etruscans and Romans worked the
copper and silver to be found here. Massa's rise to become the
chief town in the Maremma began in the 8th c., when the
Bishop of Populonia, fleeing from the malaria of the coastal
region, made it his episcopal seat. During the Middle Ages,
particularly in the 12th–14th c., handsome public buildings
were erected in the town. Pisa and Siena contended for
possession of Massa, a place of some military importance, until
it was finally incorporated in the Grand Duchy of Tuscany. But
the town could not escape the ravages of malaria, and between
the 16th and 19th c. its population fell steadily and its
importance declined. Only after the draining of the marshes and
the eradication of malaria was it able to develop and prosper
again.
Massa Maríttima was the birthplace of San Bernardino of Siena
(Bernardino Albizzeschi, 1380–1444).

The town

The Città Vecchia (Old Town), around the Cathedral, takes its
character from its 13th and 14th c. buildings. Farther east, in the
vicinity of the old castle, is the Città Nuova (New Town), most
of which dates from the 15th and 16th c.

Piazza Garibaldi

The Piazza Garibaldi, the main square of the Città Vecchia,
developed in irregular fashion over the centuries, with the
Cathedral, the Bishop's Palace (Palazzo Vescovile), the
Palazzo Pretorio, the Palazzo Comunale and other historic old
buildings.

Massa Maríttima: Cathedral

*Cathedral

On the south side of Piazza Garibaldi, approached by a broad flight of steps, is the Cathedral of San Cerbone, which dates in its present form from 1228 to 1304 and accordingly shows both Romanesque and Gothic features.

The façade, on which Giovanni Pisano (*c.* 1250–*c.* 1320) worked, has round-arched blind arcades, the lower tiers of which continue round the side walls. On the lintel of the main doorway is a finely carved relief depicting scenes from the life of San Cerbone. Abutting the left-hand side of the church rises the massive campanile, with five tiers of windows, increasing in number from the lowest to the uppermost tier so as to create a striking perspective effect. Over the crossing is an octagonal dome.

The interior (aisled) contains some notable sculpture. In the right-hand aisle is a font carved from a single block of travertine, with reliefs of scenes from the life of John the Baptist by Giroldo da Como (1267). In a chapel in the transept is an Altar-piece of the Madonna delle Grazie, modelled on the "Maestà" of Duccio di Buoninsegna and attributed to Duccio himself or one of his many pupils.

In the crypt (entrance beside the high altar) is the Arca di San Cerbone, the Shrine of St Cerbonius, with a series of magnificent reliefs of scenes from the Saint's life: the masterpiece of the Sienese sculptor Goro di Gregorio (14th c.).

Palazzo Pretorio

On the west side of Piazza Garibaldi, facing the cathedral, is the Palazzo Pretorio or Palazzo del Podestà, built entirely of travertine. Formerly the residence of successive governors and rulers of Massa Maríttima (the *podestà*, the *commissari*, the *capitani di guistizia*), it now houses the Pretura (law court). A severe Romanesque building (13th c.), it bears on its façade the coats of arms of governors of Massa and Siena from 1426 to 1633.

Casa Biserno

Adjoining the Palazzo Pretorio is the tower-like Casa dei Conti di Biserno, a Romanesque building of the 13th c. (partly rebuilt in the 19th c.).

Palazzo Comunale

Immediately adjoining the Casa dei Conti di Biserno is the Palazzo Comunale, a massive travertine structure formed out of a number of Romanesque tower houses (including the 13th c. Torre del Bargello). On the first floor is the Gabinetto del Sindaco (Mayor's Room), with 16th c. frescoes and one of the masterpieces of Sienese painting, Ambrogio Lorenzetti's "Madonna and Child with Angels and Saints" (*c.* 1330).

Città Nuova

Above the Cathedral rises the Fortezza dei Senesi, built by the Sienese around the old Castle of Monte Regio after they gained control of Massa in 1335. Notable features of this Città Nuova (New Town) are the Torre del Candeliere (1228), also known as the Torre del Orológio (Clock-Tower), and the Arco dei Senesi (1337) linking the old castle with the new Sienese structures.

Museo Archeológico

The Museo Archeológico (Archaeological Museum), in Piazza Matteotti, contains pictures of the Sienese school and archaeological material from the surrounding area.

Sant'Agostino

A little way east via the Corso Diaz is the Romanesque and Gothic Church of Sant'Agostino (1299–1313), with an aisleless interior and a handsome campanile of 1627.

Museo della Miniera

In the Museo della Miniera (Mining Museum), on the south side of the old town, the different mining techniques used in Tuscany are displayed in an old mine-shaft.

Montalcino

Province: Siena (SI)
Altitude: 564 m (1850 ft)
Population: 5,500

Situation

The little town of Montalcino, situated high above the rivers Ombrone and Asso in south-eastern Tuscany, lies some 40 km (25 miles) south of Siena.

History

There was a settlement here in Etruscan and Roman times. During the Middle Ages Montalcino was a free commune, its allegiance varying between Florence and Siena. After the Battle of Montaperti (1260), in which the Florentines were defeated by Siena and the Ghibellines, it submitted to the Sienese, who built a stronghold on the highest point of the hill.

Wine production

Montalcino lies on the edge of the Chianti (see entry) wine-producing region and in recent years gained an increasing reputation for its red wine. Brunello di Montalcino now ranks as one of the finest Italian wines, with a correspondingly high price.

The town

In the centre of the little town, still surrounded by its old walls, is the Piazza del Pópolo, in which stands the Palazzo Comunale (13th to 14th c.) with a portico, a façade decorated with coats of arms and a tall tower. To the west is the Church of Sant'Agostino (14th c.), a plain and undecorated Romanesque building (aisleless) with a Gothic doorway; the choir has 15th c. frescoes of the Sienese school. Immediately adjoining the church a former Augustinian convent houses the Museo d'Arte Sacra (Museum of Sacred Art), with a 13th c. Romanesque Crucifix, parts of a polyptych by Luca di Tommè (14th c.), a number of panel paintings and numerous polychrome wooden statues of the 14th and 15th c.

Fortezza

The massive fortezza on top of the hill, built in 1361, is in an excellent state of preservation. In the 16th c. it was the last refuge of 600 Sienese, who fled here when their city was under siege by the Emperor Charles V and established a kind of government in exile. Some of the rooms are open to the public; there is a fine panoramic view from the castle.

Museo Cívico

Housed in the same building is the Museo Cívico (Municipal Museum) with an art collection consisting mainly of works of the 13th–15th c., including terracottas from the workshop of the della Robbias, panel-paintings of the Sienese school and a 12th c. Bible illustrated with miniatures (Sienese work).

Museo Archeológico

The third museum in this complex is the Museo Archeológico with a collection of Prehistoric and Etruscan finds.

Town walls

There is a rewarding walk to be had round the town's excellently preserved medieval walls, with their six gates and (originally) 19 towers.

Madonna del Soccorso

On the north side of the town near the Piazza Cavour and Viale Roma stands the 16th to 17th c. church of Madonna del Soccorso, a popular place of pilgrimage.

Monte Amiata   D3

Provinces: Siena (SI) and Grosseto (GR)
Altitude: 1738 m (5702 ft)

Monte Amiata, Tuscany's highest peak, rises out of a tract of lower hills between the valleys of the Orcia, Fiora and Paglia in the south of Tuscany, on the boundary between the provinces of Siena and Grosseto.   *Situation*

Topography

Monte Amiata (known to the Romans as Mons Tuniae or Mons ad Meata) is an extinct volcano, with numerous springs which supply water to Siena and Grosseto. It is rich in workable minerals (mercury, antimony), which were already being exploited in Etruscan and Roman times.

On the fertile lower slopes of the hill corn, vines and olives are grown; higher up are forests of chestnut, oak and beech, traversed by attractive footpaths. In recent years an extensive winter sports area has been developed, roads (kept open in winter) constructed and hotels built.

The summit of Monte Amiata is encircled by a 13 km (8 mile) long road, some stretches of which have steep gradients, but the drive is well worth while. The road, which is most easily reached from Abbadia San Salvatore (see entry), has a track on the south side leading to the summit on which a tele-communications station has been set up and on which stands a steel cross. From here there is a magnificent panoramic view

Cross on summit

Monte Argentario   D3

Province: Grosseto (GR). Altitude: 635 m (2083 ft)

The promontory of Monte Argentario rises out of the Tyrrhenian Sea on the coast of Tuscany, 35 km (22 miles) south of Grosseto.   *Situation*

131

Monte Argentario

Monte Argentario: View of the west coast

* Topography

In prehistoric times the Argentario Promontory was an island. Then a process of silting-up led to the formation of a tongue of land, 4 km (2½ miles) long and 500–600 m (550–650 yd) wide, on which the town of Orbetello (see entry) now stands; and later still two other sandbanks were formed (the Tómbolo di Feniglia to the south, the Tómbolo di Giannella to the north), creating the Laguna di Orbetello.

Monte Argentario (Silver Hill) is 11·5 km (7 miles) long and up to 7 km (4½ miles) wide. Its highest point is Monte Telégrafo (635 m – 2083 ft).

With its beautiful scenery and varied coastline, partly flat and partly rocky, Monte Argentario is now attracting increasing numbers of holiday-makers. The main tourist resorts are Porto Santo Stéfano on the north coast, Port'Ércole on the east coast and the modern yacht marina of Cala Galera.

Porto Santo Stéfano

This little fishing village and ferry port (services to some of the islands in the Arcipélago Toscano – see entry) is beautifully situated in a valley running down to the sea. It suffered heavy damage during the Second World War. From the 17th c. rocca (castle) above the town there are beautiful views of the town and the bay.

From Porto Santo Stéfano there is an attractive drive round the west coast of Monte Argentario.

Monte Argentario: Porto Santo Stefano

Monte Telégrafo

Monte Telégrafo, the highest point on Monte Argentario (635 m – 2083 ft), lies in the south-east of the peninsula, 17 km (11 miles) from Porto Santo Stéfano by a road which branches off SS 440 (the Orbetello road), on the south. On this road, commandingly situated at a height of 275 m (900 ft), is the Convento dei Padri Passionisti, mother house of the Passionist Order founded in 1720 by Paolo Francesco Danei (St Paul of the Cross). the road ends a short distance below the summit, on which is a telecommunications transmitter with an extensive aerial system. From here there are magnificent views, extending seaward in good wether as far as the French island of Corsica and inland as far as Amiata (see entry).

Port'Ércole

The fishing port of Port'Ércole, on a site inhabited since ancient times, is the principal resort on the east coast of Monte Argentario. It is attractively situated in a small bay which is bounded on the south by a spur of hill crowned by an ancient castle. The old part of the town has preserved much of its former character.

The painter Michelángelo da Caravaggio died of malaria in Port'Ércole in 1610; his tomb is in the parish church.

To the north of the town is the new yacht marina of Cala Galera. There are boat services from Port'Ércole to the island of Giannutri (see entry).

Montecatini Terme C2

Province: Pistoia (PT)
Altitude: 27 m (89 ft)
Population: 22,000

Situation

Montecatini Terme, one of Europe's leading spas, lies in north-western Tuscany, some 30 km (20 miles) east of Lucca and 15 km (9 miles) west of Pistoia.

History

The healing power of the springs of Montecatini appears to have been recognised in ancient times, for the Terme Leopoldine have yielded Roman figurines which have been interpreted as votive offerings. In his book on Italian spas (1417) the 15th c. doctor Ugolino Simoni mentions Montecatini, referring to three bathing establishments which were then in existence. Under the Médici, who added Montecatini to their private estates in 1583, the importance of the spa declined, and it began to recover only in the latter part of the 18th c. Grand Duke Leopold I (later Emperor Leopold II) was mainly responsible for the modernisation of the town and the construction of the various spa establishments – the Stabilimento Regina, the Terme Leopoldine, the Stabilimento Tettuccio, the Palazzina Regia. The development of the spa continued when it became the property of the Benedictines of the Badía di Firenze. Montecatini is now the largest spa in Italy; its waters (temperature 19–25 °C (66–77 °F); 2592 cu. m

Montecatini Terme: Tettuccio Spa establishment

Montecatini Terme

Spa Area

SPA ESTABLISHMENTS
1 Terme Leopoldine
2 Excelsior
3 Tamerici
4 Torretta
5 Rinfresco
6 Tettuccio
7 Regina
8 La Salute
9 Terme F. Redi

A   Accadémia d'Arte (Museum)
F   Funicular to Montecatini Alto
    (Val di Niévole)

300 m
(984 ft)

(3391 cu. yd) daily) are recommended particularly for the treatment of disorders of the liver and gall bladder and diseases of the stomach and intestines.

** The spa

Montecatini Terme lies in an open basin in the Valdiniévole, surrounded by attractive hilly country. The town's main square is the Piazza del Pópolo, with the modern Church of Santa Maria Assunta; a little way west is the Kursaal. From the Piazza del Pópolo a broad avenue, Viale Verdi, runs north-east to the spa area. Along the edge of the large and beautiful park are a series of spa establishments. First comes the Stabilimento Excelsior (enlarged in 1968), on the left; then the neo-classical Terme; Leopoldine and the Stabilimento Tamerici; and beyond these again, at the end of the avenue, the Stabilimento Tettuccio (1927), an imposing structure in neo-Renaissance style with beautiful colonnades. Near by, in Viale A. Diaz, is the Stabilimento Regina. The Accadémia d'Arte, opposite, houses a small museum. North-west of the Stabilimento Tettuccio are two smaller establishments, Torretta and Rinfresco.

At the north-east corner of the park is the lower station of the funicular to Montecatini Alto (see below).
To the south-west of the town are the Stadium and the Ippodromo (Race-course).

Montecatini Alto (Montecatini Val di Niévole) C2

Situation
5 km (3 miles) NE

Funicular
from Montecatini Terme

Some 260 m (850 ft) above Montecatini Terme, on a hilltop site, is the old-world little town of Montecatini Val di Niévole (usually called simply Montecatini Alto).

Grotta Maona

On the road from Montecatini Terme to the old town is the entrance to the Grotta Maona, a stalactitic cave discovered in the 19th c.
There are only scanty remains of the old Castle of Montecatini Alto. The Church of San Pietro, originally Romanesque, was remodelled in the Baroque style; adjoining the church is a small museum of sacred art.

Buggiano C2

Situation
3 km (2 miles) W

On the road from Montecatini Terme to Pescia is the village of Borgo a Buggiano, from which a side road leads up to the old walled village of Buggiano Castello (1·5 km – 1 mile). Its most notable building is the 13th c. Palazzo Pretorio, its façade covered with 15th and 16th c. coats of arms. In the small square stands the Romanesque parish church, originally built in 1038 for a Benedictine abbey and later partly rebuilt. The aisles are separated from the nave by columns with antique capitals (on the right) and pillars (on the left); fine marble sculpture and wall-paintings.

Montecristo (İsola di Montecristo) D2

Province: Livorno (LI)
Area: 10·39 sq. km (4 sq. miles)

Situation

The little island of Montecristo lies in the Tyrrhenian Sea 40 km (25 miles) south of Elba and 45 km (28 miles) west of Giglio.

Access

No regular boat services.

The island

Montecristo, one of the islands in the Arcipélago Toscano (see entry), is almost exactly circular in form, rising to its highest point in Monte Fortezza (645 m – 2116 ft). Surrounded by a jagged rocky coast, this granite island is almost inaccessible. The only settlement is La Villa, on the west coast. The island is a nature reserve, and can be visited only with a permit from the authorities.
10 km (6 miles) west of Montecristo lies the rocky islet known as the Fórmica di Montecristo, with a lighthouse.

Monte Oliveto Maggiore, Abbazía di

See Abbazía di Monte Oliveto Maggiore.

Montepulciano   C3

Province: Siena (SI)
Altitude: 605 m (1985 ft)
Population: 14,000

Montepulciano lies in eastern Tuscany, some 70 km (45 miles)   Situation
south-east of Siena and 20 km (12½ miles) west of Lake
Trasimene (which is in Umbria).

Montepulciano is traditionally believed to have been founded   History
by Porsenna; and it seems very probable that the place was of
Etruscan origin. It first appears in the records in the 8th c. A.D.
as Mons Policianus, from which its present name is derived (as
well as the designation of its inhabitants as Poliziani). During
the Middle Ages it was alternately allied with, or subject to,
either Siena or Florence. Leading artists and architects were
attracted to the town by the noble families who retained their
influence here longer than in other Tuscan cities, and in
consequence Montepulciano can boast numbers of fine
Renaissance and Baroque buildings.
Montepulciano was the birthplace of Marcello Cervini who in
1555 as Marcellus II was pope for 21 days.

Piazza Grande

The main sqaure of the old town, still surrounded by walls, is
the Piazza Grande (officially the Piazza Vittorio Emanuele), in
which are some of Montepulciano's most important buildings.

Cathedral

On the south side of the square stands the cathedral, built on
the site of the earlier parish church, at the time when the Bishop
of Chiusi was driven by the increasing marshiness of the Chiana
Valley to transfer his episcopal seat to Montepulciano. The
present building, designed by Ippolito Scalza, was erected
between 1592 and 1630. The campanile is a relic of the earlier
church. The rough stonework of the façade shows that it was
left unfinished. There are three doorways.
Inside, to the left of the main doorway, is the recumbent figure
of Bartolomeo Aragazzi, Secretary to Pope Martin V
(1417-31). His tomb, in the style of the Early Renaissance, was
the work of Michelozzo di Bartolommeo, but was later taken to
pieces; other fragments can be seen elsewhere in the cathedral.
Behind the high altar is a triptych of the Assumption by Taddeo
di Bártolo (1401).

Montepulciano
Old Town

1 Palazzo Avignonesi
2 Palazzo Cocconi
3 Palazzo Venturi
4 Palazzo Cervini
5 Palazzo Ricci
6 Palazzo Neri Orselli
  (Museo Cívico)
7 Palazzo della Pretura
  (formerly Capitano del Pópolo)
8 Palazzo Tarugi
9 Palazzo Comunale
10 Palazzo Contucci
11 Casa del Poliziano
12 Sant' Agnese
13 San Bernardo
14 Santa Lucia
15 San Francesco
16 Church of Gesú
17 Santa Maria dei Servi

200 m
(656 ft)

Palazzo Comunale

The Palazzo Comunale, an austere and massive building on the west side of the Piazza Grande, was begun at the end of the 14th c., but was given its present form in 1424 by the Florentine Renaissance architect Michelozzo, as plans by Michelozzo found as recently as 1965 have demonstrated. The plain, clearly articulated façade with its battlemented top and the tower with its upper section are reminiscent of the Palazzo Vecchio in Florence (see entry), though the Palazzo Vecchio lacks the symmetry of Montepulciano's Palazzo Comunale. From the top of the tower (which visitors can climb) there are extensive views of the surrounding countryside.

Palazzo Contucci

Opposite the Palazzo Comunale, on the east side of the square, is the Palazzo Contucci. Like many other buildings in

Montepulciano: Palazzo Comunale ▶

Montepulciano, it was the work of Antonio da Sangallo the Elder (*c.* 1455–1534), who built it for Cardinal Giovanni Maria del Monte, later Pope Julius III. The second floor was added by Baldassare Peruzzi. The palace contains frescoes by Andrea Pozzo (1642–1709).

Palazzo Tarugi

The massive Palazzo Tarugi, on the north side of the square, is also attributed to Antonio da Sangallo the Elder, though there is some probability that it was the work of Giacomo da Vignola (1507–73). The lower part of the façade is articulated by columns supporting a balustrade; the open loggia on the ground floor originally had a counterpart on the upper floor, but this is now walled up.

Adjoining the Palazzo Tarugi is a fountain erected in 1520, incorporating two Etruscan columns; it is topped by two lions bearing the Médici coat of arms and two griffins.

Palazzo della Pretura

Set back a little from the Palazzo Tarugi is the Palazzo della Pretura (formerly Palazzo del Capitano del Pópolo), a fairly plain 14th c. building.

Santa Maria dei Servi

From the cathedral Via della Fortezza runs south past the fortezza (rebuilt about 1880 in a pastiche of its original style) to the Church of Santa Maria dei Servi, outside the town walls. Built in the 14th c., it has an exterior in Gothic style, but the interior (aisleless) was given its Baroque form by Andrea Pozzo in the late 17th c. There are some fine altar-pieces of the 13th and 14th c.

Museo Cívico

Via Ricci runs north from the Piazza Grande. At No. 11, on the right, is the Palazzo Neri Orselli (14th c.), built of brick and travertine. It now houses the Museo Cívico (Municipal Museum), which is mainly devoted to pictures of the medieval and Renaissance periods but also contains a number of fine terracottas by Andrea della Robbia.

Palazzo Cervini

North-east of the Museo Cívico, at Via di Voltaia 21, is the Palazzo Cervini, which consists of a central section set back from the street and flanked by two side wings. The palazzo was built by Antonio da Sangallo the Elder between 1518 and 1534 for Cardinal Marcello Cervini, later Pope Marcellus II, but remained unfinished.

Montepulciano: Palazzo Tarugi

Sant'Agostino

A short distance north of the Palazzo Cervini by way of Via di Gracciano is the Church of Sant'Agostino (1427). The handsome Renaissance façade by Michelozzo di Bartolommeo (with a terracotta relief, also by Michelozzo, in the tympanum) shows curious reminiscences of Gothic. The interior (aisleless) was remodelled in the late 18th c. The church contains a fine wooden Crucifix (15th c.) and a number of pictures, mainly of the 16th and 17th c.

Palazzo Cocconi

A few paces north of Sant'Agostino, on the right-hand side of the street, is the Palazzo Cocconi, which is thought to have been built by Antonio da Sangallo the Elder.

Palazzo Avignonesi

Near the north end of Via di Gracciano (No. 99, on the left) stands the Palazzo Avignonesi, the design of which is attributed to Giácomo da Vignola (real name Giácomo Barozzi, 1507–73). The Late Renaissance façade has rusticated masonry on the ground floor and two orders of windows on the upper floors, surmounted by alternate triangular and curving pediments.

Sant'Agnese

Outside the town walls, reached by the Porta al Prato at the north end of the town, is the Church of Sant'Agnese, dedicated to St Agnes of Montepulciano (Agnese Segni, d. 1317). It occupies the site of the earlier church of Santa Maria Novella built by the Saint herself. In the first chapel on the right is a fresco of the Madonna, of the school of Simone Martini; on the high altar is the Saint's reliquary. Adjoining the church is a cloister with 17th c. frescoes.

*Madonna di San Biagio

2 km (1¼ miles) south-west of Montenpulciano, finely situated at the end of a long avenue of tall cypresses, stands the Church of the Madonna di San Biagio, built by Antonio da Sangallo the Elder between 1518 and 1545 to house a much-venerated image of the Madonna. The church is on a Greek cross plan (that is with four arms of equal length), and above the crossing is a high dome borne on a drum. There are two free-standing campaniles, the one on the right being unfinished. This beautifully proportioned church, built of golden-yellow travertine, ranks among the finest examples of Renaissance architecture.

The interior is richly decorated. The presbytery has frescoes depicting the Death, Assumption and Coronation of the Virgin which are believed to be by the Zúccari brothers (16th c.). On the reredos of the high altar (1584) are four figures of Saints. The canónica (priest's house) near the church, like the fountain in front of the house, was designed by Sangallo but built after his death. It now houses a small museum devoted to St Blaise (San Biagio).

Orbetello   D3

Province: Grosseto (GR)
Altitude: 0–3 m (0–10 ft)
Population: 15,000

Situation

Orbetello lies on the coast of southern Tuscany in the middle of a lagoon (area 26 sq. km – 10 sq. miles) between (see entry) Monte Argentario and the mainland.

History

The tongue of land on which the town is built was probably settled as early as the 8th c. B.C. In the course of time the town grew in importance, and during the Middle Ages it changed hands many times. In the mid 16th c. it became the chief place in the "Stato dei Presidi" established by the Spaniards.

The tongue of land was extended to Monte Argentario by an artificial causeway constructed in 1842, thus cutting the lagoon in two.

The town

There are still considerable remains of Etruscan sea-walls and – particularly in the Piazza Quattro Novembre – of the Spanish

fortifications begun in the reign of Philip II (1557) and completed under his son and successor Philip III (1620).
The cathedral was built in 1376 on the site of an earlier church and enlarged in the 17th c. by the addition of two aisles. On the travertine façade, still in Gothic style, are a finely carved doorway and, above this, a rose-window and a bust of St Benedict.
In the Palazzo della Pretura is the Antiquarium Cívico, a museum containing archaeological material from Orbetello and the surrounding area, including Etruscan and Roman bronzes and pottery.

Pescia   C2

Province: Pistoia (PT)
Altitude: 62 m (203 ft)
Population: 20,000

The town of Pescia lies in northern Tuscany, half-way between Lucca and Pistoia. It is the principal centre in the fertile valley of the River Pescia and is famed for its asparagus, its olive oil and its flower-market.

Situation

The town

The most prominent building in the part of the town which lies on the left bank of the river is the cathedral, built in the late 17th c. on Romanesque foundations and raised to cathedral status in 1726. The façade dates from the late 19th c.; the massive campanile (1306) may be a relic of the earlier Romanesque church. The interior of the cathedral is Baroque.
The little Church of Sant'Antonio (1361) has 15th c. frescoes of scenes from the life of St Antony Abbot.
Also on the left bank of the river is the Gothic Church of San Francesco (begun 1298), with an interior partly remodelled in Baroque style. The finest work of art in the church is a panel-painting by Buonaventura Berlinghieri (1235) depicting St Francis with the stigmata and six scenes from his life.
The part of the town lying on the right bank on the river is Pescia's secular centre. In Piazza Mazzini is the Palazzo dei Vicari (13th–14th c.), with coats of arms on its façade and a tower; it is now the town hall. Near by, in Piazza Santo Stéfano, is the Museo Cívico (Municipal Museum), the main items in which are pictures of the 14th–16th c.

Collodi   C2

The village of Collodi gave its name to the author of the world-famous children's book "Pinocchio", Carlo Collodi. Born in Florence as Carlo Lorenzini (1826–90), he spent his boyhood in the village. He is commemorated by the Parco del Pinocchio, a children's amusement park (open daily 8 a.m. to 8 p.m.).
Also of interest in Collodi is the Villa Garzoni (Baroque garden).

Situation
5 km (3 miles) W

On a hill to the west of Collodi is the little village of San Gennaro, which has a charming 12th c. Romanesque church, with a fine pulpit of the same period.

San Gennaro

Segromigno   Still farther west is Segromigno, with the Villa Mansi and Villa Torrigiani. See under Lucca.

Pianosa (Ísola di Pianosa)   D2

Province: Livorno (LI)
Area: 10·25 sq. km (4 sq. miles)

Situation   The little island of Pianosa lies in the Tyrrhenian Sea some 15 km (9 miles) south-west of Elba and 70 km (43 miles) west of the coast of Tuscany.

Access   Boat services from Livorno (see entry) and Elba (see entry).

The island

As its name implies, Pianosa is relatively flat, nowhere rising more than 27 m (89 ft) above sea-level. The island is built up from Muschelkalk formations and Quaternary deposits; much of it is devoted to agriculture (wine, corn).
There is a penal establishment on the island, which can be visited only with a special permit from the Ministry of the Interior.

Pienza   C3

Province: Siena (SI)
Altitude: 491 m (1611 ft)
Population: 2500

Situation   Pienza lies in south-eastern Tuscany near the borders of Umbria, some 55 km (34 miles) south-east of Siena and 15 km (9 miles) west of Montepulciano.

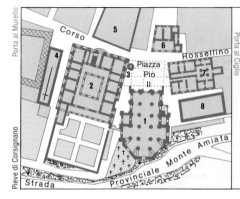

Pienza
Central Area

1 Cathedral
2 Palazzo Piccolómini
3 Fountain
4 Church of San Francesco
5 Palazzo Ammannati
6 Palazzo Comunale (Town Hall)
7 Palazzo Vescovile
  (Bishop's Palace)
8 Museo della Cattedrale
  (Museo de la Casa dei Canonici)

30 m
(164 ft)

Pienza: Piazza Pio II with cathedral and Palazzo Piccolomini

Pienza owes its position as one of the most charming art towns in Tuscany to one man, Enea Silvio (Aeneas Sylvius) Piccolómini (1405–64), who became Pope as Pius II in 1458. With the help of the architect Bernardo Rossellino he transformed the insignificant village of Corisgnano, in which he had been born, into a model town laid out on clear planning principles. Work began in 1459 and advanced so quickly that three years later, on 13 August 1462, Pius II was able to issue a Bull elevating his birthplace into a town and episcopal see named Pienza (after his Papal name). After Pius's death, however, the development of the town came to a halt.

History

** Piazzo Pio II

In the centre of the town is the Piazza Pio II, trapezoid in form. On the south side of the square stands the cathedral, on the east side the Palazzo Vescovile (Bishop's Palace), on the west side the Palazzo Piccolómini, while to the north is the Palazzo Comunale (1463), with a charming loggia.

Cathedral

The Cathedral of Santa Maria Assunta was built between 1459 and 1462 on the site of an earlier Romanesque church dedicated to the Virgin; the architect was Bernardo Rossellino. The travertine façade is articulated by pilasters and blind arcading, and on the pediment is Pius II's coat of arms, the tiara and keys of St Peter with the arms of the Piccolómini family. The light interior still shows Gothic influence; the nave and aisles are of the same height, bringing the cathedral into the category of the hall-church, a type relatively rare in Italy. The transepts are continued by a ring of chapels. The apse has extensive underbuilding, made necessary by the slope of the site. Notable features of the interior are the Gothic choir-stalls (1462) and a famous painting, the "Assumption" by Vecchietta (1412–80) in the chapel to the left of the choir. In the crypt is a font designed by Rossellino.

Palazzo Piccolómini

To the right of the cathedral is the Palazzo Piccolómini, one of Rossellino's finest works. The façade, of carefully dressed stone, is broken up by pilasters and string-courses, between which are elegant double windows. In front of the palazzo is a fountain designed by Rossellino.

The square courtyard is surrounded by porticoes. On the garden front, to the south, are three tiers of loggias, looking out on the "hanging gardens" with their retaining walls. In the interior are pictures, firearms and side-arms, old furniture, etc.

Palazzo Vescovile

Opposite the Palazzo Piccolómini, to the left of the cathedral, is the Palazzo Vescovile (Bishop's Palace), which dates in its present form from the 15th c. It was built for Rodrigo Borgia, later Pope Alexander VI.

Diocesan Museum

To the right of the bishop's palace, with its façade looking on to the side wall of the cathedral, is the Casa dei Canónici, a palazzo in restrained Renaissance style built to house the Canons of Cathedral Chapter. It is now occupied by the Museo Diocesano di Arte Sacra, also known as the Museo della Cattedrale. Notable items in the collection are two copies, on of which belonged to Alessandro Piccolómini, the other to Pius II; the latter (14th c. English work, with lively representations of scenes from the lives of Saints) was presented to Pius by Thomas Palaeologus, titular Despot of the Peloponnese.

Palazzo Ammannati

Facing the north front of the Palazzo Piccolómini, in Corso Rossellino, is the Palazzo Ammannati, built for Cardinal Giácomo Ammannati of Pavia, a friend of Pius II's.

Pieve Santi Vito e Modesto

1 km ($\frac{3}{4}$ mile) to the west, outside the town, we came to the old Pieve (Parish Church) of Corsignano, in which Enea Silvio Piccolómini was baptised. Built in the 11th–12th c., it has fine figural decoration on the doorways.

Sant'Anna in Camprena   C3

This old monastic house, founded in 1324, notable particularly for its refectory, which has frescoes (1503–07) by Sodoma (real name Giovanni Antonio Bazzi).

Situation
7 km (4½ miles) S

Monticchiello   C3

The township of Monticchiello still retains its old walls, towers and castle. The 13th c. Church of Santo Leonardo e Cristóforo, with a Gothic façade, contains an altar-piece of the Virgin and Child by Pietro Lorenzetti (c. 1280–1348).

Situation
5 km (3 miles) S

Pietrasanta   C2

Province: Lucca (LU)
Altitude: 14 m (46 ft)
Population: 26,000

Pietrasanta lies on the slopes of the Apuan Alps in north-western Tuscany. It is the chief town of the Versilia, the coastal region between Massa and Viareggio. Silver was mined in the region until 1590; the main industry is now marble-working.

Situation

The town

The main feature of interest in the town, which was founded between 1242 and 1255 by Guiscardo Pietrasanta, Podestà of Lucca, is the Cathedral of San Martino (originally 13th c.), with a campanile which remained unfinished. Beside the cathedral is the baptistery, which has a fine font of 1509 by D. Denti. Close by stands the 14th c. Church (aisleless) of Sant'Agostino, with a façade relieved by arcading. The adjoining cloister has 17th c. frescoes.

Valdicastello Carducci   C2

The hamlet of Valdicastello Carducci owes the second part of its name to the poet Giosuè Carducci (1835–1907; Nobel Prize for literature 1906), who was born here. On the road to Valdicastello is the Pieve (Parish Church) of Santi Giovanni e Felicità, originally founded in the 6th c., altered in the 13th c. and subsequently several times restored. It contains 14th c. frescoes.

Situation
4 km (2½ miles) E

Vallecchia   C2

The village of Vallecchia has a parish church (Santo Stéfano) of the 12th–14th c., with a 17th c. pulpit decorated with reliefs.

Situation
4 km (2½ miles) N

147

Piombino   D2

Province: Livorno (LI)
Altitude: 0–19 m (0–62 ft)
Population: 40,000

Situation

The port and industrial town of Piombino lies roughly half-way down the coast of Tuscany, to the north-east of the island of Elba. To the north of the town rises Monte Massoncello (286 m – 938 ft).

History

The town was a Roman foundation, under the name of Portus Falesiae. In the 6th c. A.D. the Lombards, thrusting into Italy during the Great Migrations, destroyed Populonia, long a neighbour and rival, and thus increased the importance of Piombino, which in the 12th and 13th c. became a major Pisan stronghold. Thereafter is frequently changed hands, until the Congress of Vienna in 1814 assigned it to the Grand Duchy of Tuscany.

The name Piombino comes from the Italian word *piombo* (lead), reflecting the importance of the metalworking industry to the town's economy. Iron ore from Elba was already being smelted at Populonia in Etruscan times; and when modern industry came to Piombino in the latter part of the 19th c. the use of new and efficient techniques made it possible to win iron not only from the ore of the nearby Colline Metallifere but from the huge slag-heaps left by the ironworkers of antiquity. Present-day Piombino is still a considerable industrial town, with blast-furnaces and rolling-mills as prominent landmarks.

The town

In Piazza Giuseppe Verdi, in the centre of the town, can be seen a fragment of its medieval defences, a massive 13th c. tower and a 14th c. town gate. From here the Corso Vittorio Emanuele, the principal street of the old town, leads to the Palazzo Comunale (originally 12th c., but much rebuilt), adjoining which is the late 16th c. clock-tower.

In Piazza Curzio Desideri the late 14th c. Church of Sant'Antimo contains two fine tombs of the 14th and 15th c., a marble font by Andrea Guardi (1470) and another font made from an antique column.

From the streets on the seafront there are attractive views of the island of Elba and the sea.

Pisa   C2

Province: Pisa (PI)
Altitude: 4 m (13 ft)
Population: 104,000

Situation

Pisa, chief town of its province, lies on the Arno in the northern coastal region of Tuscany. In Roman times it was a considerable port, but as a result of the silting-up of the mouth of the Arno it now lies fully 10 km (6 miles) inland.

History

In all probability Pisa was originally a Greek foundation of the 7th or 6th c. B.C. The town, which then lay on the coast, was

Pisa: Campo die Miracoli (Square of Miracles)

equipped by the Romans with a harbour which became of great military and commercial importance. In medieval times Pisa was able to maintain its importance as a port in spite of Saracen raids; and the defeat of the Saracens by Pisan and Norman forces at Messina and Palermo in 1063 marked the beginning of Pisa's rise to become mistress of the western Mediterranean. The cathedral was built in thanksgiving for these brilliant victories. The Pisans took part in the First Crusade with a large fleet and brought back huge quantities of booty. Commerce and industry flourished, and architects, sculptors and painters created works famed throughout Europe. Towards the end of the 11th c. Pisa became the first town in central and southern Italy to be governed by the townspeople themselves, political authority being exercised by a Council of Twelve.

Pisa took the Ghibelline (Imperial) side in the conflict between the Pope and the Holy Roman Emperor, and was rewarded by the Emperor Frederick Barbarossa with the grant of extensive lands in the coastal area between the present-day towns of Portovénere and Civitavecchia. But Pisa had constantly to be prepared to defend itself against attack by its rivals – the land powers Lucca and Florence, the maritime republics of Amalfi and Genoa.

At the peak of its power the Republic of Pisa was mistress of the Near East, Greece, North Africa, Sicily, Sardinia and the Balearics; but on 6 August 1284 it suffered an annihilating defeat at the hands of the Genoese in the naval Battle of Meloria and thereafter ceased to exist as a Great Power. Democratic rule alternated with dictatorship; the city was compelled to give up

149

Campo dei Miracoli   Pisa

BAPTISTERY
1 Font
2 Pulpit

CATHEDRAL
A Pulpit
B Dome

C Apse
D Sagrestia dei Cappellani
E Porta di San Ranieri

its possessions and its profitable trading activities; for a time it was held by the Visconti family of Milan, and in 1406 was captured by Florence. The Médici who now ruled Pisa took a keen interest in the town, promoting great engineering projects like the regulation of the rivers Arno and Serchio and the construction of bridges and canals. The destinies of Pisa were now increasingly bound up with those of Florence.

During the Second World War Pisa suffered considerable damage in Allied air raids, now long since made good.

Pisa is the birthplace of the mathematical and scientific genius Galileo Galilei (1564–1642).

**Campo dei Mirácoli (Piazza del Duomo)

In the Campo dei Mirácoli (Square of Miracles) or Piazza del Duomo, in the north-west of the old town, are Pisa's most celebrated sights: the cathedral, the Leaning Tower (Torre Pendente), the Baptistery (Battistero) and the Campo Santo (Cemetery).

**Cathedral

The Cathedral of Santa Maria Assunta, a five-aisled Romanesque basilica (95 m – 312 ft long, 32 m – 105 ft wide) of white marble with aisled transepts and an elliptical dome over the crossing, was begun in 1063, after the naval victory over the Saracens, to the design of a Pisan architect named Buscheto, and was consecrated, still unfinished, in 1118. Towards the end of the 12th c. a new west front was added by the architect Rainaldo and the principal apse was completed.

150

The splendid façade is clearly articulated and richly decorated. Above the lower part with its arches and pilasters and its three doorways are four orders of dwarf galleries, their disposition reflecting the section of the nave and aisles. On the highest point of the pediment is a figure of the Madonna by Andrea Pisano. The arcading on the façade is continued round the side walls. The transepts, projecting well beyond the aisles, end in small apses. The semicircular main apse is very finely worked. Over the crossing, dominating the whole church, is the finely proportioned dome, on an oval plan. The three bronze doors (1595) in the façade merit particular attention. The central door has scenes from the life of the Virgin, the smaller ones to the right and left scenes from the life of Christ.

Finer still, however, is the Porta di San Ranieri (on the east side of the south transept), through which visitors usually enter the cathedral. The bronze doors, cast about 1180, have reliefs depicting scenes from the life of Christ and the Virgin.

*Porta di San Ranieri

In the south transept can be seen the Tomb (by Tino di Camaino, 1313) of the Emperor Henry VII (1308–13), who is referred to by Dante in the "Divine Comedy".
To the right of the principal apse the Sagrestia dei Cappellani houses the Cathedral Treasury (two bronze reliquaries, gold and silver objects, etc.). On the right-hand pier at the near end of the choir is a "St Agnes" by Andrea del Sarto, on the left-hand one a "Madonna and Child" by Giovanni Antonio Sogliani and in the apse a mosaic (13th–14th c.) of Christ enthroned between the Virgin and John the Evangelist (the latter by Cimabue). The fine bronze lamp (1587) is traditionally

Pisa: Nave of cathedral

151

said to have given Galileo the idea of the swinging of a pendulum.

*Pulpit

The most celebrated work of art in the cathedral, however, is the pulpit by Giovanni Pisano (which is similar to the one in the Church of Sant'Andrea in Pistoia – see entry). It was originally created betwen 1302 and 1311, taken to pieces in 1599 and put together again, not entirely correctly, in 1926. Giovanni Pisano's vigorous style, inspired by new ideas, marked a development beyond the severe style of his father Nicola, as can be seen by comparing the angular pulpit by Nicola Pisano in the baptistery (see below) with the rounded forms of the one by his son in the cathedral. The pulpit is supported on columns (the shorter ones borne on lions) and figures of the Archangel Michael, Hercules and Christ (with the Four Evangelists round the base) and an allegorical figure representing the Church (with the Four Cardinal Virtues). On the central support are personifications of Faith, Hope and Love. Above the capitals are Sibyls, Prophets, Evangelists and Saints, and in relief panels round the pulpit lively representations of the Birth of John the Baptist, the Annunciation, the Visitation, the Nativity and the Annunciation to the Shepherds, the Adoration of the Kings, the Presentation in the Temple, the Flight into Egypt, the Slaughter of the Innocents, the Betrayal, Christ's Passion and the Last Judgment.

**Leaning Tower (Torre Pendente)

Leaning Tower of Pisa
(Torre Pendente/Campanile)

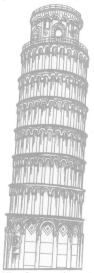

View from south-west

The Leaning Tower of Pisa, the campanile of the cathedral, is world-famous both for its architectural beauty and its structural peculiarity. Construction began in 1173 or 1174, but the original builder, Bonanus (fragmentary inscription from his sarcophagus to left of entrance), carried the work no farther than the third storey when, as a result of the instability of the subsoil, the tower began to tilt towards the south-east – notwithstanding the efforts made by the Pisans to find an area of dry and stable solid ground for the cathedral and associated buildings. It was more than a hundred years before work was resumed under the direction of Giovanni di Simone, who sought to compensate for the subsidence of the foundations (which occurred elsewhere in Pisa, as can be seen, for example, in the towers of San Nicola and San Michele degli Scalzi) and bring back the tower's axis to the vertical by altering the angle of the upper storeys. The bells were at first (in 1301) hung on the sixth storey; the present bell-chamber was added about 1350. About 1590 Galileo used the inclination of the tower to carry out his famous experiments in the effect of gravity on falling objects.

As we see it today the Leaning Tower is 56·50 m (185 ft) high on the north side but only 54·25 m (178 ft) high on the south side. The deviation from the vertical is about 8 degrees, or 4·54 m (15 ft) at the top of the tower. The tower's inclination is increasing at the rate of about 1 millimetre ($\frac{1}{25}$ in) a year, and the tower is sinking at a corresponding rate into the subsoil; it has now sunk to depth of 2·25 m (7 ft 5 in).

Owing to subsidence and the subsequent danger to visitors, the tower has been closed indefinitely.

**Baptistery (Battistero)

West of the cathedral, on the same axis, stands the bapistery –
here, as elsewhere in Italy, separate from the church to which
it belongs. Construction began in 1153, almost a hundred years
after the cathedral but still in the great days of Pisa. The first
architect was one Master Diotisalvi (inscription on pillars
flanking the entrance). The likenesses between the baptistery
and the cathedral are particularly marked in the earlier phases of
the baptistery's construction – the use of the same building
material, the patterning with different colours of stone, the
articulation of the structure by blind arcading and dwarf
galleries. Since the work of construction continued, with
interruptions, for two centuries the architecture of the
baptistery shows the transition from Romanesque to Gothic
between the lower and the upper levels. In 1260 Nicola Pisano
took over responsibility for the project, followed (1285–93) by
his son Giovanni. The roof vaulting was completed in 1358,
and the 3·30 m (11 ft) high figure of John the Baptist which
tops the dome was set up towards the end of the 14th c. Most
of the figures on the outside of the building have now been
replaced by copies; the originals are in museums.

Notable features of the interior, with its conical dome borne on
four pillars and eight columns creating an effect of light and
solemnity, are the font by Guido da Como, (1246), the figures of
Saints by pupils of Nicola and Giovanni Pisano, the altar and
above all the free-standing marble pulpit (1260), a masterpiece
by Nicola Pisano, following Etruscan and Roman models (from
the nearby Camposanto: see below). The pulpit, one of the
great master works of Romanesque sculpture, is decorated
with relief panels depicting with great artistic intensity the
Nativity, with the Annunciation to the Shepherds and Adoration by the Shepherds, the Adoration of the Kings, the Presentation in the Temple, the Crucifixion, and the Last Judgment.

The baptistery is also notable for its magnificent acoustics, as
the guides usually make a point of demonstrating.

**Camposanto

According to local legend Archbishop Ubaldo dei Lanfranchi,
returning from the Fourth Crusade, brought back several
shiploads of earth from Golgotha, so that the citizens of Pisa
might be buried in sacred soil. The construction of the
Camposanto (Sacred field), however, began only in 1278,
under the direction of Giovanni di Simone.

This cemetery enclosure, which bounds the north side of the
Campo dei Mirácoli, is a large rectangular cloister aligned from
east to west, having round-headed windows with Gothic
tracery opening into the courtyard. On the floor of the cloister
are the grave-slabs of Pisan patricians, and around the sides are
antique sarcophagi. The walls were covered with 14th and
15th c. frescoes, but as a result of a fire caused by artillery
bombardment on 21 July 1944 these were either completely
destroyed or badly damaged by molten lead running down
from the roof. The frescoes were then detached from the walls,
revealing the artists' preliminary sketches (*sinópie*: see Museo
delle Sinópie, below) in red pigment. The frescoes, now

Pisa: Camposanto

restored, are displayed in rooms in the north wing, preparatory to being restored to their original positions. Particularly notable are the "Triumph of Death" by an unknown master, one of the finest large-scale paintings of the 14th c., and a "Last Judgment" by the same artist, together with part of a Passion cycle by various painters. Among the artists involved in the work were Benozzo Gozzoli, Antonio Veneziano, Spinello Aretino, Lippo Memmi and Taddeo Gaddi.

*Museo delle Sinópie

On the south side of the Piazza del Duomo, housed in a former hospice, is the Museo delle Sinópie (opened 1979). During the restoration of the Camposanto (see above) a large number of these preliminary sketches for frescoes (*sinópie*) were discovered, and these are now displayed in the museum. These sketches were the artist's most important contribution to a fresco, specifying as they did every detail of a composition; thereafter the actual execution of the fresco was often left to pupils or assistants.

In the museum the *sinópie* are shown in conjunction with reproductions of the corresponding frescoes.

Palazzo Arcivescovile

At the east end of the Campo dei Mirácoli, in the Piazza dell'Arcivescovado, stands the 15th c. Palazzo Arcivescovile

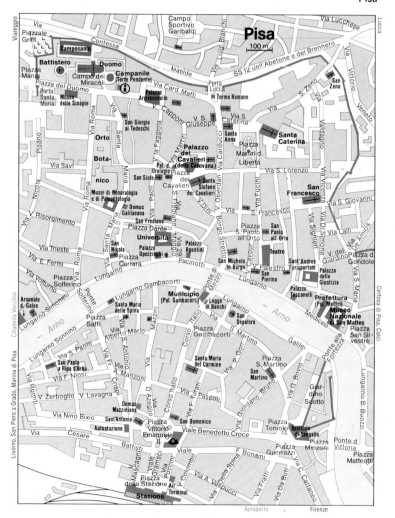

(Archbishop's Palace), which contains the Archiepiscopal Archives. The chapel on the first floor is decorated with Baroque frescoes.

Displayed in the 23 rooms of the Museo dell'Opera del Duommo, opened here in 1988, are paintings by Nicola and Giovanni Pisano and Tino di Camaino, engraved precious stones, stone facings and various small items found during archeological excavation of the Camposanto.

Museo dell'Ópera del Duomo

155

Terme Romane

Still farther east, in Via Fedeli, are the Terme Romane (Roman Baths), usually known as the Bagno di Nerone (Nero's Baths), dating from the 2nd c. A.D.

Botanic Garden

Entrance
Via Luca Ghini 5

Opening times
Mon.–Fri. 8 a.m.–12.30 p.m.
and 2–5 p.m.

To the south of the Campo dei Mirácoli, between Via Roma and Via Porta Buozzi, lies the Orto Botánico (Botanic Garden), originally laid out in 1543 by Cosimo de' Médici. It is now associated with the University; in the centre of the gardens is the Botanical Institute. Here plants from many different climatic zones flourish, either in the open air or in the various glasshouses.

Museo di Mineralogía e
  Petrografía
Museo di Paleontología
Via Santa Maria 53

At the south end of the Botanic Garden are the Museum of Mineralogy and Petrography and the Museum of Palaeontology, with collections of fosils and minerals from the various regions of Italy.

Domus Galilaeana

Location
Via Santa Maria 26
Opening times
Daily 9 a.m.–12 noon and
3–6 p.m.

Opposite the museums the House of Galileo (Domus Galilaeana) has a well-stocked library and a study centre. It is a memorial to the great scientist and mathematician Galileo Galilei, born in Pisa in 1564.

San Nicola

Location
Via Santa Maria

The Church of Santa Maria, originally built in the 12th c., was much altered in later centuries. The 13th c. campanile, like the campanile of the cathedral, leans off the vertical, but less seriously so. The lower part is cylindrical, the upper part octagonal; there is a spiral staircase to the top.

San Frediano

Location
Piazza San Frediano

The Church of San Frediano, in a square to the east of the House of Galileo, is first mentioned in the records in 1061, but was probably not finished until the 12th c. The façade with its blind arcading is Romanesque; the interior in its present day form dates from the 16th and 17th c.

*Palazzo dei Cavalieri

Location
Piazza dei Cavalieri

This palace in the Piazza dei Cavalieri, to the east of the Botanic Garden, was originally the Palazzo degli Anziani (Palace of the Elders); then in 1562 Giorgio Vasari began the rebuilding and enlargement which produced the magnificent Palazzo dei Cavalieri or Palazzo della Carovana, named after the training courses for knights (*cavalieri*) of the Order of St Stephen which were held here; the courses were known as *carovane* (caravans). The imposing façade is decorated with sgraffito ornament, coats of arms and busts of six Grand Dukes of Tuscany (from Cosimo I to Cosimo III). The effect of the building is enhanced by the wide projection of the roof and the

Pisa: Palazzo dei Cavalieri

handsome double staircase leading up to the entrance. Since 1810 the palazzo has housed the Scuola Normale Superiore, an élite college of higher education founded by Napoleon. In front of the building is a statue of Cosimo I by Piero Francavilla (1596).

Palazzo dell'Orológio

On the north side of the Piazza dei Cavalieri can be seen the Palazzo dell'Orológio, built in 1607 for the Order of St Stephen (founded 1554), incorporating the remains of two tower houses. This palazzo was also the work of Vasari, who very skilfully contrived the combination of a State prison, the Torre delle Sette Vie (named after the seven streets running into the square), and the Palazzetto dei Gualandi or Torre della Fame (Tower of Hunger). In the latter tower, as Dante recounts in the "Divine Comedy" ("Inferno" 33), Count Ugolino della Gherardesca is said to have been starved to death in 1288, having been accused – probably unjustly – of seeking to establish his personal rule during his period of office as Capitano del Pópolo.

Location
Piazza dei Cavalieri

Santo Stéfano dei Cavalieri

The Church of Santo Stéfano was also designed by Vasari. Originally built in 1565–69, it was provided in 1594–1606 with a marble façade designed by Giovanni de' Médici. The two side wings (17th c.) were originally changing-rooms for the knights

Location
Piazza dei Cavalieri

of the Order of St Stephen, who wore their ceremonial costume for services. These rooms were later incorporated in the church. Since the aisles are linked with the nave only by two doorways on each side, the first impression is of an aisleless church. In the panels of the coffered ceiling are paintings depicting the history of the Order of St Stephen, whose function was to defend the city against enemy raids, like those suffered in the 16th c., mainly at the hands of Saracens from North Africa. On the walls are numerous trophies and captured enemy flags recalling Pisa's Turkish wars. Other features of interest are the richly decorated high altar (1709), with the throne of the martyred Pope Stephen I (254–257), and the Baroque organ.

San Michele in Borgo

Location
Borgo Stretto

The little Church of San Michele, on the north (right) bank of the Arno, was built at some time before 990, perhaps on the site of a Roman Temple of Mars. Rebuilding in the 14th c. gave it a façade (by Fra Agnelli) which shows the transition from Romanesque to Gothic. The church suffered heavy damage from air raids in 1944, and during rebuilding and restoration work a 13th c. fresco of St Michael was brought to light over the left-hand doorway.

San Pierino (San Pietro in Vinculis)

Location
Piazza Cairoli/Via Palestro

A little way south-east of San Michele in Borgo, near the Lungarno Mediceo, stands the Church of San Pierino or San Pietro in Vinculis (St Peter in Chains), built between 1072 and 1119. Notable features of this aisled church are the façade with its two orders of arcading and, in the interior, a 14th c. "Annunciation" over the doorway and a 13th c. Crucifix behind the high altar. The crypt extends under the whole area of the church. The campanile, originally a tower belonging to an earlier complex of buildings, is older than the church.

Palazzo Médici

Location
Lungarno Mediceo/
Piazza Mazzini

The origins of the Palazzo Médici, at the east end of the old town, go back beyond the period of Médici rule. This imposing palazzo, now the Prefecture, was originally built in the 13th c. and was altered in the 14th, when the Appiano family ruled Pisa. Later it became the residence of Lorenzo the Magnificent. The ground floor has pillared arcading; the windows on the façade are double-arched and triple-arched.

*Museo Nazionale di San Matteo

Location
Lungarno Mediceo

Opening times
Tue.–Sat. 8.30 a.m.–
7.30 p.m., Sun. 8.30 a.m.–
1.30 p.m. Closed Mon.

The Benedictine Convent of San Matteo (dissolved 1866) now houses the Museo Nazionale (National Museum). The main part of the collection centres on sculpture and pictures of the Tuscan schools from the 12th to the 15th c.

Of particular interest are the sculptures from various churches in Pisa, brought here to preserve them from increasing environmental pollution and replaced by copies in their original

positions. The statues by Giovanni Pisano come from the baptistery, the famous "Madonna del Latte" (c. 1340) from the Church of Santa Maria della Spina.
Painting is represented by a number of 12th and 13th c. crucifixes, panel-paintings by Simone Martini, Giovanni di Nicola, Benozzo Gozzoli and others, and examples of book illumination.

San Francesco

There is evidence of the foundation of a small Franciscan church on this site, to the north of the Palazzo Médici, in the year 1211: that is during the lifetime of St Francis. The present aisleless church, however, dates from 1265 to 1270 and was probably the work of Giovanni di Simone; the façade was completed in 1603.
Numerous grave-slabs, some of them bearing coats of arms, are let into the floor. The second chapel on the right contains the remains, deposited here in 1922, of Count Ugolino della Gherardesca and his sons, who were starved to death in the Palazzo dell'Orológio (see above). The church also contains a number of pictures, including some depicting scenes from the legend of St Francis, and a marble polyptych by Tommaso Pisano (14th c.) the "Virgin and Child with Saints".

Location
Piazza San Francesco

Santa Caterina

This church, to the north-east of the central area of the town, was built for the Dominicans between 1251 and 1300 on the site of an earlier building. The Pisan-style façade with its rose-window and dwarf gallery was added about 1330, the beautiful campanile (by Giovanni di Simone) still later. Damage caused by a fire in 1651 was rather clumsily made good. The church contains a marble "Annunciation" by Nino Pisano (c. 1330) with traces of its original colouring.

Location
Piazza Santa Caterina

San Zeno

The little Romanesque Church of San Zeno, at the north-eastern corner of the old town, is one of Pisa's oldest churches, built by Benedictines between 1100 and 1180. It has a fine tufa façade decorated with arcading and preceded by a portico. Some of the columns separating the nave from the aisles have Roman capitals.

Location
Via San Zeno

Palazzo Gambacorti

The 14th c. Palazzo Gambacorti, now the Town Hall (Município), stands on the south (left) bank of the Arno in the centre of the old town. The façade, decorated with coats of arms, has double Gothic windows on the upper floors. Its one-time owner Pietro Gambacorti, then the ruler of Pisa, was murdered here by conspirators in 1393.

Location
Lungarno Gambacorti

Pisa: Santa Maria della Spina by the Arno

Logge di Banchi

Location
Piazza Venti Settembre

Facing the Palazzo Gambacorti, to the south-east, can be seen the Logge di Banchi, a grandiose loggia built in 1603–05 to house the cloth-market. The upper floor, which was added later, contains part of the State Archives.

From the Ponte di Mezzo, which spans the Arno here, there are views of the *lungarni*, the streets running along the banks of the river.

*Santa Maria della Spina

Location
Lungarno Gambacorti

The Church of Santa Maria della Spina, on the left bank of the Arno to the west of the Palazzo Gambacorti, is perhaps the best known of the smaller churches of Pisa. In its original position close to the river it suffered severe damage to its foundations, and in 1871 it was pulled down stone by stone and rebuilt higher up. Originally a small oratory, it was rebuilt in the Gothic period as a richly decorated church. It owes its name to its possession of a thorn (*spina*) from Christ's crown of thorns, brought to Pisa from the Holy Land.

The west front is surmounted by three gables and has two doorways, with small rose-windows in the gables above. In the centre is a baldachin with a statue of the Virgin and Child with Saints by G. di Balduccio. The south side of the church has a series of arches enclosing doorways and multiple windows and, higher up, an aedicule (niche) with figures of Christ and the Apostles. The building is crowned by tabernacles con-

Certosa di Pisa: Carthusian monastery

taining statues, some of them now replaced by copies (originals in the Museo Nazionale: see above): for example, the "Virgin and Child" by Nino Pisano and the figures of Apostles by pupils of Giovanni Pisano. The famous "Madonna del Latte" inside the church is also a replica.

San Paolo a Ripa d'Arno

The Church of San Paolo, in the south-west of the old town near the south bank of the Arno, was founded in 805 but was altered and enlarged in the 11th and 12th c. It was clearly influenced by the cathedral, as can be seen, for example, in the façade, which has all the characteristics of Pisan Romanesque, with its round-arched doorways and dwarf galleries. An aisled basilica, the church contains the tomb of the 12th c. scholar Burgundio, with a reused Roman sarcophagus. There is another Roman sarcophagus built into the wall above the doorway in the left transept.

To the east of the church is the little Romanesque Oratory of Sant'Ágata (12th c.).

Location
Piazza San Paolo a Ripa d'Arno

Calci

C2

The village of Calci lies on the south-western slopes of Monte Pisano in the Valgraziosa, a valley with extensive plantations of olives. In the centre of the village is the late 12th c. Pieve (Parish Church), with a two-storey façade decorated with arcading and an unfinished campanile. The nave of the church is

Situation
13 km (8 miles) E

161

separated from the aisles by antique columns. It has a fine 12th c. font with relief decoration.

Certosa di Pisa   C2

Situation
14 km (9 miles) E

Conducted tours

Close to Calci, to the east, is the Certosa di Pisa, a Carthusian house founded in 1366. The present aspect of the extensive complex of buildings results from the remodelling in Baroque style which was carried out in the 17th and 18th c.
Visitors can be shown round the monastery only on conducted tours. The main features of interest are the two cloisters (15th and 16th c.) and the church, in pure Baroque style.

*San Piero a Grado   C2

Situation
5 km (3 miles) SW

Legend has it that the Apostle Peter landed at this place, then on the coast, on his way to Rome. The church which he founded here, the Ecclesia ad Gradus (Church by the Steps), became from an early period an important staging-point for pilgrims making their way to Rome from the north.
The present aisled Romanesque basilica, under which excavation has revealed remains of an earlier church, probably dates from the 11th c. The choir apse at the east end is flanked by two subsidiary apses, and there is also an apse at the west end; there is no transept. The church has frescoes of about 1300 (lower register, portraits of Popes; middle register, scenes from the life of St Peter; upper register, the heavenly Jerusalem) which are generally attributed to Deodato Orlandi.

Pistoia   C2

Province: Pistoia (PT)
Altitude: 65 m (213 ft)
Population: 94,500

Situation

Pistoia, chief town of its province, lies on the southern slopes of the Apennines in the extreme north of Tuscany, some 50 km (30 miles) from the coast.

History

In Roman times Pistoria, as it was then known, was a small fortified settlement (*oppidum*) on the Via Cassia, the road from Rome to Florence and beyond. After the death of Countess Matilda in 1115 the townspeople declared their city independent and took the Ghibelline (Imperial) side in the conflict between the Emperor and the Pope, thus aggravating the rivalry between Pistoia and the neighbouring Guelf towns of Lucca, Florence and Prato. Until the mid 13th c. Pistoia was able to hold its ground against these rivals, and architects, sculptors and painters were offered ample scope in the embellishment of the town. Thereafter, however, Pistoia was compelled to acknowledge the superiority of Florence and Lucca, and a time of troubles, a period of family feuds and party strife, began. The town's political dependence is reflected in the fact that only the cathedral has a tower: the mansions of the burghers have none.

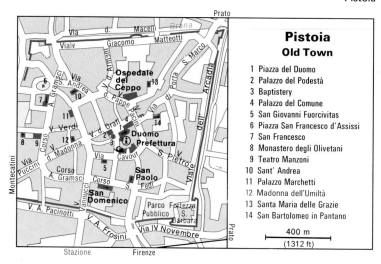

*Cathedral

In the centre of the old town, on the south side of the Piazza del Duomo, stands the Cathedral of Santi Zeno e Iácopo, built in the 12th–13th c. on the site of an earlier church dating from the 5th c. The façade, with its seven-arched portico and three doorways, was completed in 1311. The vaulting behind the central arch, which is higher than the others, is decorated with panels of majolica, and the lunette over the central doorway has a glazed terracotta relief of the Virgin and Child with two Angels by Andrea della Robbia (1505). In the centre of the façade above the portico are two orders of arcading, and above these, at the ends of the pediment, are marble figures of the church's patrons, SS. James and Zeno.

At the left-hand end of the façade rises the massive campanile, 67 m (220 ft) high, the lower part of which is said to have been a Lombard watch-tower. The upper storeys, with arcades, were added in the 13th c., the top in the 16th. With its unmistakable and characteristic form the campanile has become the emblem and landmark of Pistoia.

The spacious interior of the cathedral has pillars and columns with richly decorated capitals separating the nave from the aisles. Immediately inside the right-hand doorway is the Tomb of Cino da Pistoia (Sienese work of about 1337). A doorway in the south aisle leads into the Cappella di San Iácopo, with a silver altar which is a masterpiece of the silversmith's art. The work was carried out in stages between 1287 and 1456, and thus shows a succession of different styles from Early Gothic to Renaissance. On the front are 15 New Testament scenes (by Andrea di Iácopo d'Ognabene, 1316), on the right-hand end nine Old Testament scenes (by Francesco di Niccolò and Leonardo di Giovanni, 1361–64) and on the left-hand end nine scenes from the life of St James (by Leonardo di Giovanni,

* Silver altar

163

1367–71). The two figures of Prophets on the left-hand side of
the upper part are attributed to Brunelleschi (1377–1440).
The sacristy leads into the Museo Capitolare (Museum of the
Cathedral Chapter), with the Cathedral Treasury, the richness
of which is referred to by Dante in the "Divine Comedy"
("Inferno" 24). Its contents include reliquaries of SS. James
and Zeno, illuminated manuscripts and a terracotta "Madonna"
by Pollaiuolo (15th c.).
In front of the altar is a bronze candelabrum (1440) by Maso di
Bartolomeo. In the chapel to the left of the altar are a painting,
the "Madonna Enthroned" (1485) by Verrocchio and Lorenzo
di Credi and a stele with the figure of Bishop Donato de' Médici
by Antonio Rossellino (1475). Beside the north doorway on
the west front can be found the Monument of Cardinal Niccolò
Forteguerri (1419–73), probably by Verrocchio and his pupils,
and between the north and central doorways is a font designed
by Benedetto da Maiano.

Palazzo del Vescodado

Adjoining the south side of the cathedral is the former Palazzo
del Vescodado (Bishop's Palace; 14th c.), its façade decorated with coats of arms and containing the Museo Diocesano
(Diocesan Museum) exhibiting with pictures, gold and silver
articles, etc.

*Baptistery

Opposite the west end of the Cathedral is the baptistery
(1338–59), faced with white and green marble; it was built by
Cellino di Nese, to the designs of Andrea Pisano. In the
tympanum of the main doorway, which is surmounted by a
pediment containing a small rose-window, is a figure of the
Madonna; below this, on the lintel, are scenes from the life of
John the Baptist; and on either side of the doorway are figures
of the Baptist and St Peter. Immediately to the right of the
doorway stands a small external pulpit. The baptistery has a
font by Lanfranco da Como (13th c.).

Palazzo del Podestà (Palazzo Pretorio)

The palazzo was built in 1367 as the residence of the *podestà*,
the Florentine governor of the city, and was later used as law
courts. Of the original structure there survives, for all practical
purposes, only the courtyard, in which is the stone judicial
bench, with the Latin inscription:

| HIC LOCUS | ODIT | AMAT | PUNIT | CONSERVAT | HONORAT |
| | NEQUITIAM | LEGES | CRIMINA | IURA | PROBOS |

(This place hates illdoing, loves the laws, punishes crimes,
preserves the right, honours the righteous.)

Madonna dell'Umiltà

The Church of the Madonna dell'Umiltà, begun in 1495, was
built by Ventura Vitoni, in the manner of Brunelleschi, to house
a miraculous image of the Virgin which had begun to perform

Pistoia: Façade of cathedral

Pistoia: Silver altar in cathedral . . .

. . . and baptistery

wonders in 1490. It replaced the earlier Church of Santa Maria Forisportae.

The ground-plan of the church is highly unusual. A domed central octagon lies beyond a wider vestibule, and to the rear is a rectangular chapel. The barrel vaulting and the vaulting of the central dome over the vestibule are coffered, and the four successive levels of the central octagon are foreshortened to give an effect of perspective. On the high altar is the miraculous image of the Virgin.

San Giovanni Fuorcivitas

The building of this church (St John outside the town), on the site of an earlier (8th c.) church beyond the town walls, began in the mid 12th c. but was completed only in the 14th c. Although the west front is in plain brick, the south side of the church is faced with bands of white and green marble. It has three orders, differing in height, of blind arcading; within the arches are rhombs filled with ornament. On the lintel of the doorway in the south front is a relief, the "Last Supper" by Gruamonte (c. 1160), and in the tympanum above this is a figure of John the Baptist (14th c. Pisan school) flanked by two lions.

The most notable feature in the interior of this aisleless church is the pulpit by Fra Guglielmo da Pisa (1270), which has reliefs of the Annunciation, the Visitation, the Adoration of the Kings, the Washing of the Feet, the Crucifixion, the Descent from the Cross, the Descent into Limbo, the Ascension, Pentecost and the Death of the Virgin. The holy water stoup has representations of the Three Theological Virtues and the Four Cardinal Virtues (the latter an early work by Giovanni Pisano). To the left of the high altar is a polyptych (1353–55) by Taddeo Gaddi, and on the left-hand side altar a terracotta of the Visitation from the workshop of the della Robbias.

San Doménico

To the south of San Giovanni stands the Church of San Doménico, built in the 12th c. and enlarged about 1380. Originally the church of a Dominican friary, it shows the unadorned Gothic style of the Mendicant Orders. In the spacious interior are remains of 14th c. frescoes. Behind the first side altar on the right is the church's most notable monument, the Tomb of Filippo Lazzari by Bernardo and Antonio Rossellino (1462–68). The chapterhouse has a 13th c. fresco of the Crucifixion, and in the adjoining rooms are other frescoes of the 15th and 16th c., formerly in the church.

San Francesco

This large church dedicated to St Francis, begun in 1294 and completed about 1400, stands in the Piazza San Francesco d'Assisi. In later centuries it was converted to secular use as a store and as a barracks. The façade, banded in white and green marble, was not added until 1717.

Pistoia: Church of Sant'Andrea . . .   *. . . and pulpit by Giovanni Pisano*

The façade, banded in white and green marble, was not added until 1717.

The interior was remodelled during the Baroque period, when the 14th c. frescoes were damaged; during restoration work in 1930 many of them were again revealed. The wall-paintings (14th c.) in the principal chapel, by Lippo Memmi, Pietro Lorenzetti and Puccio Capanna (a pupil of Giotto), depict scenes from the life of St Francis. There are other 14th c. frescoes in the side chapels, and in the sacristy and chapter-house (which adjoins the cloister) there are also frescoes on the legend of St Francis.

Sant'Andrea

A little way east of San Francesco is the Church of Sant'Andrea, the origins of which go back to the 8th c. Work continued in the 12th c., but the church remained unfinished. The façade has blind arcading of white and green marble. In the main doorway are two lions flanking a statue of St Andrew in the manner of Giovanni Pisano. On the architrave is a relief depicting the Three Kings before Herod and in Bethlehem by Gruamonte and Adeodato (1166). The capitals of the pillars framing the doorway have, on the left, representations of Zacharias and the Angel and the Visitation and, on the right, the Annunciation and St Anne.

The nave is impressive: tall and narrow, with an open timber roof structure. The pulpit, one of Giovanni Pisano's finest works (1298–1301), is similar to the one in the Cathedral of Pisa (see entry). It rests on seven porphyry columns, two

* Pulpit

167

supported on lions, one on a bent human figure and the central one on a lion and an eagle. On the capitals, which are linked by arches with Gothic tracery, are figures of Sibyls and Prophets. The relief panels round the pulpit depict the Annunciation, the Nativity, the Adoration of the Kings, Joseph's Dream, the Slaughter of the Innocents, the Crucifixion and the Last Judgment. Between the panels are Old and New Testament figures. Giovanni Pisano was also responsible for the wooden Crucifix on the tabernacle in the third chapel on the left.

Palazzo del Comune

To the left of the cathedral, at the far end of the Piazza del Duomo, is the Palazzo del Comune, a bare and forbidding building which with its symmetry and solidity is of powerful effect. It was begun in 1294, during the period of office of Giano della Bella, a Florentine governor who ruled the city fairly and well, but thereafter work came to a halt; it was resumed in 1334, and the building, now enlarged, was completed in 1385. The bridge linking it with the cathedral was added in 1637. The façade is divided vertically into five sections; at the base is a portico, above this are double-arched windows, and above these again triple-arched windows. In the centre of the façade can be seen a large Médici coat of arms, with the keys of St Peter (for the Médici Popes Leo X and Clement VII). To the left of the central window is a black marble head, the significance of which has various explanations; one story is that it represents the Moorish King of Majorca who was defeated by Pisa in 1114.

The palazzo contains a series of handsome apartments with 15th and 16th c. frescoes.

In front of the palazzo is the elegant Pozzo del Leoncino (Lion Well).

San Bartolomeo in Pantano

A short distance east of the Palazzo del Comune stands the Church of San Bartolomeo in Pantano (St Bartholomew in the Marsh), so called because the site of the church (built in 1159) was an area of drained marshland. The beautiful façade, with five arcades borne on columns, has remained unchanged throughout the centuries. On the lintel of the central doorway is a relief (1167; attributed to Gruamonte), "Christ sending out the Apostles", its formal pattern based on the reliefs on Roman sarcophagi.

The most notable feature of the narrow interior is the pulpit by Guido da Como (c. 1250). Its beautifully carved but restrained figures from the New Testament reflect the transition from the simple Romanesque style to the rich and dramatic compositions of a sculptor such as Andrea Pisano (pulpit in Sant'Andrea: see above).

*Ospedale del Ceppo

This hospice, to the north of the Palazzo del Comune, was founded in the 13th or 14th c.; it takes its name from the offertory-box (*ceppo*) in which alms for the poor and sick

Pistoia: Majolica frieze of the Ospedale del Ceppo

were collected. At the beginning of the 16th c. it became a dependency of the Ospedale di Santa Maria Nuova in Florence, and, following the Florentine pattern, a portico was built in front of the façade. The splendid polychrome majolica frieze was the work of artists from the studio of the della Robbias (in particular Santi Buglioni and Giovanni della Robbia). It depicts the Seven Works of Mercy alternating with the Cardinal and Theological Virtues (from left to right: Clothing the naked; a sphinx; Taking in the stranger; Prudence; Visiting the sick; Faith; Comforting the prisoner; Charity; Burying the dead; Hope; Feeding the hungry; Justice; Giving drink to the thirsty; a sphinx). In medallions below the frieze are scenes from the life of the Virgin.

Santa Maria delle Grazie

To the north-east of the old town centre is the Church of Santa Maria delle Grazie, built between 1452 and 1484 to the design of Michelozzo. It has a plain façade with a beautiful doorway.

Pitigliano   D3

Province: Grosseto (GR)
Altitude: 313 m (1027 ft)
Population: 4000

The little town of Pitigliano lies in the extreme south of Tuscany, some 20 km (12½ miles) west of the Lago di Bolsena (which is in Latium) and 50 km (30 miles) east of the coast.

Situation

This easily defensible site was probably occupied by the Etruscans, followed by the Romans, to whom it was known as Caletra. During the Middle Ages it belonged to the Orsini, an influential Guelf family, who granted it a municipal charter. Later the town passed to the Florentine family of Strozzi, and in 1604 it was incorporated in the Grand Duchy of Tuscany.

History

*The town

Pitigliano is perched on a crag of yellowish-red tufa between the gorges of the rivers Meleta, Leuta and Prochio, in an extremely picturesque situation. The soft rock below the town

Pitigliano: Old Town

is riddled with man-made holes; some are ancient tombs, others are used as cellars for storing the excellent local wine.

In the Piazza della Repúbblica is the battlemented Palazzo Orsini, built in the 14th c. and altered and enlarged in the 15th and 16th.

In Piazza Gregorio VII stands the Cathedral of Santi Pietro e Paolo, originally a medieval building but much altered in the 18th c., with a Baroque façade and a massive campanile. It contains paintings by Francesco Zuccarelli (1702–88) and two large historical pictures of the late 19th c.

In the square is a travertine pillar with a figure of a bear (*orso*), the punning heraldic emblem of the Orsini family.

The valley is spanned by a 16th c. aqueduct with 15 arches which once supplied the town with water.

*Sorano   D3

Situation
9 km (5½ miles) NE

Just off the road to Sorano, 1 km (¾ mile) from Pitigliano, is the Parco Orsini, with the ruins of a villa.

Like Pitigliano, the little town of Sorano is built on a crag of tufa. It is still surrounded by its medieval walls.

*Sovana   D3

Situation
8 km (5 miles) NW

The tiny town of Sovana, originally founded by the Etruscans, has preserved its medieval aspect, but is now a place of little consequence, having long been overshadowed by Pitigliano. It has the beautiful little Romanesque Cathedral of Santi Pietro e Paolo, built in the 12th–13th c. on the site of an earlier (9th c.) church and altered in the 14th c. Near by is the Romanesque Church of Santa Maria, with early 16th c. frescoes and a pre-Romanesque ciborium (altar canopy).

In the valleys below the town, 1·5 km (1 mile) away, is an Etruscan cemetery area of chamber tombs (4th–2nd c. B.C.) hewn from the soft tufa.

Etruscan tombs

Poppi C3

Province: Arezzo (AR)
Altitude: 437 m (1434 ft)
Population: 6000

Poppi lies in the heart of the Casentino, some 40 km (25 miles) north of Arezzo and 55 km (35 miles) east of Florence.

Situation

The town first appears in the records, as Pupium, in 1169. After a long period of independence under the rule of the Counts Guidi it passed to Florence about 1440 and thereafter was governed by Florentine *commissari* and *vicari*.

History

Poppi: Fortress wall

171

Palazzo Pretorio

The Palazzo Pretorio, built for the Counts Guidi in the 13th c., is a plain and massive building with a tall tower; the battlements were added during the period of Florentine rule. The two-storey wing is built round an elegant courtyard with the coats of arms of Florentine governors. The chapel has 14th c. frescoes.

Adjoining the palazzo are the Torre dei Diávoli (Devils' Tower) and a large cistern.

San Fedele

The Church of San Fedele was originally a monastic church, built for the Vallumbrosan Order in the late 13th c. In the three-aisled crypt is a gilt-bronze bust of San Victoriello. The choir contains a number of 16th and 17th c. paintings.

Populonia   D2

Province: Livorno (LI)
Altitude: 181 m (594 ft)
Population: 150

Situation

The village of Populonia lies above the Golfo di Baratti some 15 km (9 miles) north of Piombino.

Populonia: The Rocca (fortress)

The site of Populonia was occupied in prehistoric times. As Pupluna it was an Etruscan town, engaged from an early period in smelting copper ore from the Colline Metallífere and iron ore from Elba. It sank into insignificance in the 7th c., when the Bishop transferred his seat to Massa Maríttima.

*Rocca

High above the Golfo di Baratti stands the massive medieval castle, the rocca, with a large cylindrical tower and a square keep, from which there are fine panoramic views.

Museo Etrusco

The Etruscan Museum (Museo Etrusco) contains numbers of grave-goods from the nearby Etruscan cemetery.

*Etruscan tombs

The Etruscan cemetery of Populonia, with tombs dating from the 9th to the 2nd c. B.C., lies below the village to the east. Until the early 20th c. the tombs were hidden below the huge deposits of slag left by the ancient metalworkers, so that although their roofs might be broken down by the weight their rich contents were preserved. Most of the material recovered can be seen in the Archaeological Museum in Florence (see

Populonia: Etruscan tombs...

... and Gulf of Baratti

entry). The slag was resmelted, using modern methods, and its high metal content rooovorod.

There are three main types of tomb: tumulus tombs roofed with "false vaults" formed of overlapping courses of stone; chamber tombs hewn from the tufa; and aedicula tombs (in niches) built of dressed stone, with saddle roofs of stone slabs.

Prato   C3

Province: Firenze/Florence (FI)
Altitude: 63 m (207 ft)
Population: 145,000

Situation

Prato lies in a basin in the Bisenzio Valley, on both banks of the river, roughly half-way between Florence and Pistoia.

History

The site of present-day Prato was probably occupied by an Etruscan settlement. Prato itself first appears in the records in the 10th c.; it received its municipal charter in 1653.

In medieval times Prato was famous for its wool, and it is still a major textile centre. The older part of the town has preserved a number of handsome and historic old buildings.

*Castello dell'Imperatore

This formidable battlemented stronghold, built by the Emperor Frederick II between 1237 and 1248 on the road to the south of Italy from the north, can be compared with his Castel del Monte in Apulia. It incorporates two older (10th c.) towers.

Santa Maria delle Cárceri

The Church of Santa Maria delle Cárceri, opposite the north corner of the castello, owes its name to a miraculous image of the Virgin painted on the wall of a prison (*cárcere*) which once stood here. To house the painting Giuliano da Sangallo built this handsome Renaissance church, on a Greek cross plan, between 1484 and 1495. The exterior is faced with coloured marble, and there is a dome over the crossing. The church contains terracotta medallions of the Evangelists by Andrea della Robbia.

Palazzo Pretorio

In the centre of the old town is the Palazzo Pretorio (formerly the Palazzo Comunale), built in the mid 14th c. and incorporating a number of 13th c. houses and towers. The complex was acquired by the Capitano del Pópolo in 1284 to provide accommodation for the civic administration. The palazzo is of severe aspect, with an old and irregular façade, a balcony and a staircase leading up to the entrance. The battlements and the small belfry were added in the 16th c.

Gallería Comunale

The Gallería Comunale (Municipal Gallery), founded in 1850, which is housed in the Palazzo Pretorio, has an interesting collection, particularly of the 14th and 15th c. Florentine schools. Items of special interest on the first and second floors

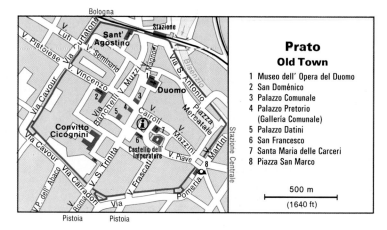

Prato
Old Town

1 Museo dell' Opera del Duomo
2 San Doménico
3 Palazzo Comunale
4 Palazzo Pretorio
   (Gallería Comunale)
5 Palazzo Datini
6 San Francesco
7 Santa Maria delle Carceri
8 Piazza San Marco

500 m
(1640 ft)

are the Tabernacle of St Margaret, by Filippo Lippi (1458; restored from fragments after destruction in an air raid in 1944); the Bacchus Fountain, by Ferdinando Tacca (1665); scenes from the legend of the Virgin's Girdle (see Cathedral, Cappella del Sacro Cíngolo), attributed to Bernardo Daddi (14th c.); a polyptych by Bernardo Daddi, "Virgin and Child with Saints" (c. 1328); a polyptych by Giovanni da Milano, "Madonna Enthroned, with Saints" (c. 1354); Filippo Lippi's "Madonna del Ceppo" (1453); Francesco Botticini's "Madonna with Saints" (15th c.); Filippino Lippi's "Virgin and Child" (1503); and a fresco of the Virgin and Child by Fra Bartolommeo (15th–16th c.).

On the third floor are works of the 16th to 18th c.

Opposite the Palazzo Pretorio is the present Palazzo Comunale, which has lost its original appearance as a result of 19th c. restoration work.

Palazzo Datini

The Palazzo Datini, to the south of the Piazza del Comune, was the residence of the merchant and banker Francesco di Marco Datini (1330–1410), one of the wealthiest men of his day. (See Iris Origo's book, "The Merchant of Prato"). After Datini's death the outside of the house was covered with frescoes depicting scenes from his life, now represented only by scanty remains of the *sinópie* (the artist's preliminary sketches).

Location
Via Ser Lapo Mazzini/
Via Rinaldesca

San Doménico

The Church of San Doménico was built between 1283 and 1322; the façade was left unfinished. Note the richly decorated doorway on the north side. The church contains a large painted Crucifix of about 1400.

In the 15th c. cloister is the entrance to the Museo di Pittura Murale (Museum of Wall-Painting), which contains frescoes

Location
Piazza San Doménico

Museo di Pittura Murale

175

and *sinópie* (preliminary sketches for frescoes) of the 13th to 17th c., together with displays illustrating the technique of fresco-painting and the various methods of restoration.

*Cathedral

The cathedral, dedicated to St Stephen, was originally known as the Church of Santo Stéfano di Borgo al Cornio (the name borne by Prato when it was a small country township), built by Guido da Como (1211 onwards) on the site of an earlier parish church. Subsequently the church was altered and enlarged, receiving the addition of a transept with five chapels between 1317 and 1368. It was raised to cathedral status in 1653, when Prato became the see of a bishop and was granted a municipal charter.

Exterior

The façade is splendidly faced with bands of white and green marble. In the lunette over the main doorway is a glazed terracotta "Madonna and Child with Saints" (1489) by Andrea della Robbia. To the right is the famous external pulpit by Donatello and Michelozzo, the Pérgamo del Sacro Cíngolo (Pulpit of the Holy Girdle). Donatello's dancing *putti* (cherubs; copies: originals in Cathedral Museum) are a marvel of harmony and gaiety. Note also the tall campanile (1340–56), with the size of the window openings increasing from storey to storey.

*Pérgamo del Sacro Cíngolo

Interior

The nave, flanked by aisles, is Romanesque; the vaulting dates only from 1676. The transept, with Gothic ribbed vaulting, was

Prato: External pulpit . . .   *. . . and interior of cathedral*

built between 1317 and 1368. The banding of green and white marble follows Pisan and Lucchese models. Notable features are the pulpit by Mino da Fiésole and Antonio Rossellino (1473), on the left-hand side of the nave; the bronze candelabrum by Maso di Bartolomeo in front of the presbytery; and the bronze Crucifix by Ferdinando Tacca (1653) on the high altar.

On the walls of the choir are two cycles of frescoes painted by Fra Filippo Lippi at the height of his artistic powers (1452–66). On the left are scenes from the life of St Stephen (to whom the church is dedicated), on the right the life of John the Baptist. In the latter series note particularly the scene of Herod's feast: the graceful figure of Salome dancing is traditionally identified as the nun Lucrezia Buti, who became Filippo's wife and bore his son Filippino.

To the right of the choir is the Cappella dell'Ángelo Cústode (Chapel of the Guardian Angel), with frescoes by two unknown 15th c. masters, and beyond this is the Cappella del Crocifisso (Chapel of the Crucifix), with 19th c. wall-paintings. There are also two chapels to the left of the choir. The first has 15th c. frescoes (legends of St James the Elder and St Margaret of Antioch); in the second is the Tomb of Filippo Inghirami (15th c.), which is attributed to the Florentine sculptor Niccolò de' Bardi.

At the west end of the north aisle is the Cappella del Sacro Cíngolo (Chapel of the Holy Girdle), constructed in the late 14th c. to house the Holy Girdle. The legend of this famous and much-venerated relic is recounted in the frescoes by Agnolo Gaddi (1392–95) in the chapel. The story goes that during her Assumption the Virgin gave her girdle to the Apostle Thomas, who presented it to a priest. Later a Prato merchant named Michele Dagonari received the relic as his wife's dowry when he married a girl named Mary in the Holy Land. He brought it back to Prato and, directed by Angels, presented it to representatives of the Church and the City. To this day, therefore, the Bishop and the Mayor of Prato each possess a key to the shrine containing the sacred relic, which can be opened only by both of them together when the relic is taken out to be displayed on feast days.

To the left of the cathedral, on the site of the Romanesque cloister of which some fragments remain, is the Cathedral Museum (Museo dell'Ópera del Duomo), with altar-pieces, missals, goldsmiths' work, including particularly the precious shrine containing the Holy Girdle, and the originals of Donatello's reliefs on the Pérgamo del Sacro Cíngolo.

Cathedral Museum

*Centro per l'Arte Contemporanea Luigi Pecci   C3

To the south of the old Town is the new Contemporary Art Centre. Opened in 1988 it has exhibitions of paintings, sculpture and design and a large collection of videos.

Location
Via della Repubblica

Poggio a Caiano

Beyond the motorway, at the foot of Monte Albano, lies Poggio a Caiano, famous for the Médici villa built by Giuliano da

Situation
8 km (5 miles) S

Sangallo about 1480. Normally only the beautiful park is open to the public.

Artimino   C3

Situation
13 km (8 miles) S

Beyond Poggio a Caiano, on the edge of the hills, is the village of Artimino, still surrounded by medieval walls. Features of interest are the Romanesque Church of San Leonardo and the Etruscan cemetery which has been excavated here since 1970. Near the village is the beautiful Villa dell'Artimino, built for Grand Duke Ferdinand I in the late 16th c.

San Galgano, Abbazía di

Abbazía di San Galgano (see entry).

San Gimignano   C3

Province: Siena (SI)
Altitude: 332 m (1089 ft)
Population: 7500

Situation

The little town of San Gimignano is prominently situated on a hill some 35 km (22 miles) north-west of Siena and 50 km (30 miles) south-west of Florence.

San Gimignano: Towers built by rival families

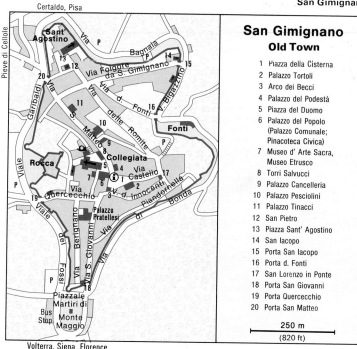

Certaldo, Pisa

Pieve di Cellole

San Gimignano
Old Town

1 Piazza della Cisterna
2 Palazzo Tortoli
3 Arco dei Becci
4 Palazzo del Podestà
5 Piazza del Duomo
6 Palazzo del Popolo
  (Palazzo Comunale;
  Pinacoteca Civica)
7 Museo d' Arte Sacra,
  Museo Etrusco
8 Torri Salvucci
9 Palazzo Cancelleria
10 Palazzo Pesciolini
11 Palazzo Tinacci
12 San Pietro
13 Piazza Sant' Agostino
14 San Iacopo
15 Porta San Iacopo
16 Porta d. Fonti
17 San Lorenzo in Ponte
18 Porta San Giovanni
19 Porta Quercecchio
20 Porta San Matteo

250 m
(820 ft)

Volterra, Siena, Florence

The hill on which San Gimignano stands was the site of an Etruscan settlement but the place – named after St Geminianus, a 4th c. Bishop of Módena – first appears in history in the Middle Ages. The town's situation on the "Franks' Road", the road to Rome from the north, brought it a profitable trade, and the growing of saffron brought great prosperity. As a free commune San Gimignano was governed by Consuls and later by a *podestà*, but in 1353 it came under Florentine rule. During its period of independence there was continual strife between two great families in the town, the Ardinghelli, who took the Guelf side, and the Salvucci, who were Ghibellines: a rivalry which left its distinctive mark in the form of the towers built by the rival factions, increasing constantly in number and in height. At one time there were more than 70 of these towers, and of these 13 still survive, giving this little walled town its characteristic aspect.

History

* *The town

When more convenient routes for traffic developed in the valleys trade abandoned the "Franks' Road" and San Gimignano declined. New building ceased, and it was all the inhabitants could do to prevent the old ones from falling into ruin. Thus San Gimignano remained almost unaltered in accordance with regulations promulgated by the municipality in

179

accordance with regulations promulgated by the municipality in 1602. In recent years restoration work promoted by UNESCO has done much to preserve these precious remains of the past.

*Piazza della Cisterna

The picturesque little Piazza della Cisterna, the town's main square, takes its name from a well constructed here in 1273. Triangular in shape, it was enlarged in 1346, and is paved with bricks laid in a herringbone pattern. Flanking the square (from right to left, beginning at the arch) are the Casa Razzi (No. 28, on the south side), with the stump of a tower; the Casa Salvestrini (No. 9), formerly the Ospedale degli Innocenti and now the Albergo della Cisterna; the Palazzo Tortoli, with the remains of a tower belonging to the Palazzo del Capitano del Pópolo; the Palazzo dei Cortesi (on the north side of the square), with the tall Torre del Diávolo (Devil's Tower); and the two Torri Ardinghelli (on the west side).

*Santa Maria Assunta

Location
Piazza del Duomo

The Collegiate Church of Santa Maria Assunta (the Assumption) stands on the west side of the Piazza del Duomo. (The name of the Piazza del Duomo – Cathedral Square – is misleading, for San Gimignano was never the see of a bishop and consequently never had a cathedral.)

Exterior

This aisled Romanesque church dates from the 12th c., but in 1457 it was enlarged by Giuliano da Maiano, who added a transept and side chapels,
The façade, left without a marble facing, has been much altered down the centuries.

Interior

On the inside of the entrance wall is a fresco by Benozzo Gozzoli (1456) depicting the martyrdom of St Sebastian. Here, too, are two wooden statues of the Annunciation (*c.* 1421) by Iácopo della Quercia.
In the right-hand aisle is a monumental cycle of frescoes by Barna da Siena (14th c.), with three registers of New Testament scenes – from the Annunciation to the Flight into Egypt, from Jesus in the Temple to the Entry into Jerusalem and from the Last Supper to Pentecost. As Vasari tells us in his life of Barna, the painter was killed by a fall from the scaffolding while painting the Crucifixion and the work was completed by his nephew and pupil Giovanni d'Asciano. This New Testament cycle has its counterpart in the left-hand aisle, where there is another great series of frescoes of Old Testament scenes by Bártolo di Fredi (*c.* 1356; much overpainted).
At the end of the right-hand aisle is the Cappella di Santa Fina, in the purest Renaissance style, by Giuliano and Benedetto da Maiano (1468). St Fina (1238–53) is San Gimignano's Patron Saint, much revered as a miracle-worker. The altar, also by Benedetto da Maiano, was several times remodelled in Baroque style, but was restored to its original form (involving some new work) in 1881.
On the altar is a tabernacle with relief decoration, and on top of this is an urn which until 1738 contained the remains of St Fina. Above is a "Madonna and Child flanked by two Angels".

In the arcades on either side of the altar are frescoes by Doménico Ghirlandaio (1475) depicting the life and death of St Fina.

Museo d'Arte Sacra/Museo Etrusco

Adjoining the Church of Santa Maria Assunta is the Museo d'Arte Sacra (Museum of Sacred Art), which contains sculpture of the 14th and 15th c., an Oriental carpet in the form of a Greek cross (16th c.) and liturgical vestments.

Location
Piazza Pécori

In the same building is the Museo Etrusco (Etruscan Museum), with a small collection of Etruscan urns, vases, coins, etc., found within the commune of San Gimignano.

Palazzo del Pópolo

To the left of Santa Maria Assunta is the Palazzo del Pópolo (also known as the Palazzo Nuovo del Podestà; begun 1288, enlarged 1323), which was the seat of municipal government from the end of the 13th c. and is still the Town Hall. The tower, known as the Torre Grossa (Fat Tower), is the tallest in the town (54 m (177 ft); fine view from top). A municipal ordinance laid down that no other tower should be higher than this one.

Within the Palazzo del Pópolo is the Pinacoteca Cívica (Municipal Art Gallery). Passing through a picturesque courtyard with a well of 1361, we come into the Sala Dante, so called after a visit to the town by the poet in 1300, when he sought to persuade the municipal councillors to join the Guelf League; the date 1299 given in an inscription in the room is incorrect. On the right-hand wall of the room is a "Maestà" (Madonna enthroned) by Lippo Memmi (1317).

Pinacoteca Cívica

The collection also includes a painted Crucifix by Coppo di Marcovaldo (13th c.), a "Madonna and Child" by Pinturicchio (1512), two tondi depicting the Annunciation by Filippino Lippi (1483) and numbers of notable works by Florentine and Sienese painters of the 13th–15th c.

Palazzo del Podestà

Facing Santa Maria Assunta is the old Palazzo del Podestà, built in 1239, incorporating houses belonging to the Mantellini family, and enlarged in 1337. On the ground floor is a loggia, and the palazzo is dominated by a 51 m (167 ft) high tower known as the Rognosa.

Torri Salvucci

To the left of the Palazzo del Podestà, at the end of Via San Matteo, are the two Torri Salvucci, which once belonged to the powerful Ardinghelli family. Farther along Via San Matteo are the Casa-Torre Pesciolini (No. 32) and the Palazzo Tinacci (Nos. 60–62).

Rocca

A little way west of Santa Maria Assunta, built against the town walls on the highest point of the hill, is the rocca (castle), erected by the Florentines in 1353 but demolished in 1555 on the orders of Cosimo I. Only a tower and fragments of the walls survive. From the top there are magnificent views of the town and surrounding countryside.

San lácopo

Near the Porta San Iácopo, the north town gate, is the little Romanesque Church of San Iácopo, built by the Templars in the 13th c. The façade (lower part brick, upper part travertine) has a Pisan-style doorway with a beautiful rose-window. The interior is aisleless, with groined vaulting. There is a fine fresco of the Crucifixion by Memmo di Filippuccio (13th–14th c.)

Sant'Agostino

A little way north of the Porta San Matteo, at the northern tip of the old town within the walls, stands the Church of Sant'Agostino, an aisleless brick church built by Augustinian Canons between 1280 and 1298 in the plain Gothic style of the Mendicant Orders.

Immediately on the right of the entrance is the Cappella di San Bártolo, with a sumptuous marble altar by Benedetto da Maiano (1494) containing the remains of San Bártolo. On the high altar is an altar-piece depicting the Coronation of the Virgin by Piero Pollaiuolo (1483).

*Frescoes

The most notable feature of the church is splendid cycle of frescoes by Benozzo Gozzoli (1464–65) in the choir. Beautifully painted in a lively narrative style, they depict in 19 scenes the life of St Augustine (354–430), one of the great Latin Fathers of the Church. In the lowest row are Augustine as a boy in Tagaste (North Africa); Augustine as a youth in Carthage; his mother St Monica praying for her son; Augustine sailing to Italy; his landing; Augustine teaching in Rome; his departure for Milan. Middle row: his audience with Bishop Ambrose of Milan and with the Emperor Theodosius; St Monica begging for the conversion of her son; disputation between Augustine and St Ambrose; Augustine reading Paul's Epistle to the Romans (13, 13) on his conversion; Augustine baptised by St Ambrose; Augustine and the Christ Child by the sea; Augustine explaining his Rule; death of St Monica. Top row: Augustine as Bishop of Hippo; conversion of a heretic; vision of St Jerome; death of Augustine. There are other frescoes in the nave: "St Sebastian Clothed", by Benozzo Gozzoli (1524); "Madonna Enthroned", by Lippo Memmi (1330); "San Bártolo giving a Blessing", by Sebastiano Mainardi (1487); "Life of the Virgin", by Bártolo di Fredi (c. 1400).

On the south side of the church, entered from the sacristy, is a 15th c. cloister and the chapter-house.

Pieve di Céllole   C2/3

Standing on a hill, surrounded by cypresses, is the Pieve
(Parish Church) of the village of Céllole, probably built at the
turn of the 12th–13th c. The façade is plain, but the outside of
the apse has rich figural decoration. The church has a beautiful
font.

Situation
4·5 km (3 miles) NW

San Giovanni Valdarno   C3

Province: Arezzo (AR)
Altitude: 134 m (440 ft)
Population: 20,000

The industrial town of San Giovanni lies in the Arno Valley
halfway between Arezzo and Florence. The Autostrada del Sole
(motorway) runs past the town on the other side of the river.
There are lignite-mines in the surrounding area. The town's
main industries are steelworking, ceramics and glass.
San Giovanni Valdarno was the birthplace of the Renaissance
painter Masaccio (Tommaso di San Giovanni di Simone Guidi,
1401–28).

Situation

The town

In the centre of the main square (Piazza Cavour and Piazza
Masaccio) is the 13th c. Palazzo Pretorio, probably built by
Arnolfo di Cambio. On the outside are numerous coats of arms
of Florentine *podestàs* and *vicari* of the 15th and 16th c., and in
front of the building is a column bearing a figure of the Marzocco, the heraldic beast of Florence. To the rear is the 14th c.
Parish Church of San Giovanni Battista, with a beautiful portico.
Behind the Palazzo Pretorio is the 15th c. Church of Santa
Maria delle Grazie, with a neo-classical façade of 1840. The
church contains an image of the Madonna (*c.* 1400) which is
revered as miraculous.
Adjoining the church is the Pinacoteca Parrocchiale, with a
small but interesting collection of pictures. Also in the square is
the 14th c. Oratorio di San Lorenzo, with two aisles of different
heights; on the high altar can be seen a large polyptych by
Giovanni del Biondo (14th c.).

*Convento di Montecarlo   C3

The Convento di Montecarlo, founded in the 15th c., is well
worth a visit. The church (San Francesco) has a beautiful
"Annunciation" by Fra Angélico (*c.* 1440) or his pupil Zanobi
Strozzi.

Situation
2 km (1¼ miles) S

Sammezzano   C3

The village of Sammezzano in the Arno Valley, reached by way
of SS 69, has a striking castello, originally founded in the
Middle Ages but completely rebuilt in neo-Moorish style in the
19th c. It is now a hotel.

Situation
20 km (12½ miles) N

San Miniato al Tedesco C2

Province: Pisa (PI)
Altitude: 156 m (512 ft)
Population: 23,000

Situation

San Miniato lies on high ground on the southern edge of the Arno Valley, 45 km (28 miles) east of Pisa.

History

Thanks to its excellent strategic situation the site of San Miniato was occupied in Roman times and later by the Lombards. Its name San Miniato al Tedesco (*tedesco* = German) reflects its connection with the German (Holy Roman) Empire; for in the Middle Ages it was an important Imperial stronghold, and in the reign of Otto I (936–973) it became the official residence of the Imperial Vicars. Frederick II (1212–50) had his counsellor Pier delle Vigne imprisoned and blinded in the tower on top of the hill, as Dante relates in the "Divine Comedy" ("Inferno" 13). In the 14th c. San Miniato came under Florentine control.

The town

In the Piazza del Pópolo is the Church of San Doménico (also called Santi Iácopo e Lucia de Forisportam), built in 1330, with a façade of unfaced stone. The aisleless church contains

San Miniato: Church of San Francesco

frescoes (c. 1700) on the life of St Dominic, also the tomb (1461) of a doctor, Giovanni Chellini, the work of Donatello and Rossellino.

Near by is the Palazzo Vescovile (Bishop's Palace), built in the 13th c. and used as the bishop's palace since 1622.

In the Prato del Duomo, a square commanding extensive views, stands the Cathedral of Assunta e San Genesio, an aisled church dating from the 12th c. but subsequently much altered. In the 15th c. a massive tower belonging to the old castle was converted into a campanile. During the Baroque period the church was again remodelled, leaving only the façade as it was. The church contains a number of 16th c. pictures.

The Church of San Francesco, a massive brick structure, was built in 1276 on the site of an earlier church dedicated to St Miniatus. It was enlarged in the 15th c.

The Palazzo Comunale, now the Town Hall, dates from the 14th c. but has a modern façade. In the Council Chamber are frescoes of the school of Giotto (14th c.).

San Quírico d'Orcia   C3

Province: Siena (SI)
Altitude: 409 m (1342 ft)
Population: 2500

The little town of San Quírico d'Orcia lies above the valleys of the Orcia and Asso, some 45 km (28 miles) south-east of Siena.

Situation

San Quirico d'Orcia: Collegiate church

History

In Roman times there was a settlement here, known as Vicus Alecinus, on the Via Cassia. During the Middle Ages the town was long the residence of an Imperial Vicar (governor); then in 1256 it came under the control of Siena. It remained with this city republic and with it passed into the Grand Duchy of Tuscany.

Collegiata

There was a church on the site of the Collegiata (also known as Pieve di Osenna as early as the 8th c. The present church was built in the 12th c., in Romanesque style, and enlarged in the 13th. The plain façade has a fine Romanesque doorway, with a carving on the lintel of a fight between monsters. The doorway on the south side was probably the work of Giovanni Pisano or his school (13th c.); it has a small porch supported on powerful Atlas figures standing on lions. The doorway in the south transept (1298) is Gothic. The interior (aisleless) has choir-stalls with intarsia decoration by Antonio Barili (1482–1502).

Palazzo Chigi

Near the church is the Palazzo Chigi, in pure Baroque style, built by Carlo Fontana about 1680. It suffered considerable damage during the Second World War.

San Salvatore, Abbadia

See Abbadia San Salvatore

Sansepolcro   C4

Province: Arezzo (AR)
Altitude: 330 m (1083 ft)
Population: 16,000

Situation

The industrial and commercial town of Sansepolcro lies in the Upper Tiber Valley, 35 km (22 miles) north-east of Arezzo.

History

Sansepolcro (Holy Sepulchre) owes its name to two 10th c. pilgrims named Arcano and Egidio who are said to have brought back from the Holy Land certain relics from Christ's tomb. An oratory was built to house the relics, and Camaldolese monks (Camáldoli – see entry) who were responsible for the care and service of the shrine built an abbey on the site. In later centuries the town frequently changed masters, but in the mid 15th c. finally fell under the control of Florence. Pope Leo X (1513–21) made it the see of a bishop.
Sansepolcro was the birthplace of the painter Piero della Francesca (c. 1416–1492).

Cathedral

In the town's main street, Via Matteotti, is the cathedral, dedicated to St John the Evangelist. It was the church of the Camaldolese Monastery (built between 1012 and 1049) but was subsequently much altered. The Romanesque façade has three doorways and a rose-window (a later addition). The aisled interior reflects the transition to Gothic, particularly in the polygonal apse. The church contains a number of works of art, including an "Ascension" from a drawing by Pérugino (1445–1523) and, in the presbytery, a terracotta tabernacle from the workshop of the della Robbias.

Palazzo delle Laudi

To the left of the cathedral is the Palazzo delle Laudi, built between 1591 and 1609 at the time of transition from Renaissance to Baroque; it has a fine arcaded courtyard and is now used by the municipal administration.

*Pinacoteca Comunale

Opposite the cathedral, also in Via Matteotti, is the old Palazzo Comunale, which now houses the Pinacoteca Comunale (Municipal Art Gallery), with some notable works of art. Of particular importance are the works by Piero della Francesca (c. 1416–1492), one of the leading painters and theorists of the Italian Early Renaissance; note particularly his "Resurrection" and the Altar of the Madonna della Misericordia. The collection also includes paintings of the 14th–16th c., including works by Luca Signorelli and Santi di Tito (a native of Sansepolcro), and terracottas from the workshop of the della Robbias. The Pinacoteca also contains a library.

San Francesco

The Church of San Francesco stands in the square of the same name. Of the original 13th c. church there remain the façade and the campanile; the rest of the structure was much altered in the Late Baroque period. The church has a Gothic high altar (1304).

Fortezza Medicea

This Médici stronghold was built on earlier foundations in the early 16th c., when Sansepolcro had long been Florentine. It may have been designed by Giuliano da Sangallo (1445–1516).

Monterchi   C4

The village of Monterchi is worth visiting for the sake of its cemetery chapel, which has a beautiful fresco of the Madonna del Parto by Piero della Francesca, and a ciborium from the workshop of the della Robbias in the parish church.

Situation
17 km (10½ miles) S

Sant'Ántimo, Abbazía di

See Abbazía di Sant'Ántimo

Siena   C3

Province: Siena (SI)
Altitude: 322 m (1056 ft)
Population: 61,000

Situation

Siena, chief town of its province, lies in the uplands of Tuscany, between the Colline Metallífere and the Chianti hills. Its soil yields a natural pigment formerly much used by painters ("burnt Sienna").

History

Siena was a place of no consequence in Roman times, when it was known as Saena Julia. After the death of Countess Matilda of Tuscia in 1115 Siena – like Pisa, Lucca, Florence and other cities – gained its independence. The government of the town remained in the hands of the local Ghibelline nobility, and this brought it into conflict with the Guelf city of Florence, its great rival in power and wealth, with which it was constantly at odds. After the fall of the Hohenstaufen Emperors, in 1270, Charles of Anjou won control of the town and made it a member of the Guelf League of Tuscan towns. In 1348 Siena was stricken by an outbreak of plague. A period of domestic troubles culminated in the establishment in 1487 of personal rule by Pandolfo Petrucci (known as il Magnífico, the Magnificent), whose strict but beneficient régime is praised by Machiavelli. In 1555 Siena was taken by the Spaniards, who ceded it in 1559 to Duke Cosimo I of Tuscany.

Art

The great period of Sienese art was in the 13th and 14th c. The cathedral and numerous palaces in the town are outstanding monuments of Gothic architecture. The good brick-earth found in the surrounding area led to the extensive use of brick in building. The Sienese painters of the 13th and 14th c. (Duccio, Simone Martini, the brothers Ambrogio, and Pietro Lorenzetti), with their delicate and graceful style, surpassed even the artists of Florence. Iácopo della Quercia (1374–1438) was one of the founders of Renaissance sculpture, whose influence was still felt by Michelángelo.

*The town

Siena lies on three hill ridges which meet in the centre of the old town, and accordingly is divided into three wards or *terzi* (thirds): to the south the Terzo di Città (with Via di Città as its main street), to the north the Terzo di Camollia (main street Banchi di Sopra) and to the east the Terzo di San Martino (main street Banchi di Sotto). The three main streets meet at what is called the Croce del Travaglio (Cross of Work), by the Loggia della Mercanzia. Since the valleys between the hills have no streets cutting conveniently across them, the route from one part of the town to another almost inevitably goes by way of the Croce del Travaglio.
The central area of Siena is closed to private cars.

Firenze
Porta Camollia

Firenze
Stazione

Arezzo
Osservanza

Viale Memmi

Siena

100 m
(328 ft)

Viale G. Mazzini

Viale D. Beccafumi

Via D. Simone Martini

Viale Don Giovanni Minzoni
MURA

V. Biagio di Montluc

Fonte-giusta

Via di Camollia

Via di Campansi

Campansi

Via G. Garibaldi

Barriera S.
Lorenzo

Viale N. Sauro

MURA

Viale A. Diaz

Santo
Stefano

Via G.

Chiesa
Inglese

San
Sebastiano

Fonte
d' Ovile

Viale R. Franci

Piazza
d' Sale

Porta
Ovile

Via Baldassarre Peruzzi

Viale C. Maccari

La Lizza

Piazza
A. Gramsci

Sant'
Andrea

Via d. Pian d'Ovile

Fonte
Nuova

MURA

Arezzo

Via di S. Francesco

San
Francesco

Forte di
Santa
Barbara

Stadio

Via XXV Aprile

Via F. Tozzi

Montanini

San Donato

Via dei Rossi

Via d. Pellegrini

Piazza
S. Francesco

Oratorio
di San
Bernardino

Stadio
Comunale

Viale

Via Comunale

Piazza
Matteotti

Palazzo
Salimbeni

Santa Maria
dei Nevi

Via Curtatone

Via d. Paradiso

Piazza
Salimbeni

San Pietro
Ovile

Santa Maria
di Provenzano

Viale dei Mille

Piazza
S. Domenico

Via Banchi di sopra

Palazzo
Spannocchi

Piazza
Prevenzano
Salvani

Museo
Archeologico

Via d. Sapienza

San
Cristoforo

San Vigilio

San Giovanni
d. Staffa

San
Domenico

Santuario
Caateriniano

Via S. Caterina

Palazzo
Tolomei

Via d. Terme

Università

Fonte
Branda

Via di Fontebranda

Croce del
Travaglio

V. Banchi
di sotto

Logge
del Papa

Via di Pantaneto

Porta
Fontebranda

Loggia d.
Mercanzie

Fonte
Gaia

Palazzo
Piccolomini

San
Martino

Via Esterna di Fontebranda

Il Campo

Torre d.
Mangia

Via di Porrione

Porta Pispini Arezzo Porta Romana

Palazzo del
Magnifico

Casato di sotto

Palazzo
Pubblico

Piazza
del
Mercato

Santo Spirito, Santa Maria dei Servi

Palazzo
Arcivesco-
vile

Via di Città

Museo
d. Opera
Metropolitana

Duomo

Palazzo
Chigi-
Saracini

Via d. Sole

Piazza d.
Duomo

Prefettura

Palazzo
Piccolomini

Casato di sopra

San
Sebastiano

Spedale di
Santa Maria della Scala

Via del Fosso

Piazza
Postierla

MURA

Pinacoteca
Nazionale
(Pal. Buonsignori)

Via Stalloreggi

San Pietro

Casato

San Giuseppe

Piano

Via Sarrocchi

Prato
S. Agostino

Sant'
Agostino

San Quirico

Via di Fontanella

Palazzo Pallini

Via di Mantellini

Santa
Lucia

Orto Botanico

Via Pier Andrea Mattioli

Porta
Laterina

San Niccolò
al Carmine

Porta San Marco
Grosseto

Porta Tufi
Monte Oliveto Maggiore, Grosseto

Siena: Cathedral and Piazza del Campo

**Cathedral

The cathedral (Santa Maria), one of the finest churches in Italy, stands on the highest point in the town, to the south-west of the Croce del Travaglio.

It is not known when a church was first built on this site. The cathedral in its present form was begun in 1229; the dome was completed in 1264; and the choir was extended eastward over the baptistery about 1317. Then in 1339 the people of Siena resolved on a gigantic enlargement of the cathedral which would have made it the largest Gothic building in Italy. The existing church was to become the transept of a new church more than 100 m (330 ft) long, the main axis of which would be turned through 90 degrees. Work on the project soon came to a halt, however, partly because the foundations were inadequate for the weight of the new building and partly because the population of the town was decimated by plague in 1348. Some idea of the vast scale of the project can be gained from those portions of the new nave which were completed.

The façade of the original building was completed only in 1380. The rich sculptural decoration was largely renewed in 1869, and the mosaics were set in place in 1877. The campanile dates from the end of the 14th c.

Exterior

The façade (by Giovanni Pisano, 1284–99) is one of the finest achievements of Italian Gothic, with a beautiful polychrome facing of white, green and red marble. Almost its whole width is taken up by three doorways of equal height surmounted by pediments, with a slender tower at each end. Above the central doorway is a rose-window. The façade is richly decorated with sculptured figures, almost all now replaced by copies. The

Siena Cathedral
Santa Maria Assunta

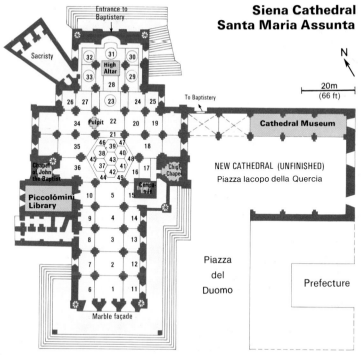

N

20m
(66 ft)

Scenes represented in the marble PAVEMENT (various dates between 1372 and 1562; partly reproductions or copies – originals in Cathedral Museum)

1 Hermes Trismegistus
2 Coats of arms of Siena (centre), Pisa, Lucca, Florence, Arezzo, Orvieto, Rome, Perugia, Viterbo, Massa, Grosseto, Volterra and Pistoia
3 Imperial Altar
4 Fortune
5 Wheel of Fortune; four philosophers
6–15 Sibyls

16 Seven Ages of Man
17 Faith, Hope, Charity, Religion
18 Jephthah defeats the Ammonites
19 Death of Absalom
20 Emperor Sigismund
21 Moses draws water from the rock
22 Dance round the Golden Calf
23 David and Goliath
24 Moses
25 Samson defeats the

Philistines
26, 27 Joshua
28 Abraham's Sacrifice
29 Wisdom
30 Moderation
31 Compassion
32 Justice
33 Steadfastness
34 Judith and Holofernes
35 Slaughter of the Innocents
36 Fall of Herod
37–49 Ahab and Elijah

mosaics in the pediments, with a gold ground, were done by Venetian artists in 1877–78.

In the angle between the nave and the right-hand transept is the Romanesque campanile; its facing of horizontally banded dark- and light-coloured marble gives it an astonishing lightness, an effect reinforced by the six orders of windows, increasing in number as they go up. In the lunette of the doorway at the foot of the tower is a bas-relief of the Virgin and

Child (the Madonna del Perdono), attributed to Donatello (15th c.).

Over the crossing of the original church, on a hexagonal drum, is the dome, which was completed before the heightening of the nave, so that the drum appears to be set into the roof of the nave. Beyond the end of the right-hand transept are fragments of the new cathedral which was never completed: the five-bayed north-eastern aisle (now occupied by the Cathedral Museum: see below), the Facciatone (Giant Façade) and three bays of the south-west wall of the nave, which enclose the Piazza Iácopo della Quercia. Much of the left-hand wall of the old cathedral is concealed by the Piccolómini Library (see below). On a column at the left-hand end of the steps leading up to the cathedral is the She-Wolf with Romulus and Remus (copy: original in Cathedral Museum).

Interior

With its regular alternation of courses of black and white marble, the interior of the cathedral (89·40 m – 293 ft long) has a rather overpowering effect, though this is relieved by the painting of the ceiling with gold stars on a blue ground. The nave is separated from the aisles by piers bearing tall round-headed arches. Above these runs a cornice with busts of Christ and 171 Popes (down to Lucius III), and in the spandrels of the arches are busts of 36 Roman Emperors (terracotta, 15th–16th c.). At the point where the nave reaches the crossing can be seen part of the dwarf gallery which encircles the drum of the dome.

The inner wall of the façade has reliefs depicting the life of the Virgin (1483) and the legend of Sant'Ansano (c. 1480); the stained glass (1549) in the rose-window depicts the Last Supper. There is also a stained-glass window in the choir (see below).

** Pavement

The pavement of the cathedral is a work of unique interest and beauty, with 56 panels depicting Sibyls, Biblical scenes, allegories, etc. Over the 200 years (from about 1370) which it took to complete the work the artists' techniques were steadily refined. At first they merely scratched out the design in the marble and then filled in the lines with asphalt, but later they increasingly tended to use different coloured marbles in intarsia or mosaic techniques.

** Piccolómini Library

In the left-hand aisle is the entrance to the Piccolómini Library. The entrance wall (by Lorenzo di Mariano, 1497) is a fine example of High Renaissance decorative sculpture. A bronze grille gives access to the library, one of the finest and best-preserved creations of the Early Renaissance. Begun in 1495, it was built for Cardinal Francesco Piccolómini (later Pope Pius III) in honour of his kinsman Enea Silvio (Aeneas Sylvius) Piccolómini (Pope Pius II, 1458–64; see under Pienza).

The colourful frescoes in the library were painted in 1502–08 by Pinturicchio and his pupils. They depict ten scenes (beginning from the right-hand window): Enea Silvio Piccolómini accompanies Cardinal Capranica to the Council of Basle (1432); he appears before King James I of Scotland as the Council's Envoy; the Emperor Frederick III crowns him as *poeta laureatus*; he submits to Pope Eugenius II; as Archbishop of Siena he presents Eleanor of Aragon to Frederick III; Pope Calixtus III creates him Cardinal; he is crowned Pope as Pius II; he seeks to unite the Christian princes against the Turks at

Mantua; canonisation of St Catherine of Siena; Pius arrives at Ancona to prepare for the campaign against the Turks.

The ceiling of the library is also covered with frescoes by Pinturicchio – the Piccolómini coat of arms, surrounded by mythological figures which are separated by bands of ornament. Round the walls of the room are displayed richly illuminated 15th c. musical manuscripts.

In the left-hand transept is the Cappella San Giovanni Battista (Chapel of St John the Baptist), with a beautiful doorway by Lorenzo di Mariano (1476–1534). In the chapel are a bronze statue of John the Baptist by Donatello (1457) and a statue of St Catherine of Alexandria by Neroccio (1487). The frescoes (scenes from the life of the Baptist and two portraits) are by Pinturicchio.

Cappella San Giovanni

The white marble pulpit by Niccoló Pisano and pupils (1265–68) is one of the finest works of art in the cathedral. Octagonal in shape, it is borne on nine columns of granite, porphyry and green marble. The outer columns stand alternately on the base and on figures of lions, the inner ones on allegories of the Seven Liberal Arts and Philosophy. Above the capitals are personifications of the Virtues. On the parapet of the pulpit are seven magnificently carved reliefs: the Nativity, the Adoration of the Kings, the Flight into Egypt, the Slaughter of the Innocents, the Crucifixion and the Last Judgment, with the Elect, and the Damned. The steps leading up to the pulpit were added in the 16th c.

*Pulpit

The presbytery is dominated by the large marble altar by Baldassare Peruzzi (1532), over which is a bronze ciborium by Vecchietta (1467–72), flanked by Angels carrying candles. The apse has frescoes by various 16th and 17th c. artists; on some of them 19th c. restoration is very evident. The carved choir-stalls, in Late Gothic style, date from 1363 to 1397; of the original 90 stalls only 36 remain. Behind the stalls are richly decorative intarsia panels by Fra Giovanni da Verona (1503).

Presbytery

A door on the left-hand side of the presbytery leads into the sacristy. In three chapels at the far end are remains of 15 c. frescoes.

Sacristy

High up in the wall of the choir is a circular window with what is believed to be the oldest stained glass in Italy, depicting the Burial, Assumption and Coronation of the Virgin, with the Four Evangelists and Siena's four Patron Saints. The window, originally made in 1288, was moved to its present position in 1365.

In the right transept is the entrance to the Cappella Chigi (Chigi Chapel) or Cappella della Madonna del Voto (Chapel of the Madonna of the Vow), which was built in 1659–62 to the design of the great Baroque architect Giovanni Lorenzo Bernini. Of the four statues in the chapel two ("St Jerome" and "The Magdalene") are by Bernini; the other two ("San Bernardino" and "St Catherine of Siena") are by his pupils.

Cappella Chigi

The campanile originally stood outside the cathedral, in the angle between the nave and the right transept, but with the enlargement of the cathedral it is now within the main structure. On the wall above the doorway leading from the last bay of the right-hand aisle into the base of the campanile is the

Campanile

Monument of Bishop Tommaso Piccolómini del Testa by Neroccio (1484).

Crypt

The crypt is reached by going round the outside of the right transept and through the doorway in the first bay of the unfinished new cathedral. The entrance to the crypt is on the first landing of the staircase. In the first room are the originals of statues on the cathedral, now replaced by copies, and in the second are remains of late 13th c. frescoes of New Testament scenes.

*Baptistery

The baptistery is a few steps lower down than the crypt. It was constructed when the choir was extended and underbuilding was necessary to compensate for the fall in the ground; the baptistery has, therefore, something of the aspect of a crypt. The groined vaulting is borne on squat pillars and is wholly covered with frescoes, originally painted about 1450 by Vecchietta (Lorenzo di Pietro, 1412–80) and other artists but now almost devoid of artistic value as a result of clumsy restoration in the late 19th c.

In front of the apse, on a stepped hexagonal base, is a marble font fashioned in 1417–30, probably by Iácopo della Quercia. The six sides of the font have bronze reliefs of scenes from the life of John the Baptist by Iácopo della Quercia, Giovanni di Turino, Lorenzo Ghiberti and Donatello. On the canopy of the font is a marble statue of the Baptist.

*Cathedral Museum (Museo dell'Ópera Metropolitana)

The Cathedral Museum is housed in three bays of the nave of the new cathedral. Practically all the items on show come from the cathedral.

Siena: Façade of cathedral

Angel of the Annunciation (Pinacoteca Nazionale)

Among the museum's many treasures are reliefs by Nicola Pisano, works by Giovanni Pisano or from his workshop, a magnificent relief of the Virgin and Child with St Antony and Cardinal Casini by Iácopo della Quercia, sculpture by Giovanni Pisano from the façade of the cathedral and a number of panel-paintings, including Duccio di Buoninsegna's famous "Maestà", Pietro Lorenzetti's "Birth of the Virgin" and the 13th c. "Madonna dagli Occhi Grossi" (Madonna with the Large Eyes). In the Treasury are reliquaries (notably the silver-gilt reliquary for the head of San Galgano and the gilt-bronze Reliquary of St Clement), sculpture in wood, etc.

Spedale di Santa Maria della Scala

The Spedale di Santa Maria della Scala stands opposite the façade of the cathedral; it takes its name from the steps (*scala*) leading up to the cathedral. The Sala del Pellegrinaggio has frescoes depicting the care of the sick in the 15th c.
Adjoining the hospital is the Church of the Santíssima Annunziata (also known as Santa Maria della Scala), which was radically rebuilt in the 15th c. It contains some works of sculpture of the 15th–17th c. and a small treasury.

Palazzo Arcivescovile

Opposite the north side of the cathedral is the Palazzo Arcivescovile (Archbishop's Palace), built in 1718–23 in 14th c. Gothic style – a surprisingly early example of neo-Gothic, designed to preserve the architectural unity of the square. The ground floor of the palazzo has the same kind of facing in two colours of marble as the cathedral.

Palazzo Piccolómini (Palazzo delle Papesse)

The Palazzo Piccolómini (1460–95), a fine example of Florentine Renaissance architecture by Bernardo Rossellino, is also known as the Palazzo delle Papesse (Palace of the Popesses) because it was built for Caterina Piccolómini, sister of Pope Pius II.

Palazzo Chigi-Saracini

The Palazzo Chigi-Saracini, constructed on a plan adapted to the bend in Via di Città, was originally built in the 12th c. and was completed in the 14th. It was enlarged in 1787 and thoroughly restored at the beginning of the 20th c. The façade with its Gothic windows and massive battlemented tower is one of the finest in Siena, with an attractive contrast between the grey stone of the two lower floors and the brick of the top floor.
Since 1930 the palazzo has been the home of the Accadémia Musicale Chigiana (Academy of Music), which in addition to its regular activities organises master classes and, in summer, concerts which are open to the public. In the interior (seen only by appointment) are pictures by Bottecelli, Neroccio, Pinturicchio, Sodoma and Spinello Aretino.

Siena

The Pinacoteca Nazionale (National Gallery) occupies one of the most elegant palazzi in Siena, the battlemented Late Gothic Palazzo Buonsignori (early 15th c.), to the south-east of the cathedral.

The gallery, the original basis of which was an 18th c. private collection, offers an excellent general impression of Sienese painting from the 12th to the 16th c., with pictures by almost all the painters working in Siena. Notable among them are works by Guido da Siena (13th c.; "Raising of Lazarus", "Entry into Jerusalem", "Transfiguration", "St Peter Enthroned"); Duccio di Buoninsegna (c. 1255–1319; "Virgin and Child", "Madonna dei Franceschani"); Ambrogio Lorenzetti (14th c.; "Virgin and Child", "Entombment", "Madonna Enthroned", "Annunciation"); Pietro Lorenzetti (14th c.; "John the Baptist", "Four Apostles", "Allegory of Sin and Salvation"); Giovanni di Paolo (1403–82; "Flight into Egypt", "Crucifixion"); Pinturicchio (c. 1454–1513; "Holy Family"); and Sodoma (Giovanni Antonio Bazzi, 1477–1549; "Flagellation", "Judith and Holofernes", "Descent into Limbo"). Also of interest are the cartoons by Beccafumi (on a scale of 1:1) for the marble inlays in the pavement of the cathedral (see above).

Sant'Agostino

Farther to the south-east, in the Prato Sant'Agostino, is the Church of Sant'Agostino, originally belonging to an Augustinian house, which was built in 1258 and altered at the end of the 15th c. and again in 1755. In the Baroque interior (aisleless) are pictures by Perugino ("Crucifixion", 1506); Matteo di Giovanni ("Slaughter of the Innocents", 1482); and Sodoma ("Adoration of the Kings", 1528).

The central feature of the old town is the Piazza del Campo, a spacious scallop-shaped square dominated by the massive façade of the Palazzo Públbico (Town Hall). Its unity and harmony make this one of the finest of all city squares. Divided by strips of light-coloured stone into nine sections of brick pavement, the square slopes up to the semicircle of houses which bounds it on the north-west. At the upper end of the central section is the Fonte Gaia (Fountain of Joy). The richly decorated rectangular fountain basin, a masterpiece by Iácopo della Quercia (1419), was restored in 1868; the original reliefs are now in the Palazzo Públbico (see below).

The harmonious effect of the Piazza del Campo is largely due to the fact that the handsome houses on the opposite side of the square from the Palazzo Públbico show very similar stylistic features to the palazzo. Particularly striking is the Palazzo Sansedoni (1216–1339), to the right of the Fonte Gaia.

**Palazzo Públbico

On the south side of the Piazza del Campo is the Palazzo Públbico (Town Hall), an imposing Gothic building of

Siena: Palazzo Pubblico and Torre del Mangia ▶

travertine and brick (1288–1309). The top floors of the lower side wings were added in 1680. The construction of the palazzo involved much upfilling and extensive underbuilding.

Exterior

The façade is relieved by rows of elegant windows and cornices of round-headed arches and topped by battlements. The black and white escutcheon of Siena, the Balzana, is constantly repeated in the arches over the windows. At either end of the central block is a bell-cote, and under its battlemented top is a roundel with Christ's monogram (IHS), the distinctive attribute of San Bernardino of Siena (1380–1444), who preached in the Piazza del Campo. In the centre of the first floor is the coat of arms of the Médici (who from 1569 were Grand Dukes of Tuscany). On the façade, and also on a column in front of it to the right, are a number of representations of the She-Wolf of the Capitol.

At the left-hand end of the building is the Torre del Mangia, one of the most daringly conceived of medieval towers. The shaft is of brick, the battlemented platform with its supporting brackets and its superstructure of travertine. The tower has a total height of 102 m (335 ft) to the tip of its metal bell-cage (with bells of 1666). It was built between 1338 and 1348 by two brothers, Minuccio and Francesco di Rinaldo; the project was regarded as so foolhardy that they were required to bear the work risk themselves. From the platform of the tower there are magnificent views of the city and the surrounding country.

At the foot of the tower is the Cappella di Piazza, built in 1352 in thanksgiving for the town's deliverance from the 1348 plague; it was considerably altered in 1463. Its Renaissance architecture, following ancient models, is in striking contrast to the restrained façade of the Palazzo Púbblico.

Interior

The interior of the Palazzo Púbblico is remarkably well preserved. It contains numerous frescoes of the Sienese school which provide an insight into the minds of the proud burgher families of 14th and 15th c. Siena. Note particularly, in the Sala della Pace, the frescoes by Ambrogio Lorenzetti depicting Good Government and Bad Government (with views of Siena), and, in the Sala del Mappamondo, a magnificent fresco by Simone Martini, "Maestà", and a picture of the Sienese General Guidoriccio Fogliani setting out for the Siege of Montemassi. Other frescoes in the Sala del Mappamondo depict the Sienese victory at Poggio Imperiale and various Saints. Adjoining this room is the chapel with its ante-chapel (which has frescoes by Taddeo di Bártolo). The chapel has stalls of about 1420 with intarsia decoration.

Museo Cívico

Also in the Palazzo Púbblico is the small Museo Cívico (Municipal Museum), with material illustrating the history of Siena and a collection of coins. On the third floor is a loggia where the original sculpture from the Fonte Gaia is displayed.

Loggia della Mercanzia

Near the Croce del Travaglio, the square at the meeting-place of the three main streets of the old town, is the Loggia della Mercanzia (1417–38), seat of the old commercial court. It shows the transition from Late Gothic to Renaissance; the upper floor was added in the 17th c. On the pillars supporting the arches, which have richly decorated capitals, are statues of SS. Peter and Paul by Vecchietta (1458–60) and SS. Victor and Ansano by Antonio Federighi (1456–63). The benches inside the loggia have figures of great Romans and allegories of the Virtues.

Palazzo Piccolómini

At the north-east corner of the Piazza del Campo, with its main front on the Banchi di Sotto, stands the Palazzo Piccolómini, built by Pietro Paolo Porrina in 1469 to the design of Bernardo Rossellino for Nenni Piccolómini, father of the future Pope Pius III. This handsome Renaissance building now houses the Archivio di Stato (National Archives), with historical documents, Government records, manuscripts, etc. Of particular interest are the *tavolette di Biccherna*, wooden panels painted by some of the most noted Sienese painters of the day as covers for the ledgers of the municipal treasury.

Logge del Papa

A little way east of the Palazzo Piccolómini can be seen the elegant Logge del Papa, a three-arched loggia by Antonio Federighi (1462) – so called because it was commissioned by Pope Pius II (Eneo Silvio Piccolómini) in honour of his family.

Santa Maria degli Servi

The Banchi di Sotto and the streets which continue in the same direction lead to the Church of Santa Maria degli Servi, at the south-east end of the old town. It was originally built in the 13th c. but was altered in the 15th–16th c. in the style of the period. The plain façade was left unfinished; the Romanesque campanile which flanks it has four orders of windows, increasing in number from level to level so as to enhance the effect of perspective.

Within the aisled church, on the right, is the "Madonna del Bordone" (depicting the Virgin and Child with two Angels), by Coppo di Marcovaldo (1261). In the second chapel in the south transept is a famous fresco, the "Slaughter of the Innocents" by Pietro Lorenzetti (*c.* 1330), and on the altar is Lippo Memmi's "Madonna del Pópolo" (*c.* 1317).

A short distance south stands the Porta Romana (1327), an imposing gate in the old town walls.

Porta Romana

Palazzo Tolomei

From the Croce del Travaglio the Banchi di Sopra and its continuation run north. On the left-hand side is the Palazzo Tolomei, one of Siena's oldest palazzi, built in 1205 and altered in 1267. The two-storey façade has double Gothic windows with elegant tracery.

Siena: Porta Romana

San Cristóforo

Opposite the Palazzo Tolomei, to the east, is the Church of San Cristóforo, originally Romanesque but completely remodelled in the 18th c. The church has a fine wooden Crucifix of the 14th c. and on the high altar a Baroque marble sculpture by B. Mazzuoli of San Bernardo Tolomei (d. 1348).

Museo Archeológico

To the north-west of the Palazzo Tolomei the Museo Archeológico (Archaeological Museum) has material ranging in date from the Stone Age to the Fall of the Roman Empire, mostly from the city and surrounding area, with a particular concentration on the Etruscans. The exhibits include marble and terracotta urns, ash-chests, bronzes and an excellent collection of coins.

Santuario Cateriniano

In a narrow lane between the Museo Archeológico and the Church of San Doménico is the birthplace of St Catherine of Siena, which has been a sanctuary and a place of pilgrimage since 1464. The handsome Renaissance doorway bears the Latin inscription "Sponsae Kristi Catherinae Domus" ("The house of Catherine, bride of Christ").

Siena: Street in the Old Town . . .   *. . . and Church of San Domenico*

San Doménico

To the west of the Museo Archeológico, near the town walls,
stands the Church of San Doménico, a severe brick building in
Cistercian Gothic style. Originally built in 1226, it was
subsequently much altered and enlarged; the battlemented
campanile, in a style alien to Cistercian architecture, was
erected in 1340.

The church has an aisleless nave with an enclosed rectangular
choir and a surprisingly high and spacious transept, from which
the two chapels flanking the choir are entered.

The effect of the interior is mainly due to its lack of decoration,
which enhances the impression of space. In the north-west
transverse wall of the nave is the entrance to a vaulted chapel
with the earliest known likeness of St Catherine of Siena
(1347–80), a fresco by Andrea Vanni (*c.* 1400). The Cappella
di Santa Caterina, built on to the right-hand wall of the nave,
contains two masterpieces by Sodoma, "The Ecstasy of St
Catherine" and "St Catherine Fainting" (both *c.* 1525), and a
marble tabernacle by Giovanni di Stéfano (1466) with the head
of the Saint, who died and was buried in the Church of Santa
Maria sopra Minerva in Rome.

On the high altar in the choir are a ciborium and two figures of
Angels bearing candelabra (*c.* 1475) by Benedetto da Maiano.
In the first side chapel on the right can be seen frescoes by
Matteo di Giovanni, and in the second chapel on the left wall-
paintings by Matteo di Giovanni and Benvenuto di Giovanni.
From one of the windows in the apse there is a superb
panoramic view of the city.

Below the apse of San Doménico is the Fonte Branda, a fountain which is mentioned in the records as early as 1081. The present form of the fountain-house with its three Gothic arches is mainly due to Giovanni di Stéfano.

Palazzo Salimbeni

A little way north of the Palazzo Tolomei along the Banchi di Sopra is the Piazza Salimbeni, with the Palazzo Salimbeni, a fortress-like Gothic building of the 14th c. Its handsome three-storey façade has the advantage of being seen from a suitable distance, which is rarely possible in the narrows streets of Siena. The Palazzo Salimbeni is now occupied by one of Italy's oldest banks, the Monte dei Paschi di Siena founded in 1472 and established in the city since 1624.

Palazzo Spannocchi

To the right of the Palazzo Salimbeni is the Palazzo Spannocchi, built by Ambrogio Spannocchi, Treasurer to Pope Pius II; the architect was Giuliano da Maiano. This elegant Renaissance building is fronted by loggias of 1880 by Giuseppe Partini.

San Francesco

To the north-east of Piazza Salimbeni stands the Gothic Church of San Francesco, a Franciscan foundation begun in 1326 but not completed until 1475. Like San Doménico (above), San Francesco shows the architectural style of the Mendicant Orders, with an aisleless nave and no apse at the east end. The campanile was added in 1765.

The interior, with its open timber roof, is painted in alternate bands of black and white, imitating the marble facing of the cathedral. Along the walls hang the banners of the old craft guilds. In the left transept are a magnificent fresco of the Crucifixion (c. 1330) by Pietro Lorenzetti and frescoes of St Louis of Toulouse (1274–97) before Pope Boniface VIII and the Martyrdom of Franciscans at Ceuta by Ambrogio Lorenzetti (c. 1330).

Oratorio di San Bernardino

This oratory, adjoining the Church of San Francesco, was built in the 15th c. on the spot where the Franciscan friar San Bernardino of Siena was accustomed to preach. On the upper floor are fine 16th c. frescoes by Sodoma, Doménico Beccafumi and Girólamo del Pacchia ("St Louis", "Presentation of the Virgin", "St Antony of Padua", "St Francis of Assisi", "Visitation", "Assumption" and "Coronation of the Virgin" by Sodoma; "Marriage of the Virgin", "Madonna with Angels" and "Death of the Virgin" by Beccafumi; "Birth of the Virgin", "San Bernardino of Siena", "Gabriel" and "Annunciation" by Pacchia).

Chiesa di Fontegiusta

In the north-west corner of the old town, at the Porta Camollia, is the Chiesa di Fontegiusta, a hall-church built in 1482–84 by Francesco di Cristóforo Fedeli and Giácomo di Giovanni. In the brick façade is a fine marble doorway by Urbano da Cortona (1489). The church contains a beautiful marble tabernacle (16th c.) and, on the left-hand wall, a fresco by Baldassare Peruzzi, "The Sibyl announcing the Birth of Christ to the Emperor Augustus" (c. 1528).

Forte di Santa Bárbara

On the west side of the town, beyond the stadium, is the Forte di Santa Bárbara, built in 1560 for Cosimo I de' Médici, from which there are fine panoramic views. In the first bastion on the left is the Enoteca Italiana, a permanent exhibition of Italian wines.

Chiesa dell'Osservanza   C 3

The Chiesa dell'Osservanza, stands outside Siena, in beautiful rolling country. It was built in 1476 and occupies the site of an earlier church founded by San Bernardino; its architect was Giácomo Cozzarelli. After suffering severe damage in air raids in 1944 it was rebuilt in its original form.

Situation
3 km (2 miles) N

The aisleless nave has eight side chapels. In the third chapel on the right is the Reliquary of San Bernardino by Francesco d'Antonio (1454), and in the fourth a beautiful triptych ("Madonna with SS. Ambrose and Jerome", 1436), by an artist known only, after this work, as the Maestro dell'Osservanza. On the pillars of the triumphal arch (between the nave and the choir) is an "Annunciation" in painted terracotta by Andrea della Robbia. The sacristy has a "Pietà" by Giácomo Cozzarelli (15th c.).
The Museo Aurelio Castelli near the church contains sculpture, pictures, prints, illuminated manuscripts, etc.

Tuscan Archipelago

See Arcipélago Toscano

Valdichiana (Val di Chiana)   C 3

Provinces: Arezzo (AR) and Siena (SI)

The Valdichiana, the Valley of the River Chiana, extends southward for some 70 km (45 miles) from Arezzo to Chiusi.

Situation

Topography

The Valdichiana is the natural continuation of the Upper Arno Valley, which in prehistoric times drained into the Tiber but was later compelled by the build-up of soil deposited by the Arno's tributary streams to turn north-west. Some of the water of the Chiana (the Roman Clanis) continued to flow south, producing the rare phenomenon of a river dividing into two. The valley then degenerated into fever-ridden marshland, until it was drained in the mid 18th c. and became one of the most fertile regions in Italy. The Tuscan Chiana discharges its abundant flow of water into the Arno by way of the Canal Maestro, while the Roman Chiana (generally called the Chiani) flows into the Paglia, a tributary of the Tiber, at Orvieto.

Verna, La

See La Verna

Vetulonia   D2

Province: Grosseto (GR)
Altitude: 345 m (1132 ft)
Population: 700

Situation

The village of Vetulonia, in the commune of Castiglione della Pescaia (see entry), lies on a hill above the plain at the mouth of the Ombrone, 20 km (12½ miles) north-west of Grosseto.

Vetulonia: Tomba della Pietrera . . .   *. . . and Tomba del Diavolino*

In Etruscan times Vatluna, as the place was then called, was a member of the Etruscan League of twelve cities. In the 7th and 6th c. B.C. the mineral wealth of the surrounding area (gold, silver, etc.) brought the town great prosperity. The reasons for its later decline are not known; but, however or whenever this took place, all trace of the once-powerful city was so completely lost that archaeologists at first looked for the Vetulonia referred to by ancient authors much farther north, in the Massa Maríttima area.

History

*Etruscan tombs

The Etruscan cemetery areas lie to the north-east and west of the ancient city, once surrounded by a wall some 5 km (3 miles) long. There are two main types of tomb, chamber tombs and tombs marked by stone circles. The finest chamber tomb is the two-storey Tomba della Pietrera (north-east of the village), which is roofed with a "false vault" reminiscent of the tholos tombs of Mycenae. Farther north is the Tomba del Diavolino, named after a statuette found in the tomb which was taken for a devil. Most of the rich grave goods found in the tombs of Vetulonia are now in the museums of Grosseto and Florence (see entries).

Viareggio

Province: Lucca (LU)
Altitude: 2 m (6½ ft)
Population: 59,000

The seaside resort of Viareggio lies at the foot of the Apuan Alps, some 25 km (15 miles) west of Lucca.

Situation

The town

With its long beach of fine sand, Viareggio is one of the leading seaside resorts on the west coast of Italy. The town is laid out on a regular plan, with straight streets intersecting at right angles. The main area of tourist and holiday activity is the part of the town close to the seafront. In the northern part of the town is an extensive area of pine woods, the Pineta del Ponente. Farther south the Canale Burlamacca flows into the sea past the yacht harbour. A pleasant walk can be taken along the pier, which extends several hundred yards out to sea. Beyond the canal is the 6 km (4 mile) long Riviera di Levante, with the stadium.

Viareggio is famous for its Carnival, in which thousands of people, wearing masks, take part in the colourful parades of gaily decorated floats along the wide seafront promenade. During the summer visitors can see the workshops in which the floats are prepared for the Carnival and the papier-mâché figures and animals are made.

*Carnival

Viareggio: Carnival procession

Parco Naturale Massaciuccoli

The Parco Naturale Migliarino-S, Rossore-massaciuccoli
extends along the coast from Viareggio to Livorno. There is a
remarkable variety of flora and fauna to be found in this area of
magnificent pine woods (herons, bitterns, birds of prey, deer of
various kinds, and wild boar . . .).

Torre del Lago Puccini   C 2

Situation
6 km (4 miles) S

The Torre del Lago Puccini, on the Lago di Massaciúccoli, is so
called because the popular Italian composer Giácomo Puccini
(1858–1924) lived here for many years.

Vinca

See under Émpoli

Volterra   C 2

Province: Pisa (PI)
Altitude: 531 m (1742 ft)
Population: 14,000

Situation

Volterra lies in a region of much-eroded hills some 50 km
(30 miles) from the coast of the Maremma and 65 km
(40 miles) south-east of Pisa.

History

Excavations have shown that the hill between the rivers Cécina
and Era was already occupied by a settlement in prehistoric
times. This was succeeded by the Etruscan town of Velathri, a
member of the Etruscan League of twelve cities, which covered
an area about three times the size of the present town. In the
3rd c. B.C. the town became a Roman *municipium* under the
name of Volaterrae. In the Middle Ages it was a free commune,
which contrived to retain its independence until it was brought
under Florentine protection in 1361. It is famous as a centre of
alabaster-working, a craft which was revived in the 19th c.

Palazzo dei Priori

In the Piazza dei Priori, the central square of the medieval town,
stands the Palazzo dei Priori (1208–54), now the Town Hall –
the oldest in Tuscany. It was the official residence of the
podestà and later of the Florentine *priori* and *commissari*, as

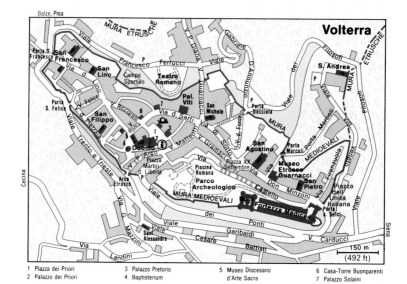

1 Piazza dei Priori	3 Palazzo Pretorio	5 Museo Diocesano	6 Casa-Torre Buonparenti
2 Palazzo dei Priori	4 Baptisterium	d'Arte Sacra	7 Palazzo Solaini

207

the coats of arms on the façade bear witness. The front of the palazzo is relieved only by a few irregularly disposed windows and narrow horizontal cornices. At either end of the façade are columns bearing the heraldic lion of Florence, the Marzocco. The Council Chamber, identifiable from the outside by a series of windows on the first floor set closer to each other than on the rest of the façade, is decorated with frecoes, most of which are in the "Historical" style of the 19th c.

Palazzo Pretorio

Opposite the Palazzo dei Priori is the 13th c. Palazzo Pretorio, which until 1511 was the seat of the *capitano del Pópolo*. It incorporated a number of earlier buildings, and is dominated by the battlemented Torre del Podestà. On top of the tower is the figure of an animal, popularly known as Porcellino (Piglet).

*Cathedral

Behind the Palazzo del Pópolo, to the west, is the cathedral (consecrated 1120), which was enlarged in Pisan style in 1254. The campanile, which commands extensive views, was rebuilt in 1493 after its collapse, but later, for greater stability, had the top storey removed.
The interior of the church, which is aisled, was remodelled in the 16th c., and in its present aspect is predominantly

Volterra: Cathedral . . .   *. . . and Etruscan arch*

Renaissance. Notable among the works of art it contains are, on the inside of the entrance wall, a beautiful antependium (altar frontal) with eight panels from the Romanesque altar; in the first chapel in the right transept the Reliquary of Sant'Ottaviano by Raffaele Cioli (1522); in the choir, flanking the altar, two Angels bearing candelabra and, on the altar, a splendid marble ciborium, for reservation of the Eucharist, by Mino da Fiésole (15th c.); between the seventh and eighth columns on the left an impressive pulpit made in the 17th c. from fragments of varying origin (12th c. reliefs of Old and New Testament scenes); and in the Cappella dell'Addolorata (in the left-hand aisle) a coloured terracotta group of Mary and Joseph with the Infant Jesus, in front of a background fresco by Benozzo Gozzoli depicting the arrival of the Three Kings, and opposite it a polychrome terracotta group of the Adoration of the Kings.

Baptistery

Opposite the façade of the cathedral is the baptistery, a two-storey building on an octagonal plan erected in the 13th c. but subsequently much altered. The side facing the cathedral is clad with bands of white and green marble and has a Romanesque doorway with figural decoration. The interior, roofed with an early 16th c. dome, is plain. There is a beautiful font by Andrea Sansovino (1502) carved with reliefs.

*Arco Etrusco

From the centre of the town a stepped lane, Via Porta all'Arco (many alabaster workshops), runs south-west to the Arco Etrusco (Etruscan Arch), a gate in the ancient circuit of walls. The dressed stones flanking the gateway and the three much-weathered heads on the arch date from the 4th–3rd c. B.C.; the arch itself was rebuilt in Roman times, and the masonry on either side of the gate is medieval. A similar gateway is depicted on an Etruscan ash-chest of the 1st c. B.C. (No. 371) in the Museo Etrusco Guarnacci (see below).
A commemorative tablet records that during the Second World War the people of Volterra prevented the gate from being blown up by German troops.

Museo Diocesano d'Arte Sacra

The Diocesan Museum of Sacred Art is housed in part of the cloister to the north-west of the cathedral. It contains ecclesiastical and liturgical objects from the diocese of Volterra, including a glazed terracotta bust of St Linus (first successor of St Peter) by Andrea della Robbia; a Reliquary of Sant'-Ottaviano, of beaten silver by Antonio del Pollaiuolo (15th c.), and a Reliquary of St Victor, of enamelled silver (Sienese workmanship, 14th c.); a wooden tabernacle decorated with miniatures (Umbrian school, 15th c.); a gilt-bronze Crucifix by Giambologna (16th c.); and valuable priestly vestments of the 16th to 18th c.

Casa-Torre Buonparenti

To the north of the cathedral, at the intersection of Via Roma and Via Ricciarelli, is the 13th c. Casa-Torre Buonparenti. There are other characteristic medieval tower houses to be seen in the vicinity – Torre Martinoli (13th c.), Casa Nannatti e Miranceli, Torre Buonaguidi (12th c.). In Via Ricciarelli are the Palazzetto della Sbarba (No. 24) and the Casa Ricciarelli (Nos. 34–36; note the small windows for children below the main windows).

Gallería Pittórica

The Gallería Pittórica (Picture Gallery) has works by Florentine, Sienese and Volterran artists. Of particular interest are Rosso Fiorentino's "Descent from the Cross" (1521), Luca Signorelli's "Annunciation" and "Virgin and Child with Saints" (1491), two triptychs by Taddeo di Bártolo (14th–15th c.). Benvenuto di Giovanni's "Nativity" (1470) and Ghirlandaio's "Christ with Saints" (15th c.).

Teatro Romano

Just outside the medieval walls, at a re-entrant curve on the north side of the town, can be seen a Roman theatre of the 1st c. A.D., the remains of which have been excavated since 1951. Lower down are the remains of Roman baths of the 3rd c. A.D.

Parco Archeológico

Outside the west end of the fortezza (see below) lies the Parco Archeológico (Archaeological Park), where remains of the ancient acropolis were excavated in 1926. The remains include the foundations of two temples of the 2nd c. B.C. and a cistern known as the Piscina.

Fortezza

On the highest point of the hill is the massive fortezza, one of the mightiest Renaissance strongholds in Italy (now a penal establishment; not open to the public). The Rocca Vecchia (Old Castle) at the east end was built in the 14th c., the Rocca Nuova (New Castle) in 1472–75 for Lorenzo de' Médici. The central round tower of the New Castle (built 1472 onwards) is known as the Maschio (Male), the semi-elliptical tower of the Old Castle as the Femmina (Female).

Museo Etrusco Guarnacci

In Volterra and the surrounding area rich finds of Etruscan material have been made, and the Guarnacci Etruscan Museum has a remarkable collection of this material. It owes its existence to a local prelate, Mario Guarnacci (1701–85), who bequeathed his collection to the town; this, together with a collection of Etruscan urns assembled by another ecclesiastic, Canon Franceschini, in the years before 1732, formed the basic stock of the museum, which also contains prehistoric and Roman material. The Etruscan section of the museum gives an excellent view of the life and culture of this people about whom so little is known. It contains more than 600 cinerary urns of tufa, alabaster or terracotta, mostly dating from the 4th to 1st c. B.C. Of particular interest are two urns with reliefs depicting the Siege of Thebes, on one of which (No. 371) is an arched gateway resembling the Arco Etrusco. Other items include a crater (wine-mixing vessel) from Attica, funerary stelae, jewellery, coins, etc.

Etruscan walls

Around the town are considerable remains, picturesquely overgrown with ivy, holm-oaks and stunted cypresses, of the walls built by the Etruscans to defend the prosperous city of Velathri. The topography of the site meant that the walls enclosed an area of very irregular outline much larger than that of the medieval town, extending for a considerable distance to the north and north-west. In some places the walls rise as high as 11 m (36 ft). There is a particularly fine stretch by the little Church of Santa Chiara.

Volterra: Roman theatre

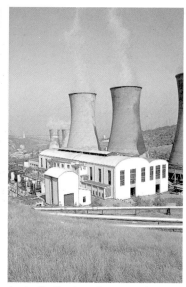

Larderello: Geothermal power station

* Balze   C2

Immediately north-west of the town are the Balze, a barren and inhospitable terrain of hills scarred and gullied by erosion. As a result of the continuous wearing away of the soil numbers of Etruscan tombs, a section of the ancient walls and a medieval church have been carried away in quite recent times.

Situation
NW of Volterra

Larderello   C2

Situation
35 km (22 miles) S

The village of Larderello lies on Monte Cérboli (691 m – 2267 ft), a little off the road from Volterra to Massa Maríttima. The *soffioni* (jets of steam of volcanic origin) which come to the surface here, sending white columns of vapour into the air, are put to use in two ways; the boric acid and other substances which they deposit in large underground reservoirs of water (*lagoni*) can be recovered, and the steam is harnessed to produce power.

Practical Information

Warning

Visitors to Italy should keep a careful eye on their property and take sensible precautions against theft, particularly in the larger towns. Handbag-snatching and the theft of other portable articles of value such as cameras, binoculars, watches and jewellery, as well as more substantial items including suitcases, are a constant hazard, and particular care should be taken in public places – hotels, restaurants and cafés, shops, trains, petrol stations. Even a car slowing down at traffic lights is a possible target for attack. Cars may be broken into, robbed or stolen if left unattended, caravans and minibuses are particularly vulnerable, but even touring coaches and hired cars with Italian registration are not immune.

It is important, therefore, to carry all objects of value – papers, money, travellers' cheques, bank and credit cards, keys, etc. – on your person and never to leave them in an unattended car. The glove compartment, and if possible the boot as well, should be left empty and unlocked. Overnight your car should be kept in a lock-up garage if one is available, preferably with a safety lock or similar device. The Italian police are always ready to help, but are almost powerless in face of this type of crime, often carried out by organised gangs. After a break-in or robbery by violence they can frequently do no more than take particulars of the offence (which is in any event an essential part of the procedure for making a claim against your insurance company).

If you lose travellers' cheques, a bank card or a credit card you should at once inform the bank or other agency concerned by telegram so they they can stop payment.

Air services

The principal airport in Tuscany is the Pisa/Florence airport (Galileo Galilei Airport). The Leonardo da Vinci Airport at Rome/Fiumicino is of international importance. Apart from Pisa/Florence there is no airport in Tuscany used by scheduled services.

Airports

Alitalia, the Italian national airline, flies both international and domestic services. It has desks at all Italian airports and the principal foreign airports.

Airlines

Alitalia:
Lungarno Acciaioli 10–12r,
Florence. Tel. (055) 26 30 51

British Airways:
Via della Vigna Nuova 36r,
Florence. Tel. (055) 21 86 55–59

TWA:
Piazzo Santa Trínita 2,
Florence
Tel. (055) 29 68 56

Bathing beaches

The beaches of Tuscany are predominantly flat, with fine sand, but there are stretches of rocky coast at Piombino and Populonia and on Monte Argentario. The most popular bathing resorts are (from north to south): Marina di Carrara, Marina di Massa, the Riviera della Versilia (with Forte dei Marmi, Lido di Camaiore, Viareggio, etc.), the Riviera degli Etruschi (between Livorno and Piombino; less crowded) and the coast of the Maremma (with Punta Ala, Castiglione della Pescaia, the Monti dell'Uccellina nature reserve and the Promontorio dell'Argentario). The islands are, of course, popular with water-sports enthusiasts.

Camping

Italy has large numbers of camping sites, particularly in the areas most frequented by visitors and holiday-makers. Sites in Tuscany are among the best looked after and best equipped in the whole Italian peninsula. Most of them are on the coast and are, therefore, crowded or overcrowded during the main holiday season; advance booking is accordingly advisable.
Camping on public land is not permitted (with the exception of a one-night stand in a motor caravan or trailer). Before camping

Bathing beach at Canara and the Apuan Alps

on privately owned land the owner's permission should be obtained.

Lists of camping sites can be obtained from ENIT (the Italian State Tourist Office) and from the Federazione Italiana del Campeggio. Casella Postale 23, Via Vittorio Emanuele 11, I-50041 Calenzano/Firenze.

Car ferries

Cars are carried on the ferry services between Piombino and the island of Elba (Portoferraio) and between Porto Santo Stéfano and the island of Giglio.

Car hire

Via Borgognissanti 128r   Avis
I–50100 Firenze (Florence)
Tel. (055) 26 30 10

Via Garibaldi 49
I–57100 Livorno
Tel. (0586) 88 00 90

Via Manin 8
I–51016 Montecatini Terme
Tel. (0572) 7 29 46

Aeroporto San Giusto
I–56100 Pisa
Tel. (050) 4 20 28

Via Roma 54
I–50047 Prato
Tel. (0574) 4 27 00

Via Margherita 48
I–55049 Viareggio
Tel. (0584) 4 61 11

Banchina IV Novembre 17
I–5736 Porto Azzurro/Elba
Tel. (0565) 9 50 00

Via Borgognissanti 53r/55r   EuropCar
I–50100 Firenze (Florence)
Tel. (055) 29 34 44

Aeroporto Galileo Galilei
I–56100 Pisa
Tel. (050) 4 10 17

Via Mantana 33
I–55049 Viareggio
Tel. (0584) 4 65 14

Via Maso Finiguerra 33
I–50100 Firenze (Florence)
Tel. (055) 29 82 05

Via Mastacchia 59–63
I–57100 Livorno
Tel. (0586) 41 05 15

Via U. Dini 13
I–57025 Piombino
Tel. (0565) 3 24 66

Via Vespucci 106a
I–56100 Pisa
Tel. (050) 4 08 78

Via Cimabue 2
I–50047 Prato
Tel. (0574) 2 10 55

Coach tours

In the larger towns coach tours in the surrounding area are
often run by local companies. Information about such tours can
be obtained from local tourist information offices (Aziende
Autónome di Soggiorno, Associazioni Pro Loco).

Consulates

See Diplomatic and consular offices.

Conducted tours

At all the principal tourist sights there are likely to be numbers
of guides ready to show the visitor round. Visitors who do not
know Italian will do well to check that a guide's English is
adequate before accepting his help. He will, of course, expect a
tip.
The local people may not like it if a party of visitors bring their
own guide with them, and will sometimes make that displea-
sure very evident.

Currency

Currency

The Italian unit of currency is the *lira* (plural *lire*). There are
banknotes for 500, 1000, 2000, 5000, 10,000, 20,000, 50,000 and
100,000 lire and coins in denominations of 5, 10, 20, 50, 100, 200
and 500 lire.

Exchange rates

Exchange rates fluctuate and can best be obtained from banks
or by reference to the National press.

Currency regulations

There are no restrictions on the import or export of foreign
currency into Italy, but it is advisable to declare large amounts
of currency on the appropriate form (*modulo V2*) at the frontier.
It is advisable to carry currency in the form of travellers'
cheques or Eurocheques, or to make use of credit cards.

Customs regulations

Visitors can take into Italy, without liability to duty, personal effects, sports gear, etc., as well as the usual duty-free allowances of alcohol, tobacco and perfume (varying for EC nationals, US visitors, other European nationals and overseas residents).
Video apparatus must be declared on entry. The import of sheath-knives and large multi-purpose knives is prohibited.

Entering Italy

On leaving Italy visitors can take out without payment of duty articles they have bought to the value of 500 US dollars. For the export of antiques and modern *objets d'art* a licence must be obtained from the Export Department of the Ministry of Education.

Leaving Italy

Diplomatic and consular offices

Embassy:
Via XX Settembre 80A
I–00187 Roma
Tel. (06) 4 75 54 41 and 4 75 55 51

United Kingdom

Consulate:
Palazzo Castelbarco
Lungarno Corsini 2, I–50123 Firenze
Tel. (055) 21 25 94, 28 41 33 and 28 74 49

Embassy:
Via Veneto 119A, I–00187 Roma
Tel. (06) 46 74

United States

Consulate:
Lungarno Amerigo Vespucci 38,
I–50100 Firenze
Tel. (055) 29 82 76

Embassy:
Via Zara 30, I–00198 Roma
Tel. (06) 8 44 18 41–46

Canada

Emergency calls

The following telephone numbers apply throughout Italy:

Police and ambulance (Pronto Soccorso): dial 113

Police and ambulance

Breakdown assistance (Soccorso Stradale): dial 116 provided by ACI (Automobile Club d'Italia)
It is advisable to keep a few telephone tokens (*gettoni*) handy in case of emergency.

Breakdown assistance

Events

Viareggio, Pisa: parades

Carnival

Many places: San Giuseppe (St Joseph's Day)

19 March

Food and drink

Palm Sunday	Many places (particularly Florence): consecration of palms, with religious procession
Wednesday before Easter	Many places: Mercoledí Santo (Lamentations, Miserere)
Thursday before Easter	Many places (particularly Florence): Washing of the Feet, Entombment
Good Friday	Many places (particularly Florence): Adoration of the Cross
Easter Saturday	Many places (particularly Florence): Lighting of the Sacred Fire
Easter Day	Florence: Scoppio del Carro ("Explosion of the Cart")
1 May	Florence: Gioco del Calcio (historic game of football)
May	Florence: Maggio Musicale (Musical Festival)
May/June	Torre del Lago: Puccini Opera Season
Ascension	Florence: Festival del Grillo (Festival of the Cricket)
Corpus Christi	Many places: religious processions
1st Sunday in June	Pisa: Gioco del Ponte (Bridge Festival: historical regatta)
Mid June	Many places: Corpus Domini (Ascension processions)
Beginning of July	Siena: Palio delle Contrade (horse-race in medieval costume, parade)
15 August	Many places: Assumption (procession, fireworks)
Mid August	Siena: Palio delle Contrade (horse-race in medieval costume, parade, torchlight procession)
1st Sunday in September	Arezzo: Giostra del Saracino (Saracen's Joust)
Beginning of September	Florence: Rificolone (night festival of lanterns)
2nd Sunday in September	Sansepolcro: crossbow contest
Mid September	Lucca: Luminaria di Santa Croce
22 November	Many places: Santa Cecilia (St Cecilia's Day)
Mid December to mid January	Many places: Christmas cribs (*presepi*, Nativity groups)
Note	In general, Catholic ceremonies, particularly on the occasion of a church's patronal festival or the festival of a town's patron saint, feature prominently in the annual festival programme. At many places, too, there are Passion plays and pilgrimages, especially during Holy Week.

Food and drink

Cuisine	Tuscany has for centuries been famed for its agricultural produce; and here, as elsewhere in Italy, more importance is attached to the natural taste of the food than to elaborate

dressings and refinements. It would not be far from the truth to say that the farmer plays a more important part in Tuscan cuisine than the chef.

Apart from the numerous pasta dishes, served in infinite variety and with a wide range of different sauces or dressings, the Tuscan menu includes many excellent fish dishes. Much use is made of olive oil in cooking. The famous Italian pizza was originally a flat dough cake spread with tomatoes, herbs and oil – a simple, cheap and tasty alternative to bread. The numerous variations with ham, salami, cheese, mushrooms, artichoke hearts, etc., developed later with increasing prosperity and under the influence of tourism.

The standard drinks with all meals are wine and mineral water. Beer is found everywhere, both the light Italian beer and foreign brands (mostly from Germany, Holland and Denmark).

Italian eating habits differ in some respects from those of more northerly countries. Italians take little in the way of breakfast; but the hotels have adapted themselves to northern European customs, accompanying the breakfast coffee with bread, butter and jam, plus eggs, sausage and cheese if desired. Lunch (*pranzo*) usually consists of several courses. Spaghetti and other forms of pasta are merely a substitute for soup, not a main dish. They are often preceded by an *antipasto* (hors d'œuvre). The pasta (the *primo* or first course) is followed by the *secondo*, a meat or fish dish; and this in turn may be followed by cheese and fruit or a sweet of some kind. Lunch ends with an *espresso* (strong black coffee), which some Italians prefer *corretto* – "corrected" by the addition of grappa (Italian brandy) or cognac. The evening meal is usually also a substantial one.

Restaurants are generally open for lunch from 1 to 3 p.m. and for dinner from 7 to 10 p.m.

Customs

Every restaurant is required to give the customer a receipted bill, which must be produced to an Inland Revenue official if requested in the vicinity of the establishment (i.e. within 50 metres). Failure to do so may result in an on-the-spot fine. It is obviously desirable, therefore, to keep the receipted bill in case of a spot check outside the restaurant.

Note

Getting to Tuscany

It is a long way from Britain or northern Europe to Tuscany. Motorists will be well advised, therefore, to use motorways and main trunks roads as far as possible. The distance from the Channel ports to Florence is about 850–900 miles. Car sleeper services operate in summer from Boulogne, Brussels and Paris to Milan.

By car

The only international airport in Tuscany is Pisa/Florence (Galileo Galilei Airport), to which there are direct scheduled flights from London, with connecting flights from other British towns. An alternative is to fly to Rome/Fiumicino (Leonardo da Vinci Airport), which has more numerous international connections, and take a domestic flight from there.

By air

The fastest route from London to Florence takes just over 25 hours. Florence is on the inland route from Pisa to Rome; the

By rail

coastal line runs from Pisa via Livorno and Grosseto to Rome. There are branch lines from Émpoli via Siena to Grosseto, from Siena to Chiusi, from Asciano to Grosseto and from Cécina to Volterra.

Hotels

Hotels of the higher categories in large towns and holiday centres offer the usual international standards of comfort and amenity, but in the more remote areas the accommodation available will often be of a more modest standard. In the larger towns and in spas and seaside resorts there are numerous *pensioni*, singular *pensione* (guest-houses).

Categories

Hotels *alberghi*, singular *albergo* are officially classified in five categories. In the following lists they are designated:
L luxury; **** 1st category; *** 2nd category; ** 3rd category; * 4th category.

no rest. = without a restaurant

Tariffs

Tariffs vary considerably according to season, and are substantially higher in large towns and popular holiday areas than in the rest of the country. Changes in the value of the lira also affect prices.

Warning

Hotel bills, like restaurant bills, should be kept, as they must be produced to an Inland Revenue inspector on request, and failure to do so may result in a fine.

Pensioni are also classified but only in three categories. Since there are so many they have not been included in this guidebook; their names and addresses may be obtained from tourist offices (see entry).

Abbadia San Salvatore

***

Adriana
Aurora
Giardino
Italia
Kappadue
Milano
Tondi

**

Fabbrini
Gambrinus
Garden
Il Cacciatore
Olimpia
Roma

Arezzo

***

Continentale, Piazza Guido Monaco 7
Etrusco, Via Fleming
Europa, Via Spinello 45
Minerva, Via Fiorentina 4

**
Astoria, Via Guido Monaco 54
Cecco, Corso Italia 215
Truciolini, Via Pacinotti 6

*
Michelangelo, Via Michelangelo 26
Milano, Via M. del Prato 83
Roma, Via Vittorio Veneto 46

*Lo Spiedo **Asciano**

*** **Bagni di Lucca**
Alberghi Termali, Via del Paretaio 1
Silvania, in the Lugliano district

**
Bernabo, Via delle Terme
Bridge, Piazza Ponte a Serraglio 5A
Corona, Via Serraglia 78
La Frantoia, Via Tovani 26
Svizzero, Via C. Casalini

*Savoia, Piazza San Martino

Primavera, Via Cassia 38 **Barbarino Val d'Elsa

****Il Ciocco, in the Castelvecchio Pascoli district **Barga**

***La Pergola, Via San Antonio

**
Alpino, Via Mordini 16
Gorizia, in the Fornaci di Barga district
Villa Libano, Via del Sasso 6

***Brogi, Piazza Mazzoni **Bibbiena**

**
Amorosi Bei, Via Dovizi 18
Giardino, Piazza Palagi

*Verdi Colli, Piazza Garibaldi

Milano, in the Socciglia district **Borgo a Mozzano

*Il Pescatore, Via I Maggio 2

*Villa Ebe, in the Ferracciano district **Borgo San Lorenzo**

***Il Rustichello, Via del Corniolo **Camaldoli**

*Camaldoli, Via Camaldoli

****La Mandola (no rest), Via della Mandola 1 **Capraia**

***
Da Beppone, Via Assunzione 63
Il Saracino, Via Lamberto Cibo 40
Residence La Vela, (no rest), Via Genova 3
Residence Milano (no rest), Via Vittorio Emanuele 20

Hotels

Caprese Michelangelo

***Fonte Galletta, in the Fonte Galletta district

**Buca di Michelangelo, Via Roma 51

Carrara

***Michelangelo, Corso Fratelli Rosselli 3

**

Carrara, in the Avenza district
Da Roberto, Via Apuana 5
Dei Marmi, in the Avenza district

In the Marina di Carrara
****Maestrale, Via Fabbriccotti

***

Mediterraneo, Via Genova
Miramare, Viale Cristoforo Colombo 23
Panoramic, Viale Cristoforo Colombo
Paradiso, Viale Cristoforo Colombo

**

Anana, Via Garibaldi 4
Atlantic, Viale Amerigo Vespucci 36
La Pineta, Viale Cristoforo Colombo 119 B
Margherita, Via Venezia 22
Tenda Rossa, Viale Cristoforo Colombo 14

Castelfiorentino

**Lami, Piazza Gramsci 27

Castelnuovo di Garfagnana

**

Da Carlino, Via Garibaldi 15
Vittoria, Piazza Umberto 6

*La Laterna, Via N. Fabrizi 26

Castiglione di Pescaia

****

David, in the Poggiodoro district
L'Approdo
Riva del Sole, in the Riva del Sole district

***

Kinda
Lucerna
Miramare
Piccolo Hotel
Roma
Sabrina

**

Anfora
Aurora
Corallo
Gli Archi
Il Gambero
Iris
Macchiascandona
Mirella
Perla
Rossella
Souvenir
Tirreno
Villa Gina

At Punta Ala
****

Cala del Porto
Gallia Palace Hotel
Golf Hotel
Piccolo Hotel Alleluja

***

Il Pozzino
Punta Ala

***Park   **Castiglion Fiorentino**

**La Nave, in the La Nave district

**   **Certaldo**

Il Castello, Via della Rena 6
La Speranza, Borgo Garibaldi 80

****   **Chianciano Terme**

Alba
Alexander Palme
Ambasciatori
Atlantico Palace Hotel
Continentale
Grande Albergo Fortuna
Grande Albergo Le Fonti
Grande Albergo Milano
Grand Hotel Boston
Grand Hotel Capitol Garibaldi
Grand Hotel Excelsior
Grand Hotel Il Club
Grand Hotel Plaza
Grand Hotel Terme
Majestic
Michelangelo
Moderno
President
Quisisana
Raffaello
Taormina

***

Adriatico
Angiolino
Ardea
Astoria
Astra
Aurora
Bagni
Bellaria
Bosco
Carlton Elite
Chianciano
Columbia
Conte
Cosmos
Cristallo
Cristina
Etruria

Hotels

Europa
Firenze
Giotto
Grande Albergo San Marco
Igea
Iris
Irma
Italia
Kursaal
Macerina
Margherita
Mediterraneo
Minerva
Miralaghi
Montecarlo
Panorama
Park Hotel
Patria
Posta
Ricci
Rossana
San Giorgio
San Paolo
Sanremo
Sant'Agostino
Santa Chiara
Sestriere
Sole
Susy
Tiffany
Torino
Universo
Villa Alda

**

Anna
Ariston
Bellavista
Bruna
Casa Immacolata
Domus Pacis
Flora
Franca
Giorni
Le Sorgenti
Lucy
Massarelli
Miramonti
Nanda
Niagara
Nisi
Reali
Risorgimento
Rosati
Salus
Sant'Antonio
Santa Caterina
Suisse
Villa Gaia
Villa Maria

Villa Rosa
Villa Verde

***

                                        Chiusi

Centrale, in the Scalo district
Moderno, in the Scalo district

**La Sfinge

***

                                        Colle di Val d'Elsa

Arnolfo
La Vecchia Cartiera
Villa Belvedere

**Nazionale

At Monteriggioni:
***

Anna
Casalta
San Luigi Residence

***

                                        Cortone

Miravalle, in the Torreone district
Oasi, in the Le Contesse district
Portole, in the Portole district
Sabrina, Via Roma
San Luca, Piazza Garibaldi
San Michele, Via Guelfa 15

**

Farneta, in the Farneta district
Firenze, in the Camucia district
Nuovo Centrale, Via I. Scotoni 5

****

                                        Elba (Island of Elba)

At Portoferraio
Airone Residential Hotel (no rest), in the San Giovanni district
Biodola, in the Biodola district
Fabricia, in the Magazzani district
Hermitage, in the Biodola district
Picchiaie Residence, in the Monte Orello district
Villa Ottone, in the Ottone district

***

Acquabona Golf Hotel, in Acquabona, (no rest.)
Acquaviva Park Hotel, in Acquaviva,
Adriana, in Padulella
Casa Rosa, in Biódola
Danila, in Scaglieri
Garden, in Schioparello.
Il Caminetto, in San Martino
La Valdana, in Valdana (no rest.)
Mare, in Magazzini
Massimo, Calata Italia 23
Nuovo Padulella, Viale Einaudi
Paradiso, in Viticcio
Park Hotel Napoleone, in San Martino
Residence San Giovanni, in San Giovanni (no rest.)
Touring, Via Roma 13
Villa Ombrosa, Viale De Gasperi 3

**

Al Tromonto, in Viticcio
Clara, in Bagnaia
Grotte del Paradiso, in Le Grotte
L'Alpe Elbana, Salita C. de'Médici 2
Nobel, Via Magnanaro 72
Scoglio Bianco, in Viticcio
Tirrena, in Magazzini
Villa Mare, in Bagnaia (no rest.)

In Marina di Campo:
****

Iselba Residence Hotel, Viale Etruschi 28, (no rest.)
Montecristo, Viale Nomellini 11
Select, Via Mascagni 2

***

Acquarius, Via Mascagni 2
Aviotel Residence, in La Pila (no rest.)
Bahia, in Cávoli
Barcarola 2, in San Mamiliano
Barracuda, Viale Elba 2
Eden Park, in Lammia
Galli, in Fetovaia
Hotel dei Coralli, Viale Etruschi
Residence Le Formiche, Colle di Cávoli
Lilly, Viale Etruschi 53
Lo Scirocco, in Fetovaia
Marina 2, in Sagagnana
Meridiana, Viale Etruschi 69
Punto Verde, Viale Etruschi 23
Residence La Quiete, in Lammia (no rest.)
Riva, Via degli Eroi 11
Santa Caterina, Viale Elba
Tre Colonne, Via Fattori 6
Villa Nettuno, Viale Etruschi 30

**

Da Fine, in Seccheto
Elba, Via Mascagni
La Stella, in Seccheto
Lorenzo, in Cávoli
Montemerlo, in Fetovaia
Villa Etrusca, Via Etruschi 19

In Capolíveri:
****Hotel della Lacona, in Lacona

***

Al Pozzo Residence, in Morcone (no rest.)
Antares, in Lido
Belvedere, in Castagni (no rest.)
Capodistella, in Lacona
Capo Sud, in Lacona
Costa dei Gabbiani, in Ripalte (no rest.)
Drago Residence, in Morcone (no rest.)
Elba International Hotel, in Naregno
Frank's, in Naregno
Le Acacia, in Naregno
Residence Fiorenzo, in Sálici (no rest.)

Residence Punta Morcone, in Punta Morcone (no rest.)
Stella Maris, in Pareti
Villaggio Turistico Innamorata, in Innamorata (no rest.)

**

Anfora, in Naregno
Baia del Sole, in Lido (no rest.)
Da Pilade, in Mola (no rest.)
Dino, in Pareti
Elba Residence, in Naregno (no rest.)
Giardino, in Lacona
La Scogliera, in Morcone (no rest.)
Le Grazie Est, in Madonna delle Grazie (no rest.)
Mini Hotel, in Lacona (no rest.)
Romana, in Naregno
Villa Rodriguez, in Naregno

In Marciana:
****

Desirée, in Procchio
Residenza del Golfo Hotel, in Procchio

***

Brigantino, in Procchio
Cernia, in San Andrea
Delfino, in Procchio
Fontallecchio, in Procchio
Gallo Nero, in San Andrea
Hotel di Procchio, in Procchio
La Perla, in Procchio
L'Edera, in Procchio
Píccolo Hotel Barsalini, in San Andrea
San Andrea, in San Andrea
Valle Verde, in Procchio

**

Bel Tramonto, in Patresi
Da Giacomino, in San Andrea
Da Ilio, in San Andrea
Monna Lisa, in Procchio

In Marciano Marina:
***

Gabbiano Azzurro, Viale Amedeo 49
La Conchiglia, Via Venti Settembre 31
La Primula, Via Carducci
Marinella Viale Margherita 38
Sainte Claire, Via Aldo Moro (no rest.)

**

Anselmi, Viale Amedeo 37
Imperia, Viale Amedeo 12

In Porto Azzurro:
***

Belmare, Banchina Quattro Novembre
Cala di Mola, in Mola
Lido, in Lido, Il
Residence della Luna, in Lo Stipito (no rest.)

Hotels

**
Due Torri, Viale Venticinque Aprile
Gavila's Residence, in Sassi Turchini (no rest.)
Plaza, Punta Fanaletto
Residence Porto Azzurro, Via d'Alarcon 58, (no rest.)
Residence Reale, in Reale (no rest.)
Residence Sud-Est, in Mola (no rest.)
Residence Via Giulia, in Lido (no rest.)
Rocco, via Kennedy 36

In Rio Marina:
***
Club Capo d'Arco, in Capo d'Arco
Ortano Mare, in Ortano
Rio, Via Palestro 31

In Cavo:
Cristallo
La Pineta
Marelba,
Maristella
Pierolli

**Ginevra

In Rio nell'Elba:
***
La Feluca, in Bagnaia
La Ginestra, in La Ginestra

Émpoli

***
Commercio, Piazza O. Ristori 16
Il Sole, Piazza Don Minzoni 18
Tazza d'Oro, Via G. del Papa

**Maggino, Canto Ghibellino 1

*
Plaza, Piazza Vittoria 11
Vittorio, Via Carducci 105

Fiésole

**Dino, Via Faentina 329

Florence

L
Excelsior, Piazza Ognissanti 3
Grand Hotel, Piazza Ognissanti 1
Grand Hotel Villa Cora, Viale Machiavelli 18
Regency Umbria, Piazza d'Azeglio 3
Savoy, Piazza della Repúbblica 7
Villa Médici, Via il Prato 42

****
Alexander, Viale Guidoni 101
Anglo-American, Via Garibaldi 9
Astoria Pullman, Via Giglio 9
Atlantic Palace, Via Nazionale 12
Augustus & dei Congressi, Piazzetta dell'Oro 5
Berchielli, Lungarno Acciaiuoli 14
Bernini Palace, Piazza S. Firenze 29
Continental, Lungarno Acciaiuoli 2
Crest Hotel, Viale Europa 205

Croce di Malta, Via della Scala 7
De la Ville, Piazza Antinori 1
Della Signoria, Via delle Terme 1
Executive, Via Curtatone 5
Fenice Palace, Via Martelli 10
Grand Hotel Baglioni, Piazza Unità Italiana 6
Grand Hotel Majestic, Via del Melarancio 1
Grand Hotel Minerva, Piazza Santa Maria Novella 16
Jolly Carlton, Piazza Vittorio Véneto 4A
Kraft, Via Solférino 2
Laurus, Via Cerretani 8
Londra, Via Jácopo da Diacceto 18/20
Lungarno, Borgo San Jácopo 14
Michelangelo, Viale Fratelli Rosselli 2
Milano Terminus, Via Cerratani 10
Mirage, Via Barraca 231
Monginevro, Via di Nóvoli 59
Monna Lisa, Borgo Pinti 27
Montebello Splendid, Via Montebello 60
Nord Florence, Via Baracca 199A
Park Palace, Piazzale Galileo 5
Pierre, Via Lamberti 5
Plaza Hotel Lucchesi, Lungarno della Zecca Vecchia
Príncipe, Lungarno Vespucci 34
Queen Palace Hotel, Via Solférino 5
Raffaello, Viale Morgagni 19
Relais Certosa, Via di Colle Ramole 2
Ritz, Lungarno della Zecca Vecchia 24
Rivoli, Via della Scala 33
Torre di Bellosguardo, Via Roti Michelozzi 2
Villa Belvedere, Via Castelli 3
Villa Carlotta, Via Michele di Lando 3
Villa sull'Arno, Lungarno Cristóforo Colombo 1

***

Adriático, Via Maso Finiguerra 9
Ambasciatori, Via Alamanni 3
Auto Park Hotel, Via Valdegola 1
Bonciani, Via Panzani 1
Capitol, Viale Améndola 34
Caravel, Via Alamanni 9
Castri, Piazza Indipendenza 7
Cavour, Via del Procónsolo 3
Concorde, Viale Luigi Gori 10
Corona, Via Nazionale 14
Firenze Nova, Via Panciatichi 51
Fleming, Viale Guidoni 87
Helvetia e Bristol, Via dei Pescioni 2
Mediterráneo, Lungarno del Tempio 44
Paris, Via dei Banchi 2
Porto Rossa, Via Porta Rossa 19

**

Autostrada, Viale Luigi Gori 30
Capri, Via Ventisette Aprile 3
Careggi, Via T. Alderotti 43
Delle Nazioni, Via Alamanni 15
Nuovo Atlantico, Via Nazionale 10
Panorama-Angelico, Via Cavour 60
Splendor, Via San Gallo 30

Hotels

*

Firenze, Piazza Donati 4
Imperia, Via Rosina 7
Residenza Universitaria Fiorentina, Viale Don Minzoni 25
Universo, Piazza Santa Maria Novella 20

Forte dei Marmi

L Augustus, Viale Morin 169

****

Adam's Villa Maria, Lungarno Itálico 110
Alcione, Viale Morin 137
Areion, Via Caio Duilio 1
Atlantico, Via Torino 2
Augustus Lido, Viale Morin
Byron, Viale Morin 146
California Park, Via Colombo 32
Grand Hotel, Via Giorgini 1
Hermitage, Via Cesare Battisti
Il Negresco, Viale Itálico 82
La Pineta al Mare, Via G. Mazzini 65
Méssico, Via Corsica 9
President, Via Caio Duilio 4
Príncipe, Viale Morin 67
Raffaelli Park Hotel, Via Mazzini 37
Ritz Forte dei Marmi, Via F. Gioia 2
St Mauritius, Via Venti Settembre
Versilia Holidays, Via G.B. Vico 142

***

Acapulco, Via Raffaelli 6
Alpemare, Viale Itálico 104
Astoria Garden, Via Leonardo da Vinci 10
Astor Victoria, Via Caio Duilio 6
Bandinelli, Via Torino 3
Belvedere, Via Nove Novembre 5
Bijou, Via Salvador Allende 31
Etruria, Via Matteo Civitali 13
Florida, Viale Morin 44
Franceschi, Via Venti Settembre 19
Giada, Via Repúbblica 7
Goya, Viale Carducci 69
Ines, Viale Morin 45
Kyrton, Viale Raffaelli 14
La Primula, Via Venti Settembre 10
La Versilia, Via G. Páscoli 5/7
La Pleiadi, Via Matteo Civitali 51
Maria Luigia, Via Crispi 10
Marsiliana, Via Nazario Sauro 58
Mignon, Via Carducci 58
Miramonti, Via Raffaelli 74
Nettuno, Viale della Repúbblica 3
Olimpia, Via Marco Polo
Paradiso al Mare, Via Macchiavelli 2
Patroni, Viale Itálico 8
Píccolo Hotel, Viale Morin 24
Raffaelli Villa Angela, Via Mazzini 64
Righel, Via Colombo 19
Sonia, via Matteotti 42
Tirreno, Viale Morin 7
Villa Mia Cara, Via Crispi 11
Viscardo, Via Cesare Battisti 4

**

Bellariva, Via Gabriele d'Annunzio
Imperiale, Via Mazzini 20
La Pace, Via N. Sauro 15
Villa Cristina, Viale Mazzini 153

In Campese: **Giglio**
***

Campese
La Marina del Giglio

**

Da Giovanni
Giardino delle Palme
La Lampara

In Giglio Porto:
***

Arenella
Castello Monticello
Demo's Hotel
Il Saraceno

**

Bahamas
Da Ruggero
La Pergola
Pardini's Hermitage

****   **Grosseto**

Bastiani, Piazza Gioberti 64
Lorena, Via Trieste 3

***

Motel Agip, Via Aurelia at km 179
Nalesso, Via Senese 35
Ombrone, Via Matteotti 69

**

Leon d'Oro, Via San Martino 46
Maremma, Via Fulceri Paolucci
Quattro Strade, Via Aurelia Sud

*

Casa dello Studente, Via S. Lavagnini
Tirreno, Via Damiano Chiesa 50

In Marina di Grosseto:
***

Lola Píccolo Hotel, Via Ventiquattro Maggio
Mediterráneo, Via Ventiquattro Maggio
Nettuno, Via Ventiquattro Maggio
Rosmarina, Via delle Colonie 35

**Gondoletta, Via Ventiquattro Maggio 82

In Princina a Mare:
****Príncipe

***Grifone

Hotels

In Talamone:
***
Capo d'Uomo
Telamonio

La Verna

In Chiusi della Verna
*La Verna

Livorno

****Palazzo, Viale Italia 195

***
Atleti, Via del Pensieri 50
Boston, Piazza Mazzini 40
Excelsior, Via D. Cassuto 1
Gennarino, Viale Italia 301
Giappone, Via Grande 65
Gran Duca, Piazza Micheli 16
Touring, Via Goldini 61

**
Belmare, Viale Italia 109
Etruria, Via Italia 231
Giardino, Piazza Mazzini 85
Mini Hotel, Via Buontalenti 57

*Corsica, Corso Mazzini 148

In Antignano:
***
Rex, Via del Littorale
Universal, Viale Antignano 4

**La Capinera, Via del Castello 32

In Montereno:
**Montallegro, Piazza di Montenero 3

In Quercianella Sonnino:
***
Il Romito, Via del Littorale 247
Villa Margherita, Via M. Puccini 44

Lucca

****
Napoleon, Viale Europa 1
Villa la Principessa, in Massa Pisana

***
Celide, Via Giusti 27
Universo, Piazza Puccini 1

**
Bernardino, Via di Tigloi 109
Di Poggio, Via di Poggio 9
Il Giardinetto, in Ponte a Moriano, Via Nazionale 173
Ilaria, Via del Fosso 20
La Luna, Corte Compagni 12
Moderno, Via V. Civitali 38
Stipino, Via Romana 95
Villa Casanova, in Balbano

***Gallerian, Viale della Democrazia 2   **Massa**

**Annunziata, Via Villafranca 4

In Marina di Massa:
****Excelsior, Via Cesare Battisti 1

***

Daisy, Via Verona 12
Eco del Mare, Via Verona 1
Giulia, Via Áscoli 3
Roma, Piazza Pellarano 16

**

Anna, Via Verona 9
Argene, Via Padova 4
Bologna, Via Lungofrigido Ponente 3
Columbia, Via Cristóforo Colombo 37
Cristallo, Via P. Rossi 15
Dany, Via del Falasco 4
Eucalipto, Via delle Pinete 10
Euromar, Via dei Sálici 3
Fioravanti, Via San Leonardo 458
Frisco, Viale Roma 410
Gabrini, Via Sturzo 13
Lido, Viale Roma 426
Luna, Via Tornabuoni 17
Matilde, Via Tagliamento 4
Michela, Via Vicenza 5A
Milano, Piazza Betti 214
Miramonti, Via Monte Grappa 7
Nevada, Via Podenzana 4
Olgadanila, Via Arno 5
Parmamare, Via delle Pinete
Peselli, Via Rocortola 90
Piera, Via Casamicciola 77
Roby, Via Casamicciola 3
Scandinavia, Via Zolezzi 4
Sole, Via delle Pinete 106
Tiffany, Via Fosdivino 12
Tilly, Via Lungofrigido Levante 1
Tiziana, Via delle Pinete 106A
Virginia, Via delle Pinete 5

*Villa Serena, Via Mura dei Frati 26

**   **Massa Maríttima**

Duca del Mare
Girifalco

**   **Montalcino**

Giardino
Il Giglio

In Porto Santo Stefano   **Monte Argentario**
****Filippo 2, in Calvello

***

Il Girasole
La Caletta
Villa Domizia, in Santa Liberata
Vittoria

Hotels

**

Belvedere
La Lucciolla
Miramare, in Pozzarello

In Port'École:
****
Il Pellicano
Villa Letizia

***Don Pedro

**Stella Marina

Montecatini Terme

L
Grand Hotel Bellavista Palace & Golf, Viale Fedeli 2,
Grand Hotel & La Pace, Via della Torretta 1A

****
Ambasciatori Grand Hotel Cristallo, Viale Quattro
    Novembre 12
Cristallino, Viale A. Diaz 10
Du Parc et Regina, Viale Diaz 8
Grand Hotel Croce di Malta, Viale Quattro Novembre 18
Grand Hotel Plaza e Locanda Maggiore, Piazza del Pópolo 7
Grand Hotel Tamerici e Príncipe, Viale Quattro Novembre 2
Grande Bretagne, Viale Don Minzoni 3
Nizza et Suisse, Viale Verdi 72
Panoramic, Viale Bustichini 65
Tettuccio, Viale Verdi 74
Vittoria, Viale della Libertà 2A

***
Adua, Viale Cavallotti 100
Ambrosiano, Corso Matteotti 65
Ariston, Viale Manzoni 30
Astoria, Viale Fedeli 1
Augustus, Viale Manzoni 19
Belvedere, Viale Fedeli 10
Biondi, Viale Quattro Novembre 83
Boston, Viale Bicchierai 16
Buonamici, Viale Bicchierai 31
Cappelli-Croce di Savoia, Viale Bicchierai 139
Centrale, Piazza del Pópolo 20
Colombia, Corso Roma 19
Corallo, Viale Cavallotti 116
De la Ville, Viale San Francesco d'Assisi 5
Ercolini & Savi, Via San Martino 18
Firenz, Viale Bicchierai 68
Florida, Via Michelangelo 16
Francia & Quirinale, Viale Quattro Novembre 77
Hermitage, Via Baragiola 31
Imperial Garden, Viale Puccini 20
Impero, Viale Bicchierai 83
Lago Maggiore, Corso Matteotti 70
La Pia, Via Montebello 30
Lido Palace, Viale Quattro Novembre 14
Locarno Lugano, Viale Bicchierai 13
Maestoso, Viale Puccini 63

Manzoni, Viale Manzoni 28
Margherita, Via Garibaldi 32
Massimo d'Azeglio, Corso Matteotti 42
Mediterráneo, Via Baragiola 1
Metropole, Via Torretta 13
Michelangelo, Viale Fedeli 15
Minerva, Via Cavour 14
Nord America, Corso Roma 97
Nuovo Excelsior, Viale Cavallotti 115
Nuovo Hotel Felsinea, Viale Bicchierai 67
Parma e Oriente, Viale Cavallotti 135
President, Corso Matteotti 118
Reale, Via Palestro 7
Rigoletto, Via Baragiola 5
Salus, Viale Marconi 5
San Marco, Viale Rosselli 3
Santa Barbara, in Macchio
Savona, Via Leopardi 10
Select-Petrolini, Viale Verdi 15
Settentrionale Esplanade, Viale Grocco 2
Terme Pellegrini, Piazza del Pópolo 34
Tonfoni e Mafalda, Via delle Saline 42
Torretta, Viale Bustichini 63
Universo, Corso Matteotti 51
Villa Ida, Viale Marconi 55
Zenith, Via Cavour 20

**

Arnolfo, Via Trento 4
Brasile, Viale Bicchierai 53
Brennero e Varsavia, Viale Bicchierai 72
California, Via Trieste 19
Casa F.A.C.I., Viale Bicchierai 82
Casa Rossa, Viale Fedeli 68
Cavallotti, Viale Cavallotti 103
Concordia, Via della Salute 16
Continentale, Via Puccini 18
Corona d'Italia, Viale Verdi 5
David, Viale Puccini 73
Florio, Viale Montebello 41
Giglio, Viale Bicchierai 99
Granduca Leopoldo, Via Venezia 11
La Querceta, Via Peloni 19
La Quiete-Fabiani, Via Puglie 42
Lazzerini, Viale Cavallotti 78
Le Fonti, Viale San Francesco d'Assisi 4
Londra, Parco della Rimembranza 1
Miramonti, Viale Marconi 44
Moschini, Via Trípoli 21
Niky, Corso Matteotti 96
Nuovo Savi, Corso Matteotti 85
Paradiso, Via Ventisette Aprile 2
Reggio, Via Balducci 16
Rinascente, Via Gioberti 10
San Giorgio, Via Trieste 23
Savoia e Campana, Viale Cavallotti 10
Tiffany, Viale Bicchierai 37
Touring e Internationale, Viale Cavallotti 66
Trinacria, Via Montebello 47
Umbria, Via delle Saline 19

Hotels

Valtorta, Viale Cavallotti 92
Villa Anna, Viale Rosselli 33
Villa Hermada, Via Torino 10
Villa Rita, Viale Marconi 10

*

Giusti, Via Salsero 7
Marina, Viale Cavallotti 31

Montepulciano

***
Il Grifo
Palio
Panoramic, in Boscatti

**
Duomo
Il Borghetto
Il Marzocco
Il Poliziano
La Terrazza
Tiziana

In San Albino:
***
Tre Stelle
Villa Ambra

**
Ada
Marvin
Sangallo

Orbetello

***
I Presidi
Sole

In Albinia:
***Corallo

**Da Renato

In Ansedonia:
**Vincio

In Fonteblanda:
****Corte dei Butteri, Via Aurelia at km 156

***Cali di Forno

In Quattrostrade:
***
Il Cacciatore, Via Aurelia at km 146
Vecchia Maremma

Pescia

***Villa delle Rose

**Hotel dei Fiori, Via Otto Settembre 9

Pienza

***Corsignano

Pietrasanta

***
Derby, Via Aurelia 100
Grappolo d'Oro, in Strettoia

**

Da Piero, Via Traversagna 3–5
Italia, Via Oberdan 9
Palagi, Via Carducci 23

In Marina di Pietrasanta:
L Palazzo della Spaiggia, Lungomare Roma

****

Ermione, Viale Roma 183
Lombardi, Viale Roma 27
Verdemare, Via Cipro 27

***

Airone, Via Catalani 46
Ambasciatori, Viale Roma 271
Andrea Neri, Via Catalani 56
Arianna, Viale Roma 47
Battelli, Via Versilia 189
Coluccini, Piazza d'Annunzio
Eden Park, Piazza d'Annunzio 7
Esplanade, Viale Roma 235
Il Caravaggio, Viale Carducci 127
Il Cavallino, Viale Carducci 204
Joseph, Via Roma 323
King, Via Tolmino 14
L'Alba Hotel, Via Colombo
Le Ginestra, Viale Italia 51
Mirage Versilia, Viale Roma 215
Mistral, Via Tolmino 5
Mondial, Via Ricasoli 18
Motel Europa, Via Apua 199
Niagara, Via Duca della Vittoria
Oceano, Viale Roma 347
Poseidon, Via Dalmazia 1
Rigatti, Via Livorno 50
Ritz, Via Dalmazia 13
San Carlo, Viale Roma 161
Savoy, Via Italia 1
Suisse, Viale Versilia 197
Tierre Brasilia, Via Roma 333
Tirreno, Via Cavour 7
Tiziana, Via Cavour 67
Venezia, Via Firenze 48

**

Apuana, Via Leonardo da Vinci 49
Azzurra, Via Manzoni 22
Cometa, Viale Catalani 52
Elizabeth, Via Tagliamento 36
Globe, Viale Roma 317
Grande Italia, Via Torino 5
Happy, Lungomare Roma 291
Imperiale, Via Don Bosco 8
Le Focette, Via Trípoli 20
Le Giraffe, Via Don Bosco 21
Le Rondini, Via Duca della Vittoria 53
Milano, Via Cortona 11
Milton, Via G. Puccini 15
Miosotis, Via Savoia 1

Hotels

Naviglio, Viale Roma 77
Nettuno, Viale Versilia 193
Oasi, Viale Roma 225
Orione, Via Carducci 29
Patria, Via Roma 185
Nuovo Sabrina, Via Foscolo 11
Villa Alk, Viale Roma 265
Villa I Tamerici, Via Don Bosco 31
Villa Marzia, Via Corridoni 1
Villa Ombrosa, Via Cavour 21
Villa Signori, Via Dalmazia 29

Piombino

****Centrale, Piazza Verdi 2

***

Collodi, Via Collodi 7
Esperia, Lungomare Marconi 27

**

Ariston, Via Ferrer 7
Il Piave, Piazza Niccolini 18
Italia, Via Venti Settembre 39
Tuscania, Via A. Costa 8

Pisa

****

Cavalieri, Piazza della Stazione 2
D'Azeglio, Piazza Vittorio Emanuele 18b
Grand Hotel Duomo, Via Santa Maria 94

***

Ariston, Via Cardinale Maffi 42
Arno, Piazza della Repúbblica 6
Capitol, Via Enrico Fermi 13
La Pace, Via Gramsci, Galleria B
Mediterráneo, Via Turati 35
Roma, Via Bonanno 111
Royal Victoria, Lungarno Pacinotti 12
Terminus e Plaza, Via Colombo 45
Touring, Via G. Puccini 24
Villa Kinzica, Piazza Arcivescovado 4

**

Bologna, Via Mazzini 57
Fenice, Via Catalani 8
La Torre, Via Cesare Battisti 17
Leon Bianco, Piazza del Pozzetto 6

In San Giuliano Terme:
****California Park Hotel, Via Aurelia at km 338

In Tirrenia
****

Atlantico
Continental
Grand Hotel Golf

***

Bristol
Florida
Il Gabbiano

Le Baleari
Mediterráneo
Medusa
Tirrenia Villa Laura

**
Italia
Vittoria

***   **Pistoia**

Il Convento, Via San Quírico 33
Le Rose, Viale Adua 89
Leon Bianco, Via Panciatichi 2
Milano, Viale Pacinotti 10
Patria, Via F. Crispi 6
Charleston, in Masotti

**Appennino, Via Venti Settembre 21

**   **Pitigliano**

Corano, in Corano
Guastini
Valle Orientina

In Badía Prataglia: **Poppi**
**

Bellavista, Via Nazionale 35
Bosco Verde, Via Nazionale 8
Giardino
La Foresta, Via Nazionale 13
Mechelli, Via Sassopiano 3
Mimosa, Via Nazionale 57
Verdeluna

****   **Prato**

Palace, Via Pier della Francesca 71
President, Via Simintendi 20

***

Flora, Via Cairoli 31
Milano, Via Tiziano 15
Moderno, Via C. Balbo 11
San Marco, Piazza San Marco 46
Villa Santa Cristina, Via Poggio Secco 58

**

Giardino, Via Magnolfi 2
Stella d'Italia, Piazza Duomo 8

***   **San Gimignano**

Belsoggiorno
La Cappuccina, in La Cappuccino
La Cisterna
La Steccaia, in La Steccaia
Leon Bianco
Le Renaie, in Pancole
Pescille, in Pescille

***   **San Giovanni Valdarno**

Bianca, Viale Don Minzoni 38
River, Via F. Cervi 10

Hotels

San Miniato al Tedesco ***Miravalle

San Quirico d'Orcia ***Palazzuolo Tuscany Club

Sansepolcro ****
Borgo
La Balestra, Via dei Montefeltro 29

***Fiorentino, Via L. Pacioli 60

**Orfeo, Viale A. Diaz 12

Siena L Park Hotel, Via Marciano 16

****
Athena, Via Mascagni 55
Jolly Hotel Excelsior, Piazza la Lizza 1
La Certosa, Via di Certosa 82
Villa Patrizia Hotel, Via Fiorentina 58
Villa Scacciapensieri, Via di Scacciapensieri 10

***
Castagneto Hotel, Via dei Cappuccini 39
Continentale, Via Banchi di Sopra 85
Duomo, Via Stalloreggi 38
Garden, Via Custozza 2
Italia, Viale Cavour 67
La Toscana, Via Cecco Angiolieri 12
La Minerva, Via Garibaldi 72
Moderno, Via B. Peruzzi 19
Palazzo Ravizza, Pian dei Mantellini 34
Santa Caterina, Via Piccolomini 7
Vico Alto, Via delle Regioni 26

**
Cannon d'Oro, Via Montanini 28
Centrale, Via Calzolería 24
Chiusarelli, Via Curtatone 9
Píccolo Hotel Il Palio, Piazza del Sale 19
Villa Terraia, Via dell'Ascarello 13

Viareggio ****
Astor Hotel, Viale Carducci 54
De Russie e Plaza, Viale Manin 1
Excelsior, Viale Carducci 88
Grand Hotel e Royal, Viale Carducci 44
Palace Hotel, Via Flavio Gioia 2
Príncipe di Piemonte, Piazza G. Puccini 1

***
American Hotel, Piazza Mazzini 6
Belmare, Via Carducci 5
Bristol, Viale Manin 14
Caracas, Via Bertini 146
Eden, Via San Martino 1
Garden, Viale Foscolo 70
Liberty, Lungomare Manin 18
London, Viale Manin 16
Lukas, Piazza G. Puccini
Marchioni, Piazza G. Puccini 3
Miramare, Via Carducci 27

San Francisco, Via Carducci 68
Stella d'Italia, Via Foscolo 57

**

Bella Riviera, Viale Manin 34
Bonelli, Via Regia 96
Flamingo, Via Buonarroti 219
Katy, Via Flavio Gioia 12
Kursaal, Via Mentana 19
Turismo, Via Buonarroti 97

****San Lino   **Volterra**

***
Etruria
Nazionale
Villa Nencini

Information

Italian State Tourist Office (Ente Nazionale Italiano per il
Turismo, ENIT)

Head office:
Via Marghera 2
I–00185 Roma
Tel. (06) 4 97 11

1 Princes Street   United Kingdom
London W1A 7RA
Tel. (071) 408 1254

500 North Michigan Avenue   United States
Chicago, IL 60601
Tel. (312) 644 0990–91

630 Fifth Avenue, Suite 1565
New York, NY 10111
Tel. (212) 245 4822–24

360 Post Street, Suite 801
San Francisco, CA 94108
Tel. (415) 392 6206–07

Store 56, Plaza 3, Place Ville Marie   Canada
Montreal, Quebec
Tel. (514) 866 7667

Within Italy information can be obtained from regional tourist   Within Italy
offices (Assessorati Regionali del Turismo) in the regional capitals (in Tuscany, Florence), provincial tourist offices (Ente Pro-
vinciali per il Turismo), spa administrations (Aziende
Autónome di Cura) and local tourist offices (Aziende Autónome
di Soggiorno e Turismo).

Azienda Autonoma di Soggiorno   **Abbadia San Salvatore**
Viale Matteoti 29
I–53021 Abbadia San Salvatore
Tel. (0577) 77 86 08

Information

Arezzo	Ente Provinciale per il Turismo Piazza Risorgimento 116 I–52100 Arezzo Tel. (0575) 23 952
Bagni di Lucca	Azienda Autonoma di Soggiorno e Cura Via Umberto 1 I–55021 Bagni di Lucca Tel. (0583) 87 246
Bibbiena	Azienda Autonoma di Soggiorno Via Berni 29 I–52011 Bibbiena Tel. (0575) 59 30 98
Carrara	Ente Provinciale per il Turismo di Massa-Carrara Piazza 2 Giugno 14 I–54033 Carrara Tel. (0585) 70 668
Castiglione della Pescaia	Azienda Autonoma di Soggiorno e Turismo Piazza Garibaldi I–58043 Castiglione della Pescaia Tel. (0564) 93 36 78
Chianciano Terme	Azienda Autonoma di Soggiorno e Cura Via Giusseppe Sabatini 7 I–53042 Chianciano Terme Tel. (0578) 63 538
Chiusi	Associazione Pro Loco Via Petrarca 4 I–53043 Chiusi Tel. (0578) 2 10 60
Colle di Val d'Elsa	Associazione Pro Loco Piazza Arnolfo di Cambio 5 I–53034 Colle di Val d'Elsa Tel. (0577) 92 16 92
Cortona	Azienda Autonoma di Soggiorno Via Nazionale 72 I–52044 Cortona Tel. (0575) 60 30 56
Elba	Azienda Autonoma di Cura, Soggiorno e Turismo dell'Isola d'Elba Calata Italia 26 I–57037 Portoferraio Tel. (0565) 9 26 71
Émpoli	Associazione Pro Émpoli Piazza Farinata degli Uberti 4 I–50053 Émpoli Tel. (0571) 7 61 15
Fiésole	Azienda Autonoma di Soggiorno e Turismo Piazza Mino da Fiésole 45 I–50014 Fiésole Tel. (055) 59 87 20

Regione Toscana (Giunta Regionale)
Dipartimento Attività Produttive Turismo e Comercio
Via di Nóvoli 26
I–50127 Firenze
Tel. (055) 43 93 11

Ente Provinciale per il Turismo
Via A. Manzoni 16
I–50100 Firenze
Tel. (055) 2 47 81 41

Azienda Autonoma di Soggiorno
Via de' Tornabuoni 15
I–50100 Firenze
Tel. (055) 21 65 44

Azienda Autonoma di Soggiorno
Piazza Marconi
I–55042 Forte dei Marmi
Tel. (0584) 8 00 91

Forte dei Marmi

Ente Provinciale per il Turismo
Viale Monterosa 206
I–58100 Grosseto
Tel. (0564) 2 25 34

Grosseto

Ente Provinciale per il Turismo
Piazza Cavour 6
I–57100 Livorno
Tel. (0586) 3 31 11
Information office in port area:
Tel. (0586) 2 53 20

Livorno

Ente Provinciale per il Turismo
Piazza Guidiccioni 2
I–55100 Lucca
Tel. (0583) 4 12 05

Lucca

See Carrara

Massa

Assessorato al Turismo
I–58024 Massa Maríttima

Massa Maríttima

Associazione Pro Loco
Via Mazzini 41
I–53024 Montalcino
Tel. (0577) 84 82 42

Montalcino

Azienda di Soggiorno e Turismo
della Costa d'Argento
Corso Umberto 55a
I–58019 Porto Santo Stéfano
Tel. (0564) 81 42 08

Monte Argentario

Azienda Autonoma di Cura e Soggiorno
Viale Verdi 68
I–51016 Montecatini Terme
Tel. (0572) 7 01 09

Montecatini Terme

Information

Montepulciano	Ufficio Turistico Palazzo Comunale I–53045 Montepulciano Tel. (0578) 75 70 80
Pisa	Ente Provinciale per il Turismo Lungarno Mediceo 42 I–56100 Pisa Tel. (050) 20 3 51
Pistoia	Ente Provinciale per il Turismo Corso Gramsci 110 I–51100 Pistoia Tel. (0573) 3 43 26
Prato	Azienda Autonoma di Soggiorno Via Cairoli 48–54 I–50047 Prato Tel. (0574) 2 41 12
San Gimignano	Associazione Pro Loco Piazza del Duomo 1 I–53037 San Gimignano Tel. (0577) 94 00 08
Siena	Ente Provinciale per il Turismo Via di Città 5 I-53100 Siena Te. (0577) 4 70 51
Viareggio	Azienda Autonoma di Soggiorno Viale Carducci 10 I–55049 Viareggio Tel. (0584) 96 22 33
Volterra	Associazione Pro Volterra Palazzo dei Priori Via Turazza 2 I–56048 Volterra Tel. (0588) 8 61 50

Insurance

Car insurance

Although not a legal requirement for citizens of EC countries it is nevertheless advisable to carry an international insurance certificate ("Green card"). The insurance should be fully comprehensive and additional short-term cover against legal costs should be taken out unless already included. Italian insurance companies tend to be slow in settling claims.

Health insurance

Like other EC citizens British visitors to Italy are entitled to health care on the same basis as Italians (including free medical treatment, etc.). They should apply to their local social security office, well before their date of departure, for a certificate of entitlement (form E111). It is advisable to take out additional insurance against medical expenses as well however. Non-EC citizens should, of course, arrange appropriate insurance cover.

The risk of theft makes adequate insurance against loss of, or damage to, baggage highly desirable.

Baggage insurance

Maps and plans

Visitors planning a journey which will take them into country well off the main roads should provide themselves with suitable maps, in addition to the general map included in this Guide. The following is a selection.

Bartholomew World Travel series: Italy	1:1,250,000
TCI (Touring Club d'Italia): Carta Fisico-Politica d'Italia Hallwag Road Map of Italy Michelin: Italia, Le grandi strade	1:1,000,000
RV Reise- und Verkehrsverlag: Italy	1:800,000
RV Reise- und Verkehrsverlag: Tuscany	1:300,000
TCI (Touring Club d'Italia): Toscana	1:200,000

Visitors planning a stay of some days in Florence will find it worth their while to have Baedeker's pocket guide to Florence (160 pages, 102 photographs and plans, large town plan).

Motoring

In Italy, as in the rest of continental Europe, traffic travels on the right, with overtaking on the left.
Seat belts must be worn when driving.
Motor-cycle trailers are prohibited in Italy.

Traffic regulations

Priority belongs to main roads only if they are marked with the priority sign (a white or yellow square, corner downwards, in a red or black and white frame); otherwise, even at roundabouts, traffic coming from the right has priority. On narrow mountain roads the ascending vehicle has priority. Vehicles on rails always have priority.

Right of way

Drivers moving from one lane to another, even for the purpose of overtaking, or pulling in to the side of the road must give warning of their intention by the use of their direction indicators.

Lane change

The horn must be sounded before overtaking outside built-up areas, and also before intersections, side roads, blind curves and other danger spots; after dark the headlights should be used instead. In towns of any size the use of the horn is prohibited (indicated by a sign showing a horn with a bar through it or the words "zona di silenzio").

Warning signal

On roads or streets with good lighting sidelights only may be used. In tunnels and galleries dipped headlights must be used. Watch out for cyclists riding without lights or rear reflectors.

Lighting

On zebra crossings pedestrians have absolute priority.

Zebra crossing

245

Motoring organisations

Road signs

International road signs are in general use.

Speed limits

New regulations were introduced in 1988. Maximum speeds.
– on ordinary roads: 90 km p.h. (56 m.p.h.)
– on motorways: weekdays 130 km p.h. (80 m.p.h.); Sat. and Sun. 110 km p.h. (69 m.p.h.)
Heavy fines are imposed for exceeding these limits!

The maximum speed for cars with trailers is 80 km p.h. (50 m.p.h.) on ordinary roads and 100 km p.h. (62 m.p.h.) on motorways.

Motor-cycles with side-cars or trailers are not allowed on motorways.

See also Car ferries, Motoring organisations, and Roads.

Petrol coupons

Italian petrol prices are above the European average and are subject to much variation. Foreign visitors can obtain petrol coupons for the purchase of petrol at reduced prices, usually issued in a "package" with vouchers for the tolls on Italian motorways. Information can be obtained from motoring organisations and the Italian State Tourist Office.

Motoring organisations

Touring Club Italiano (TCI)

The Touring Club Italiano (TCI) exists to promote the mutual interests of various other motoring organisations and the tourist industry. It offers a number of useful services. For further information contact:

Head office:
Corso Italia 10
I–20122 Milano
Tel. (02) 85 26 72

Automobile Club d'Italia (ACI)

Members of UK motoring organisations are able to call upon the services of the Automobile Club d'Italia (ACI):

Head office:
Via Marsala 8
I–00185 Roma
Tel. (06) 4 99 81

The Club provides a breakdown and recovery service and operates a 24-hour emergency telephone service for assistance within Italy: ACIAT (Automobile Club International Assistance Centre), tel. 06 42 12.

ACI regional offices in Tuscany

In Florence:
Viale Amendole 36
Tel. (055) 24 861

In Pisa:
Via San Martino 1
Tel. (050) 47 333

In Arezzo:
Via Le Signorelli 24a
Tel. (0575) 23 253

In Siena:
Viale Vittorio Veneto 47
Tel. (0577) 49 001

ACI has branches in all provincial capitals, in major tourist
centres and at the main frontier crossings.

Opening times

Summer: 9 a.m.–1 p.m. and 4–8 p.m.; closed Sat. afternoon   Shops
Winter: 9 a.m.–1 p.m. and 3–7 p.m.; closed Mon. morning

Summer: Mon.–Fri. 8.30 a.m.–12.30 p.m. and 4–8 p.m.; closed   Chemists
Sat. afternoon
Winter: Mon.–Fri. 8.30 a.m.–12.30 p.m. and 3.30–6.30 p.m.;
usually closed Mon. morning

Open to the public Mon.–Fri. 8.20 a.m.–1.20 p.m. and 2.45–3.45   Banks
p.m.

Mon.–Fri. 8.15 a.m.–2 p.m. Sat. 8.15 a.m.–12 noon, head post   Post offices
offices all day. On 14 Aug, 24 and 31 Dec. they closed at 11.30
a.m.

Usually closed 12.30–3.30 p.m. and from 8 p.m.; in winter   Petrol stations
usually from 7 p.m.

9 or 10 a.m. to 1 or 2 p.m. and 2 or 3 p.m. to 5 or 6 p.m.,   Museums
occasionally to 7 p.m. In winter the hours are usually shorter,
but without a lunchtime break. All museums are closed on
Sunday afternoons and on public holidays, and most of them
also close on Mondays or (rarely) Fridays. In addition there are
often closures as a result of staff shortages, strikes, renovation,
etc.; it is advisable, therefore, before visiting a museum, to
check that it will be open.

The larger churches are usually open until 12 noon and from 4   Churches
or 5 p.m. until dusk. Some of the principal churches are open all
day.
Visitors should always be suitably dressed, avoiding sleeveless
or unduly revealing blouses or dresses, sleeveless shirts,
shorts, etc.; if inappropriately dressed they may be refused
admittance. Visitors should not look round the interior of a
church during a service.

Postal, telegraph and telephone services

Post offices are usually open from 8.15 a.m. to 2 p.m., except on   Opening times
Sundays and public holidays. On Saturday they close at 12
noon.

Stamps can be bought from tobacconists (indicated by a large   Stamps
T above the door) as well as in post offices.

Letter boxes in Italy are painted red.   Letter boxes

Most bars have public telephones (indicated by a yellow disc   Telephoning
over the entrance to the box), operated by tokens (*gettoni*),

from which local calls can be dialled. If the yellow disc bears the legend "teleselezione" or "interurbana" international calls can be dialled – though for this purpose you must be sure you have an adequate supply of tokens.

Some of the more recently installed public telephones accept 100 or 200 lire coins as well as tokens.

There are also public telephones in post offices and branches of SIP, the state telephone corporation.

International dialling codes

To the United Kingdom: 0044
To the United States: 01139
To Canada: 01139

In a call to the United Kingdom the initial zero of the local dialling code should be omitted.

Public holidays

1 January (New Year's Day)
6 January (Epiphany)
25 April (Liberation Day, 1945)
Easter Monday
1 May (Labour Day)
Ascension
Corpus Christi
2 June (proclamation of the Republic; celebrations on following Saturday)
15 August (Ferragosto, the feast of the Assumption; the peak of the Italian holiday period)
1 November (All Saints)
4 November (Day of National Unity; celebrations on following Saturday)
8 December (Immaculate Conception)
25 and 26 December

Rail travel

The main railway line between Firenze (Florence) and Roma (Rome) runs through eastern Tuscany. Secondary lines provide services along the coast from Pisa to Livorno and from Grosseto to Rome. There is also a line connecting Pisa via Florence with Rome.

Important regional branch lines link Émpoli and Siena with Grosseto, Siena with Chiusi, Asciano with Grosseto, and Cecina with Volterra.

Italian State Railways offer a number of special tariffs from which visitors to Tuscany can benefit. Each represents excellent value for money:

– the BTLC tourist ticket (1st or 2nd class) covers a number of countrywide journeys of unlimited mileage within a set period (8, 15, 21 or 30 days);

– the kilometric ticket (valid for up to two months) allows individuals or groups (up to 5 people on one ticket) a combined total of 3000 km by rail with a maximum of 20 stops. This is without question the best buy;

– the Inter-Rail ticket for the under 26s, 2nd class, valid for 1 month;

– the Rail Europ Senior (RES) card, backed by an agreement between 18 European countries, entitles senior citizens (women aged 60, men aged 65) to reduced rates on international journeys.

The nearest destinations for motorail services are Milan, Verona and Rimini, none of which are in Tuscany.   Motorail

Restaurants

Ristorante Sella	**Abbadia San Salvatore**
Vinicio	**Ansedonia**
Buca di San Francesco, Piazza San Francesco 1 Spiedo d'Oro, Via Crispi 12 Tastevin, Via de' Cenci 9	**Arezzo**
Circolo dei Forestieri, Piazza Verraud La Ruota, 2.5 km out of town	**Bagni di Lucca**
Il Cedro, at Moggiona	**Camáldoli**
Buca di Michelángelo Fonte della Galletta, 6 km out of town	**Caprese Michelángelo**
Soldaini, Via Mazzini 11 Da Gero, in Marina di Carrara, Viale Venti Settembre 305	**Carrara**
Da Rómolo, Corso della Libertà 10	**Castiglione della Pescaia**
Osteria del Vicario	**Certaldo**
La Casanova, Strada della Vittoria 10 Al Casale, Via delle Cavine 36 Il Morellone, Strada del Morellone 8	**Chianciano Terme**
La Fattoria, 3.5 km out of town	**Chiusi**
Cartiera, Via Oberdan 5 L'Antica Trattoria, Piazza Arnolfo 23 Arnolfo, Via Campana 8	**Colle di Vall d'Elsa**
La Loggetta, Piazza Peschería	**Cortona**
In Portoferraio: Al Braciere La Ferrigna In Marina di Campo: Bologna La Triglia Da Gianni In Rio Marina: La Canocchia	**Elba**
Bianconi, Via Tosco Romagnola 70	**Émpoli**
Trattoria le Cave di Maiano, at Maiano	**Fiésole**

Restaurants

Florence
(Firenze)

Sabatini, Via de' Panzani 9a
Paoli, Via dei Tavolini 12 r
Al Campidoglio, Via dol Campidoglio 8 r
Enoteca Pinchiorri, Via Ghibellina 87
Buca Lapi, Via del Trebbio 1 r
La Loggia, Piazzale Michelángiolo 1
13 Gobbi, Via del Porcellana 9 r
Da Dante – Al Lume di Candela, Via delle Terme 23 r
Harry's Bar, Lungarno Vespucci 22 r
Gourmet, Via Prato 68 r
Lorenzaccio, Via Rucellai 1a
Barrino, Via de' Biffi 2 r
La Posta, Via de'Lamberti 20 r
Il Paiolo, Via del Corso 42 r
Da Noi, Via Fiesolana 46 r
Buca Mario, Piazza Ottaviani 16 r
Pierot, Piazza Taddeo Gaddi 25 r
Leo in Santa Croce, Via Torta 7 r
Il Profeta, Borgo Ognissanti 93 r
Mamma Gina, Borgo Sant' Jacopo 37 r
Le Fonticine, Via Nazionale 79 r
La Geppia, Lungarno Ferrucci 8
Cibreo, Via dei Macci 118

Forte dei Marmi

La Barca, Viale Itálico 3
Lorenzo, Via Carducci 61

Grosseto

Buca di San Lorenzo, Via Manetti 1
La Maremma, Via Fulceri Paolucci de' Calboli 5
Canapone, Piazza Dante 3

Livorno

Gran Duca, Piazza Micholi 1
Gennarino, Via Santa Fortunata 11
La Gargotta del Buongustaio, Via San Carlo 7
Il Fanale, Scali Novi Lena 15
La Barcarola, Viale Carducci 63
Hostaria da Norma, Via Provinciale Pisana 60
La Parmigiana, Piazza Luigi Orlando

Lucca

Buca di Sant'Antonio, Via della Cervia 1/5
Antica Locanda dell'Angelo, Via Peschiera 21
Giglio, Piazza del Giglio

Massa

Manfredi, Piazza della Liberazione 21

Montecatinin Terme

Gourmet, Viale Amendola 6
San Francisco, Corso Roma 112
Chez les Amis, Viale Bovio la

Montepulciano

Il Cantuccio, Via delle Cantine 1/3

Orbetello

Osteria del Lupacante, Corso Italia 103
Il Cacciatore, in Orbetello Scalo
Da Egisto, Corso Italia 190

Pescia

Cecco, Via Forti 84
La Fortuna, Via Colli per Uzzano 18

Piombino

Centrale, Piazza Edison 2

Pisa

Sergio, Lungarno Pacinotti 1
Emilio, Via Roma 28

Buzzino, Via Cammeo 44
Da Bruno, Via Bianchi 12
Ristoro dei Vecchi Macelli, Via Volturno 49
Da Ivaldo, Via Toselli 11a

Cúcciolo della Montagna, Via Panciatichi 4   **Pistoia**
La Valle del Vincio, Via di Vignano 1
Rafanelli Sant'Agostino, Via Sant'Agostino 47
Il Boschetto, Via Adena 469

Il Paraña, Via Valentini 110   **Prato**
Villa Santa Cristina, Via Poggio Secco 58
Tonio, Piazza Nercatale 61
Pietro, Via Balbo 9a

La Griglia   **San Gimignano**
La Stella

Nello – La Taverna, Via del Porrione 28   **Siena**
Guido, Vicolo Pettinaio 7
Al Marsili, Via del Castoro 3
Le Campane, Via delle Campane 6
L'Angolo, Via Garibaldi 15
Mariott – Da Mugolone, Via dei Pellegrini 8
Tullio ai tre Cristi, Vícolo Provenzano 1
Il Campo, Piazza del Campo 50

Il Patriarca, Viale Carducci 79   **Viareggio**
Montecatini, Viale Manin 8
Tito del Molo, Lungomolo Corrado del Greco 3
Margherita, Lungomare Margherita 30
Gusmano, Via Regia 58–64
Da Romano, Via Mazzini 120
Mirage, Via Zanardelli 12–14

Il Porcellino, Vicolo delle Prigioni 16   **Volterra**
Etruria, Piazza dei Priori 8
Da Beppino, Via delle Prigioni 15

Restaurants are required to give their clients receipted bills,   Note
which must be produced to an Inland Revenue inspector on
request in the vicinity of the restaurant. Failure to do so may
result in a fine.

See entry   Food and drink

Roads

The Italian road system is extensive and generally good. It
consists of motorways, national highways, provincial roads
and secondary roads.

Practically all the major Italian towns are served by motorways   Motorways
(*autostrade*), mostly subject to tolls. Within Tuscany the motorway from Carrara via Lucca to Florence and on via Arezzo and
Chiusi to Rome is used by through traffic as well as being
convenient for touring in Tuscany. The sections of motorway
between Viareggio and Livorno and between Florence and
Siena are also much used by visitors to Tuscany.

Souvenirs

National highways

The national highways (*strade statali*), identified by numbers with the prefix SS, also serve important trunk routes and are generally well built and maintained. Many of them have names as well as numbers (often those of the old Roman roads such as the Via Aurelia, Via Cassia and Via Emilia), which are frequently better known than the numbers.

Provincial roads

The provincial roads (*strade di grande comunicazione*), which are unnumbered, are also of good quality. Local connections are provided by the seconary roads (*strade secondarie*).

Souvenirs

Visitors to Tuscany can still find a wide range of traditional arts and crafts – good shoes, leather articles and textiles, basketwork and sometimes, particularly in Florence, fine gold and silver jewellery. Volterra is famous for its alabaster workshops; much of their output, no doubt, is mass produced, but it is also possible, by looking around, to pick up individual items of quality. This is true also of articles made of wood (including olive wood) and ceramics. Local specialities include the gold jewellery, wrought-iron work, cabinet-making and pottery of Siena and the painted ceramic dishes of San Gimignano.

Other attractive buys are various kinds of sweets including *panettone*, candied fruits, the coloured sweets known as "Arno pebbles" and Siena *panforte* (a cross between nougat and cake), as well as the local wines (see Wine) and spirits.

Warning

Street traders often sell watches, jewellery, etc., at what appear to be bargain prices. Almost invariably these are of inferior quality. Gold and silver assay marks are frequently forged.

It is important to keep the receipt for purchases of any value or for major repairs to a car, since spot checks by Inland Revenue inspectors are not infrequent.

VAT rates in Italy are 38% on luxury goods (jewellery, furs, etc.) and 19% on food, hotels, restaurants, wine, aperitifs and off-the peg clothes.

Purchases totalling more than 500,000 lire in a single shop can be free of VAT. The exemption is not automatic however, depending on the shopkeeper.

Spas

Tuscany has a large number of spas, including not only the two widely famed resorts of Chianciano Terme and Montecatini Terme but numerous smaller places which attract visitors mainly from their own region. The officially recognised spas in Tuscany are the following (with name of province in brackets): Bagni delle Galleraie (Siena), Bagni di Lucca (Lucca), Bagni di San Filippo (Siena), Bágnore (Grosseto), Bagno Vignoni (Siena), Casciana Terme (Pisa), Chianciano Terme (Siena), Cortona (Arezzo), Equi Terme (Massa-Carrara), Gambassi Terme (Firenze/Florence), Monsummano Terme (Pistoia), Montecatini Terme (Pistoia), Rapolano Terme (Siena), San Carlo Terme (Massa-Carrara), San Casciano dei Bagni (Siena), San Giuliano Terme (Pisa), Terme del Bagnolo (Grosseto), Terme di Caldana

(Livorno), Terme di Firenze (Firenze/Florence), Terme di Montepulciano (Siena), Terme di Petriolo (Grosseto), Terme di Sa-
turnia (Grosseto), Terme San Giovanni (Livorno).

Time

Italy observes Central European Time (one hour ahead of
Greenwich Mean Time, six hours ahead of New York time).
From April to October Central European Summer Time (one
hour ahead of CET) is in force.

Tipping

Tipping in Italy is usual on similar occasions and on a similar
scale as in other Western countries. Tips (*Mancia*) should of
course be given only where some service has been rendered;
not for unwanted services.

Travel documents

British visitors to Italy require only a passport or British Visi-   Personal papers
tor's Passport, without a visa. Citizens of the United States,
Canada, Ireland and many other countries require only a passport, without visa.

British, United States and other national driving licences are   Vehicle papers
recognised in Italy, but must be accompanied by an Italian
translation (obtainable free of charge from the Automobile
Association). Motorists should also take the registration docu-
ment of their car. Foreign cars must display an oval nationality
plate.
It is advisable to have an international insurance certificate
("green card").

It is a good idea to have photocopies of your travel documents   Note
with you. This makes it easier to have them replaced in case of
loss.

Walks

With its gentle valleys and undulating hills the Tuscan countryside is well suited to walking, all the more so because places of
interest are seldom far apart. Maps can be bought at book-
shops in the larger towns and tourists centres. Strong walking
shoes are recommended.

Water sports

The main facilities for water sports are concentrated on the
coasts of the mainland and the offshore islands. All the seaside
resorts offer opportunities for wind-surfing and in many cases
for sailing.

Scuba-divers will find plenty of scope on the rocky coasts of Monte Argentario, round Piombino and on the islands. Around ports and river mouths, however, over-fishing and intensive underwater hunting have combined with man-made pollution to decimate the marine fauna and flora.

The Tuscan Archipelago is a favourite with sailing enthusiasts. Before undertaking an island cruise, however, it is advisable to inquire about the regulations, since it is not permitted, or permitted only with official permission, to call in at some of the islands.

There are yacht harbours at Port'Ércole, Porto Santo Stéfano, Cala Galera, Ansedonia and other ports.

When to go

The best times to visit Tuscany are the late spring and early summer (beginning of May to end of June) and the autumn (beginning of September to end of October). During the main holiday season there are swarms of visitors, making it difficult to find accommodation, and in August (Ferragosto, Assumption) half of Italy seems to be on the move.

At the height of summer the main stream of visitors and holidaymakers is to the seaside resorts, since in August the sea is at its warmest – an average of 24 °C (75 °F). Visitors who can choose their time should at least avoid the school and factory holiday periods if their programme takes them to the most popular tourist centres.

Wine

Wine has been made in Italy since time immemorial, and Italy is still the world's largest producer of wine. Tuscany is one of the best-organised wine-producing regions in Italy, and Tuscan experience played a major part in the formulation of the new wine law which came into force in 1963.

Red wines

Chianti – sign of quality

The best-known wine in Tuscany – perhaps in the whole of Italy – is the red wine of Chianti. Chianti Clássico, produced within a closely defined area, is unquestionably one of the finest Italian wines, recognisable at once by the black cockerel on the label; and Chianti Putto, identifiable by the cherub (*putto*) on the label, is in no way inferior. But the very fact that the name Chianti has become in effect a synonym for Italian red wine has sometimes led, outside the true Chianti area, to mass production of wine, with a consequent decline in quality.

Connoisseurs of Italian wine particularly prize the red Brunello di Montalcino, a fine wine with a correspondingly high price. The wine of a good year ages well and develops a delicate bouquet.

From the same area comes Rosso dei Vigneti di Brunello, made with the same grape, but from young vines or a rather poorer vintage. It is dry and velvety, with a full bouquet, and is drunk young.

A third renowned red wine is the Vino Nobile of Montepulciano, in south-eastern Tuscany. It is somewhere between pomegranae and brick-red in colour, dry, with a bouquet reminiscent of violets. Only the very best years are left to mature in the cellars.

The Wines of Tuscany

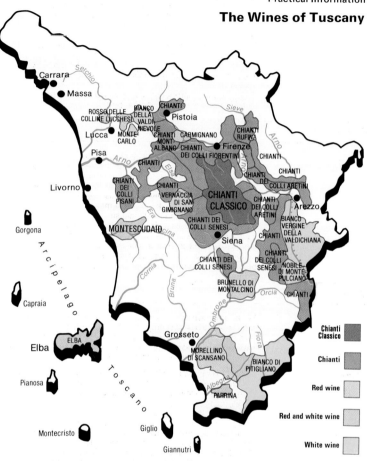

Chianti Classico

Chianti

Red wine

Red and white wine

White wine

Strictly speaking, only red wines can be called Chianti, but white wines are also produced in the Chianti area. They are mostly light and dry, but fruity wines can be produced by appropriate treatment.

One of the best white wines of Tuscany is Montecarlo, produced in an area to the east of Lucca. It is made from different kinds of grape, and accordingly can vary in character between one producer and another. It is usually drunk young. Another white wine with a long-established reputation is Vernaccia di San Gimignano. Depending whether it is fermented with or without the grapeskins, it can be full and darker in colour or fresh and flowery. It too is usually drunk young.

White wines

255

Apart from these wines with a reputation extending beyond the region in which they are produced there are numerous other wines, all over Tuscany, which are drunk locally.

The language of the wine label

There is hardly any part of Italy where wine is not produced on a greater or lesser scale. There are innumerable local wines, usually drunk only in the immediate area where they are made, and as a rule excellent of their kind; for they are mostly still made by the old natural methods, since any special method of treatment is not worth anyone's while.

Under the new Italian wine law of 1963 Italian wines must satisfy specified requirements to qualify for certain statutory designations.

Denominazione semplice, the lowest grade, is the mark of a good table wine. No specific standards of quality are prescribed.

Dennominazione di origine controllata (DOC), the next grade, means that the wine comes from an officially recognised wine-producing area and meets defined quality standards. Such wines must bear a special DOC label.

Denominazione di origine controllata e garantita (DOCG), the highest grade, is a designation granted only to wines of fine quality made by particular producers. Such wines must be bottled by the producer or some other recognised agency and must carry a Government seal guaranteeing the bottling.

The names on the wine label are not necessarily very informative about the nature of the wine: they may be place-names or varieties of grape, but they are often invented names or brand names. It is not uncommon to find red and white wines of quite different character being sold under the same name.

Youth Hostels

Youth Hostels (*alberghi ostelli per la gioventù*) provide accommodation at very reasonable prices, particularly for younger visitors. Priority is given to young people under 30 travelling on foot. If the hostel is full the period of stay is limited to three nights. Advance booking is advisable during the main holiday season and for groups of more than five. Hostellers are not allowed to use their own sleeping-bags: the hire of a sleeping-bag is included in the overnight charge. Foreign visitors must produce a membership card of their national Youth Hostels Association.

Information

Associazione Italiana Alberghi per la Gioventù
Via Cavour 44
00184 Roma
Tel. (06) 46 23 42
Within Tuscany there are Youth Hostels at Abetone, Arezzo, Cortona, Florence, Lucca, Marina di Massa and Siena.